W0036045

SAGE was founded in 1965 by Sara Miller McCune to support the dissemination of usable knowledge by publishing innovative and high-quality research and teaching content. Today, we publish over 900 journals, including those of more than 400 learned societies, more than 800 new books per year, and a growing range of library products including archives, data, case studies, reports, and video. SAGE remains majority-owned by our founder, and after Sara's lifetime will become owned by a charitable trust that secures our continued independence.

Los Angeles | London | New Delhi | Singapore | Washington DC | Melbourne

THE CINEMA OF BIMAL ROY

THE CINEMA OF BIMAL ROY

An 'Outsider' Within

SHOMA A. CHATTERJI

Los Angeles | London | New Delhi
Singapore | Washington DC | Melbourne

First published in 2017 by

SAGE Publications India Pvt Ltd
B1/I-1 Mohan Cooperative Industrial Area
Mathura Road, New Delhi 110 044, India
www.sagepub.in

SAGE Publications Inc
2455 Teller Road
Thousand Oaks, California 91320, USA

SAGE Publications Ltd
1 Oliver's Yard, 55 City Road
London EC1Y 1SP, United Kingdom

SAGE Publications Asia-Pacific Pte Ltd
3 Church Street
#10-04 Samsung Hub
Singapore 049483

Published by Vivek Mehra for SAGE Publications India Pvt Ltd, typeset in 10/12 pt Adobe Garamond by Diligent Typesetter India Pvt Ltd, Delhi and printed at Saurabh Printers Pvt Ltd, Greater Noida.

Library of Congress Cataloging-in-Publication Data Available

ISBN: 978-93-860-6286-4 (PB)

SAGE Team: Supriya Das, Sudeshna Nandy, Apeksha Sharma and Ritu Chopra

To my late mother, Sumita Gangopadhyay, who had
her first book of poems published when she was 48
and already a grandmother, for triggering in me
the spirit of creation and competition

And

To my late father, Ashok Kumar Gangopadhyay, who
introduced me to the world of cinema by taking me
for Sunday morning shows every week when I was
barely 4 to watch Mickey Mouse and Donald Duck
cartoons on the wide screen followed by the silent
movies of Charlie Chaplin.

CONTENTS

PREFACE
(ON A PERSONAL NOTE...)

Bimal Roy, the 'Silent Master of Indian Cinema', ushered in the golden age of Indian Cinema in the 1940s. As a socially committed director, his films had the power to inspire and move audiences. *Do Bigha Zamin*,[1] made more than 50 years ago, is an eloquent portrait of displaced peasants, while *Sujata* took up the ever-burning issue of caste and the tragedy of a woman born into a low caste but brought up in a high-caste environment. With each film, from Saratchandra's *Parineeta*, produced under the banner of Ashok Kumar Films, to the poignant *Devdas* with the porcelain-like beauty of Suchitra Sen or the dusky Nutan in and as *Sujata*, Bimal Roy was synonymous with the aesthetics of cinema that embraced every department of cinema—technique to direction to acting to casting to production design and music—with such intimate affection and distanced dignity that his films appealed all Indian audiences everywhere. He evolved into a legend in his lifetime. He was that rare species among human beings who also contributed by training and gifting to cinema some of its finest of craftsmen for posterity. Among these are Gulzar, Basu Bhattacharya, Hrishikesh Mukherjee, Salil Chowdhury, Asit Sen and others, who began their careers in films under the guidance and care of Bimal Roy.

---

[1] The English equivalents of the titles of his films are given in the filmography at the end of this book.

Bimal Roy won two Filmfare hat-tricks as best director (in two spells of three consecutive years each) and one best picture award (a total of eight Filmfare awards). When Bimal Roy went on stage to accept his Filmfare trophies for *Do Bigha Zamin* in dhoti, kurta and chappals, Bombay's upscale film coterie raised a hue and cry. However, Bimal Roy was only expressing his signature: simplicity and minimalism. *Do Bigha Zamin* won a special mention at the Cannes and Karlovy Vary film festivals (1955–1956). At least 12 of his films—*Udayer Pathey, Hamrahi, Do Bigha Zamin, Biraj Bahu, Parineeta, Devdas, Madhumati, Usne Kaha Tha, Kabuliwala, Sujata, Parakh* and *Bandini*—represent one of the most brilliant epochs of Indian cinema.

This book is a humble tribute to a filmmaker who formed a major slice of my growing up years from girlhood to womanhood. My mother was a close friend of Manobina Roy, Bimal Roy's talented and beautiful wife. I knew Bimal Roy personally for over 10 years, somewhere between the ages of 11 and 20. But we exchanged few words because he was a man of silence. It was difficult to find out what he was thinking, when and about whom. He spoke so little that even his family had to poke him with questions to get answers. The sharply edged picture one can recall about him is a tall, well-built, handsome man with a receding hairline and a cigarette held in his hand all the time, smoke from which rose to draw arc-like circles in the air around him. His Hindi was really bad but that did not deter him from giving directions to his actors, be it Dilip Kumar or Nutan or Vyjayanthimala. He was very clear in his mind about what he wanted out of his actors.

The only concession he made to the mingling of his film friends and his family is when he decided to celebrate his only son Joy's *annaprashan*[2] quite elaborately in their Hill Road bungalow apartment. I was hardly 8 or 9 then and was thrilled to be introduced to Baby Tabassum, then a young girl, and her parents. She had no starry airs though she was at the peak of her career as a child artiste and had played one of the two leads in Bimal Roy's *Baap Beti*. Among other celebrities I can vaguely recall was Shobha Ganguly, Ashok Kumar's beautiful wife, who had come wearing a bright red sequined sari along with her two lovely daughters—Bharati, the eldest daughter, in a sari and Roopa, the middle daughter, in a frock. People who regularly dropped in and out of the Roy bungalow and had an impromptu lunch cooked and served by Manobina *Mashima*[3] were

---

[2] *Annaprashan* means a ceremony celebrating a baby's first ritual tasting of rice—*anna* meaning rice and *prashan* meaning celebration for the first intake.

[3] *Mashima* is the Bengali form of address used for one's maternal aunt or mother's friend extended to close friends of the family.

Hrishikesh Mukherjee and his wife; Salil Chowdhury and his wife, Jyoti; Bimal Roy's two main cameramen Dilip Gupta and Kamal Bose; screenplay writer Nabendu Ghosh and his family; Kanu Roy, who scored the music for Basu Bhattacharya's *Anubhav* (1971);[4] Basu, who was assistant to Bimal Roy; Debu Sen, another assistant; and Anjana Rawail, Rahul Rawail's mother, who was a Bengali and a close friend of Manobina Roy.

I once went to Mohan Studios during the shooting of *Bandini* along with Jarasandha (Charu Chandra Chakraborty), the writer on whose novel the film was based. It was a scene with Nutan, a child actor who did a small cameo in the film, and Raja Paranjape who played Nutan (Kalyani)'s father in the film. Bimal Roy asked Paranjape to step into the compound of the small bungalow, take a given number of steps and call out to Kalyani. When Kalyani would not respond, he was to take a few steps more and call out to Kalyani again. But Paranjape could not give an okay shot several times over because his counting went wrong and Nutan would come out before he called out her name the second time. Bimal Roy, without losing patience, persuaded him to repeat the shot till he got it right. Bengali was the lingua franca on the sets of any Bimal Roy's film because almost his entire technical crew, including the excellent make-up man Babu, was Bengali. The ones who were not Bengali had picked up a smattering of Bangla over time and Bimal-da would insist on talking to them only in Bangla. It is no surprise, therefore, to see the Bengali identity deeply ingrained in every film directed by Bimal Roy. He lived in Mumbai (then Bombay) for most of his life beginning with a small rented apartment in Malad to shift later to the Hill Road bungalow where he breathed his last, but at heart, he remained a true-blooded Bengali and liberally allowed his films to be soaked in Bengali culture minus the language.

At the entrance of Mohan Studios was a corner shop that sold the most delicious lassi[5] with half the glass frothing over with thick cream bubbles. It was heavenly and no one would leave the place without having a glass of lassi. Half a glass cost 0.50 paise[6] and a full glass went out for ₹1.00. I never saw or knew of Bimal Roy drinking alcohol. It did not go with his personality, though the cigarette did. A memorable celebration every year at Mohan Studios was Saraswati Pooja on Vasant Panchami, the day

---

[4] *Anubhav* means experience. It is the name of a film directed by Basu Bhattacharya who married Bimal Roy's eldest daughter Rinki.

[5] Lassi is a drink made of buttermilk which is very thick in consistency and is covered with a layer of cream on top and usually served sweet. It is very popular in the northern parts of India.

[6] Paise is the name of the denomination of Indian coinage after it changed to the decimal system, and till today, one Indian rupee is equal to 100 naya paisa. The plural is paise.

Bengalis worship Goddess Saraswati. A stage would be put up for a night of entertainment of the purely traditional kind—including classical dance numbers, songs sung by famous and not-so-famous singers and the works. The idol of the goddess would be sculpted by the art department of Bimal Roy films. This was one day when Bimal Roy would allow his family to his studios. Dresses for the dance numbers would be generously borrowed from the studio wardrobe from earlier films.

Once, an abstract from Tagore's dance drama *Chandalika* was presented by three dancers drawn from an amateur group. The choreography was done by the famous Manipuri dance scholar Guru Bipin Sinha. *Chandalika*[7] incidentally formed a segment of Roy's *Sujata*, a deviation from the literary original, as a metaphor for the drama of casteism and untouchability that formed the core of the film. The three performers who did the roles of the untouchable Prakriti, her mother and Anando, the disciple of Buddha who transformed the young girl stigmatized by untouchability, did a fantastic realization of the Tagore piece. After the performance, Bimal Roy came backstage, patted the girls gently on their backs and said just one word, 'Good.' It made my evening unforgettable. I was the teenaged dancer who performed Prakriti.

I happened to be a house-guest along with my sister Onija at the well-appointed, spic-and-span Roy home at Mount Mary Road, Bandra, for a fortnight in 1962. My mother had to rush off to Delhi with my little brother to attend to my father, then posted in Delhi, who was sick. Manobina Mashima insisted that we go along with her instead of living alone in our Shivaji Park flat. She saw to it that we did not feel alienated and made all arrangements to keep us entertained during our stay. I had some important class tests and would study deep into the night to prepare. One morning, I was instructed by Bina Mashima not to keep awake at night to study. She said, "Your uncle noticed that the lights were on in the hall. When he asked me if I had forgotten to switch off the lights, I told him that you were preparing for your exams. He said that if a student did not prepare during the day, he or she had no right to study keeping awake at night." "She will fall asleep during the test," she quoted him as having said. I was touched by his observation. But I also wished he had told me himself.

---

[7] *Chandalika* is the name of a famous dance-drama written by Rabindranath Tagore on an untouchable girl whose life changes when Ananda, a disciple of Gautama Buddha, asks her for water and explains to her that there is no difference between human beings and she is equal to him and to everyone else.

One evening, when he came home earlier than usual, we had an early dinner because the kids—Rinki, a little older, and Jashodhara, my age—wanted to watch some reels from *Madhumati*. Bubuni (Aparajita) was just in primary school, while Joy was in nursery. In a song sequence, we saw Dilip Kumar wearing a coat over his shirt, and in the next shot, the coat was missing. Rinki noticed this lapse and told her father, "Baba, what is this? What was the continuity man doing?" Her father smiled quietly, took a puff off his cigarette and walked away into his small 'cabin' that was an extension of the main apartment. The room was decorated with the straw caps the 'peasants' had worn in *Do Bigha Zamin*.

The most touching incident happened on the night of *Bandini's* premiere at Bombay's Opera House. We got two cards to attend the star-studded premiere. As my mother was not well, after some hesitation, she packed me off with my younger sister to see the premiere show—the first in our lives. I was around 18 then and my sister was 14. We took a BEST bus (84 Express) from Cadell Road (now Veer Savarkar Marg) and got off at the Opera House stop. Opera House was not a normal venue for film premieres so the streets all around were lined with people of all classes waiting to catch a glimpse of the stars. The screening ended at around 11.30 PM. The bus service had stopped.

Another noted filmmaker, a contemporary of Bimal Roy, who had also cut his teeth in New Theatres and was a close friend of my family, had earlier promised that he would drop us home. But when the show ended, I was shocked to see him wave at us cheerfully and ride away in a friend's car. I stood there with my sister, panic stricken. We were stranded in a neighbourhood close to a notorious red-light area. The streets around were spilling over with pimps and muscle-men; I had a growing lump of fear in my throat and a bottomless pit in my stomach. Bimal Roy was the last man about to leave. "Aren't you Shoma? What are you doing here at this time of night?" he asked. I said we did not have transportation to get back home. He looked at my kid sister and then at me but did not say anything. He turned around and waved to the driver of a passing car, asking him to stop. It was one of the Roys' several cars. He quietly told us to get in and asked the driver to take us to Shivaji Park, right till our home. We reached home well past midnight. Maa almost desperate with fear and anxiety was waiting at the gate. That was the last time I saw Bimal Roy in person because I got married a couple of years later. He could not attend the reception though his family did.

Mount Mary Road is a hilly road where the beautiful, two-storied Parsi bungalow is situated, which Bimal Roy resided with his family till he passed away in 1966 and his family continued to live after his death.

Roy's residence was in the villa, later razed to make way for a high-rise. He had purchased a house on an adjoining plot where his son Joy Bimal Roy now resides. "Back then, the villa was called the Godiwala Bungalow where I and my siblings grew up. However, now that I live in the adjacent house, I will be able to keep a watch on the lane. My attempt is to beautify the entrance to the lane as much as possible," said Joy. The decision to rename the road Bimal Roy Path followed a representation to the chairperson of the local ward committee by corporator Karen D'Mello. Aakif Habib, secretary of Mount Mary ALM, said it would be befitting to have the lane named after Roy considering that he was a resident of the area and his family continues to live there. A plaque was unveiled at the entrance of the lane on 8 January 2017 that coincided with the filmmaker's 51st death anniversary. Bimal Roy had moved in with his family to this bungalow from their modest apartment in Malad in 1954. "It was an important time in his life because that's when he started his first production, 'Do Bigha Zamin'. It's a huge honour," said Joy.

My greatest regret about my relationship with the Roy family is that I was nowhere around when Bimal Roy passed away after struggling with lung cancer for months together. I was already married and settled in Kolkata and my mother would feed me with the latest on this great man. She said he spoke much more in his sickness than he had probably spoken all his life. Then, one morning in January 1966, the front page of *The Statesman* announced his passing away. Strangely, Bimal Roy's famous silence was a strong bonding factor. He spoke very little, but his silent personality had the power to hold people together. After his passing away, our bonding with the Roy family faded away, leaving us with fond memories of a man who was a great filmmaker, true, but a much greater human being.

ACKNOWLEDGEMENTS

This book was something I just had to write. I owed it not only to the person Bimal Roy and his cinema, which I practically grew up with and on, but also to his family and, most importantly, to his wife, the beautiful, sophisticated yet warm and friendly, Bina Mashima. I owe it to the younger generation of readers and film buffs and students of cinema who are not very familiar with the black-and-white magic era of Bombay cinema when story ruled supreme, the actors had to fit themselves into the story and the director was the superhero.

My first note of thanks goes to everyone at SAGE India who gave the nod to my proposal. Among the ones who tolerated my ceaseless queries and answered my questions patiently are Elina Majumdar who first introduced me to SAGE and even though she has moved on while I was writing this book, still keeps in touch; Shambhu Sahu, who, till recently, was a Commissioning Editor at SAGE (Books) and has now moved on; Rudra Narayan Sharma who replaced Mr Sahu recently and has moved on; Supriya Das, Associate Commissioning Editor; Sudeshna Nandy, Manager – Editorial (Books) and of course, Sharmila Abraham, Vice President of SAGE India. Just a two-word phrase of appreciation cannot do justice to the way they have helped in taking this book on its long journey from conception to publication.

Joy Bimal Roy, the only son of the late Bimal Roy who made a moving documentary on his father deserves a strong mention because he gave me the necessary authorization for the use of the images of his father in this book. Film archivist Subhash Chheda and his wife Aarti Chheda deserve a round of applause for giving me images from some of Bimal Roy films and also written authorizations to use them in this book. Another archivist and poster collector is SMM Ausaja who I need to thank for some images and an authorization letter though the images he had guided me with could not be used later. Without these close friends, this book would not have been what it now is. These close friends have given the images for use without any monetary consideration whatsoever and this give-and-take is based purely on the relationship factor and on our bonding based on our common passion for Hindi cinema.

I must express my deepest gratitude to my young friend, art curator and collector Sounak Chakraverti for preparing the filmography of Bimal Roy for use in this book without any other consideration but our friendship. My gratitude extends to reach out to journalist, festival curator and organizer Ratnottama Sengupta who added her personal comments as the daughter of Bimal Roy's consistent script and story-writer, the late Nabyendu Ghosh. I also extend my gratitude to the late Ms Champa Roy, daughter of the late Dilip Gupta, one of the two leading cameramen of Bimal Roy films. She helped me a great deal by gifting the book she edited on her father, which gave me a lot of source material to work with. I am also grateful to Bimal Roy's eldest daughter Rinki Roy Bhattacharya for her two books on her father, one edited by her and the other that she wrote herself. I did not have any direct interaction with her or even with Joy because I did not wish to be influenced by their perspectives of their father as a filmmaker.

Over the years, I have written dozens of articles, profiles, analyses and explorations on Bimal Roy and his films. I extend my thanks to the editors of these print and online publications such as *Screen*, www.indiatogether.org, www.thecitizen.in, *One India One People*, *The Tribune*, *Vogue India*, *Swagat*, *Vidura*, *The Times of India* and many others.

My husband Ajoy has always hovered in the backdrop helping me by just being there and allowing me to explore my space the way I wanted to; having shared 51 stormy and not-so-stormy years together, I must concede that without his help nothing of this or the other books I have authored would have seen the light of day. My grandson, Ishaan Agarwal, all of 16 who has just cleared his 'O' levels, has cheered me up with his lightning spells of mischief every now and then, though these were more to annoy and irritate me which they did.

I owe readers who will read this book a generous dose of gratitude for bearing with my very individual explorations of the works of an actress I have never met or interacted with in any way.

INTRODUCTION

BACKGROUND

There have been books written on classic filmmakers in Hindi cinema such as Mehboob, Sohrab Modi, V. Shantaram, Raj Kapoor, Guru Dutt, B.R. Chopra, Yash Chopra and several others. But till now, there has been no 'auteur' critique of the cinema of Bimal Roy. He belonged to an era where Hindi cinema had created its distinct identity, different from what we find today within its changed tautological innovation called Bollywood. This came to be known as the Golden Era of Hindi Cinema.

The author felt it necessary to do a textual and contextual analysis of the cinema of Bimal Roy not only because there is no significant work done on his cinema but also because his career began in colonial India in 1944 and ended two decades later in 1963, much after India had officially become a sovereign, democratic republic. His space and time in cinema overlaps the colonial cultural and political ambience and the ambience in Independent India where his choice of source also transcends the colonial era to step into Independent India. During his tenure as a director, Bimal Roy directed 15 feature films and 4 documentaries. He also produced some films under his Bimal Roy Productions banner which he did not direct himself.

Bimal Roy's 'cinema' embraces much more than the images we see flashed on the screen shot and projected on 35 mm which might have become a fossilized symbol of the past by the time this book is published. Why 'cinema' and why not 'films'? Because the word 'films' has a concrete image of actual footage, while 'cinema' is a much broader term that charts the map of much more than the images we watch on screen, the songs and dialogues we hear being sung or spoken and the sound effect and the time and space leaps happening in brief moments of time. 'Cinema' encompasses an entire sociocultural history in itself. When attached to the 'cinema' created by a given filmmaker, it reflects the sociocultural backdrop the filmmaker belonged to, the geography he or she shifted to if he or she did shift and the evolution of his or her mindset as he or she shifted from one sociocultural backdrop to another and from one film to the next and the next. Bimal Roy's cinema is also a representation of a certain kind of cinema where ideology and positive values run like an undercurrent in his films without being loud, aggressive or lavishly mounted. In other words, the director's ideology comes across through his selection of the source material for his films, be it literature or a poem or an Indianized adaptation of a film from a different land.

The 'great four'—Mehboob, Bimal Roy, Guru Dutt and Raj Kapoor—made the major films of the 1950s. These directors had seen traumatic time in their formative years, the 1930s and 1940s that encompassed major events in the subcontinent: the struggle for independence, famines, changing social mores, the global fight against fascism and so on. All these events shaped their ethos and vision. Iqbal Masud has noted the common traits in the works of these filmmakers.

> There are many common traits in the works of these directors. The foremost is that much abused word, humanism.... In the 40s 'humanism' had a specific connotation. It was fuelled by outrage against India's savage poverty and inequalities (exacerbated by the rise of the black market in the Second World War). A second element was its deep awareness of India's past and present cultures—both 'high' and 'popular'. A third was the skill in communicating its outrage and call for change to the masses. This last element has been called 'entertainment'. But in the 40s and 50s this had an aspirational touch about it which has vanished long ago from our cinema.[8]

---

[8] Iqbal Masud, 'The Great Four of the Golden Fifties', in *Frames of Mind: Reflections on Indian Cinema*, Aruna Vasudev, ed. (New Delhi: UBSPD, 1995). Quoted by Amir Ullah Khan and Bibek Debroy, 'Indian Economic Transition through Bollywood Eyes: Hindi Films and How They Have Reflected changes in India's Political Economy' (working paper 2, August 2002).

Roy belonged to a period in Indian cinema when the vocabulary that dotted Indian cinema was different. The term 'Bollywood' did not exist, 'post-modern' cinema, 'globalization' and 'diaspora' were words completely unknown within the sphere of Indian cinema. Even 'parallel cinema' was an unknown term because this came in sometime after Bimal Roy became an established name. Colour in cinema was very sparsely used, digital technology was an unknown entity and technique was considered secondary to content, with skill and challenges making up for gimmickry and modernization. His filmmaking as a director began a little before Satyajit Ray's *Pather Panchali*[9] which created a benchmark that divided meaningful Indian cinema into two time-periods roughly defined as *before Pather Panchali* and *after Pather Panchali*. Therefore, Bimal Roy's cinema and his style, treatment, approach and presentation were unique in defining the filmmaker without bringing in any comparative analysis of his cinema and the cinema that came after Ray made his historic debut.

Neither music could be replicated nor its 'rights' could be sold separately from the film before it was released; marketing and publicity hypes were confined to pre-release advertisements in the press; and, most importantly, television had not made its entry into Indian homes. There was almost no experiment done with the form of cinema at the time, and all challenges and explorations were attempted through and within the storylines themselves. The 'locations' were more often 'sets' constructed within studio floors than actually taking the cast and crew to a distant location. Roy did a lot of actual location shooting for *Madhumati*, but most of his films too were shot indoors on sets created by his talented art directors.

These are not taken as drawbacks but as integral to the working of cinema in India at the time. These were the realities filmmakers like Bimal Roy and his talented peers had to work with, and they did not consider them to be limitations because the modernized options simply did not exist. Though an established cameraman himself, Bimal Roy's films show that he never felt constrained by 'absences' he was not aware of and took his storyline as the basic structure to build his films on. So, the story and the script were the commanders and he steered them in the direction he wished his films to flow with the help of his technical team through characterization, music, song, dialogue, art direction and editing. Looking back, borrowing a phrase from economics, he and his dedicated team made the maximum use of minimum resources to obtain ideal results that would give the films a shelf-life, perhaps, to be saved in the film archives forever.

---

[9] *Pather Panchali*—Song of the road, directed by Satyajit Ray.

Filmmakers are creative artists and craftsmen rolled into one, so they cannot be trapped within a single time–space–language–culture paradigm. Yet, with a considerable output of films, they can be marked out for their 'signature' over a group of films that identify each one as made by a given filmmaker. For example, a single scene from a Guru Dutt film spells out the name of its maker without the viewer knowing who directed it. One shot from a Bimal Roy film impacts the cinebuff in the same way. A line from a song or a track from a music score also reveals who the filmmaker is without knowing the credits.

The problem with focusing on a single filmmaker who belonged to a particular sociopolitical backdrop of Indian cinema is the dilemma about whether the work should focus on an 'auteur' critique of his or her works, or whether it should be a historical study, in which case the director and his or her works must be placed in perspective alongside his or her contemporaries in cinema and also against the historical backdrop to which he or she belonged during the time the person was seriously engaged in directing films. One cannot separate the artist from the environment in which he or she grew up and the environment where his or her creative juices were ideally expressed through films. The writer feels that it is very difficult to separate the auteur from his or her historical circumstances. So, though the subject—Bimal Roy—demands an auteur criticism both in terms of the number of films he directed and the quality of these films, the backdrop he grew up in and his shifting mobility from Bangladesh to Calcutta to Bombay also played a significant role in the shaping of the filmmaker, his choice of subjects from literature and without for his films, his approach, style and treatment of the subjects and his evolution and growth as a filmmaker.

A three-pronged approach would emerge from this. First, the 'cinema' that is the films directed by Bimal Roy; second, creating a filmography for this work by making a list of the films included in this study which would function as the 'history' of his films and his filmmaking and, third, discovering the 'auteur' in Bimal Roy through a content analysis of his films. The first is pre-selected depending on the genres the films are divided into, not arbitrarily but in keeping with the choice of the writer. The second would emerge from within the third, and the three together would constitute an in-depth and retrospective study of the cinema of Bimal Roy.

MAJOR AIM

The major aim of this work is to remap the history of a phase in Hindi cinema that may be termed, for the sake of convenience and clarity, the 'Bimal Roy Era' through detailed content analysis of the films and to substantiate the argument that Bimal Roy's films mainly revolved around the concept of the 'displaced outsider' who does not belong to the 'mainstream' within the respective films in the study, whether created by any one or more of the following:

1. Circumstances of birth (*Parineeta, Sujata*)[10]
2. Circumstances beyond one's control (*Baap Beti*)[11]
3. Basic survival needs (*Do Bigha Zamin*)[12]
4. Social outcast becomes a murder accused (*Bandini*)[13]
5. Depiction of tragedy through villainy (*Biraj Bahu*)[14]
6. Voluntary movement from being within the mainstream to moving without and vice versa (*Devdas*)[15]
7. 'Outsider' through clash of values (*Udayer Pathey*).[16]

This 'displaced outsider-ness', if one can call it thus, is not based on gender, class, age or place but taken as 'given', and the arguments take place after that.

WHO IS AN 'OUTSIDER' IN BIMAL ROY'S CINEMA?

An 'outsider' in the cinema of Bimal Roy is 'one who does not belong to the mainstream' and is, therefore, defined by distinct characteristics that may or may not be in common with the other members of the group. From a given point of view, almost all the major characters in Bimal Roy's films are 'outsiders' by virtue of their migration from their roots, their displacement within their roots or both. They are 'off mainstream' in essence even if they appear to be 'mainstream' to begin with when a particular film opens and the narrative begins to unfold. In *Parineeta*, Lalita is an orphan brought up in the home of her maternal uncle and his family. She is within the family. But cracks open up when the family is in dire straits and she finds herself in the horns of a strange dilemma.

In *Do Bigha Zamin*, Shambhu is a farmer who lives in a village with his aged father, wife and a boy. He has a small piece of land that the draught forces him to mortgage to a landowner. But poverty dogs the family and Shambhu is forced to leave his family, his land and his home behind in

---

[10] *Parineeta*—The wedded woman; *Sujata*—Proper noun; name of the protagonist.
[11] *Baap Beti*—Father–daughter.
[12] *Do Bigha Zamin*—Two acres of land.
[13] *Bandini*—Title of the film which means 'the imprisoned woman'.
[14] *Biraj Bahu*—The name of the protagonist and the title of the film.
[15] *Devdas*—Name of the protagonist and the title of the film.
[16] *Udayer Pathey*—Towards the light.

search of an alternative livelihood in Calcutta. He is an 'outsider' as a villager who has migrated to the city. In the city, he is an outsider because he joins an occupation he knows nothing about—pulling a hand-pulled rickshaw for a living. His growing son learns the job of a cobbler. So, occupationally, both father and son are 'outsiders'. When he comes back to his village, he finds he is an 'outsider' in the village because his two *bighas* of land have been usurped by the zamindar. He stands outside the barbed wire fencing where a new factory is coming up where his land once was and literally becomes the 'outsider'.

Merriam-Webster's Dictionary defines the 'outsider' as (a) a person who does not belong to or is not accepted as part of a particular group or organization or (b) a person or animal that is not expected to win a race of a competition. Does this suggest that the 'outsider' is always an underdog in a Bimal Roy film? Not necessarily, because Devdas in the story and the film is not an underdog. He is not expected to win any race, not because he cannot but because he will not. He has given up the race even before it began and chose to step outside the group he was born into and grew up in by going away from his home, developing a strange love–hate relationship with Chandramukhi, a singing woman, and allowing himself to be destroyed by and through drinking under the excuse of love lost.

In contemporary thinking, however, the 'outsider' is one who is in conflict with the 'insider', or rather, to put it bluntly, a rebel, a renegade or one who raises one's voice or flag or fist against the 'insider' who is part of an accepted group. The 'outsider' is not a victim by choice or by circumstance. The outsider was considered to be a part of the margin, ignored or sidetracked or rendered 'invisible' by the mainstream insider in earlier decades. But today, the 'outsider' will strike out by creating his or her own sphere or space along with others of his or her ideology or belief to start a splinter group. Sometimes, this splinter group might even be appropriated by the insider group or vice versa as we see around us in the new formation of political parties created by small groups that break away from the party they belong to, not to join another but to create their own.

There is nothing even remotely rebellious in these displaced characters in Bimal Roy's cinema, except Anup Lekhak in *Udayer Pathey*. They exist or unwittingly move into spaces that are not their own, which allows them space to exist and express, but only up to a given point—spatially, socially and culturally. These 'outsiders' are not out there to prove a point, and if there is a point, they probably are unaware of it. If and when they 'are' victims, there is no inclination, overt or covert, to place their victim status at stake and win brownie points for being any kind of 'martyr' to the cause, any cause.

The concept of the 'outsider' in Bimal Roy's cinema could also be interpreted through a point-of-view perspective of each character looking at another one in a given film. In *Devdas*, Devdas keeps insulting the courtesan Chandramukhi, calls her a prostitute to her face and considers her an 'outsider'. From Chandramukhi's point of view, it is Devdas who is the 'outsider' because he returns to her haveli time and again not to hear her sing, watch her dance or be entertained by her in other ways such as sex but only to find a place to drown his woes in drinking bouts. If one were to consider Parvati's point of view, Devdas is the 'outsider' who, in her view, can fall desperately in love with a childhood sweetheart but lack the courage to accept her proposal to elope with her at the cost of incurring the wrath of his family, her parents and the entire village.

The concept of 'homelessness' described so lucidly by Ranjani Mazumdar[17] in her seminal essay does not apply to the 'outsider' as interpreted in and through the characters in the cinema of Bimal Roy. 'Homelessness' does not characterize men and women such as Devdas in *Devdas*, Lalita in *Parineeta*, Kalyani in *Bandini* or Sujata in *Sujata*. These characters are not homeless. They either do not really belong to the 'home' they are brought up in, such as Sujata and Lalita, or try to move out to seek something else in spaces other than their 'home', such as Devdas. Mazumdar cites examples of homelessness from films made at a much later date, decades after the Bimal Roy phase was over, and the entire ideology of occupying, coming to occupy or moving out and in from old to new spaces had manifested itself differently in the cinema of the kind she has elaborated on, barring Raj Kapoor's *Awaara*,[18] as the following paragraph shows.

> Homelessness evokes a certain morality and power. Homelessness has the ability to capture a contemporary imagination by situating the city as the site of ruin from within which a range of discourses can emerge. Homelessness has always had a powerful appeal in India's literary and cinematic traditions for it magnifies the experience of loss, deprivation and anger. The 'footpath' in the city is the imagined space of homelessness where millions without a home sleep. It is the imaginary reference point of many narratives where the experience of childhood on the streets provides the moral justification for the protagonist's actions (*Awaara*, 1951; *Deewar*,[19] 1975; *Muqaddar Ka Sikandar*,[20] 1978). In the 'angry man' films

---

[17] Ranjani Mazumdar, 'Figure of the Tapori: Language, Gesture and the Cinematic City', *Economic and Political Weekly* 36, no. 52 (29 December 2001): 4872–4880.

[18] *Awaara*—The vagabond; title of a film.

[19] *Deewar*—The wall.

[20] *Muqaddar Ka Sikandar*—King of his destiny.

of the 1970s, homelessness connected to memory became the vehicle for the articulation of anger and revenge.

This theory of 'the outsider' also sheds light on the concept of 'the other'. This 'other' is that which bourgeoisie ideology can neither recognize nor accept. It is dealt with in one of two ways: by rejecting, or, if possible, annihilating it, or by rendering it safe and assimilating it, converting it as far as possible into a replica of itself.[21] This concept of 'otherness' can be theorized in many ways and on many levels. Its psychoanalytic significance resides in the fact that it functions not simply as something external to the culture or to the self, but also as what is repressed in the self and projected outwards in order to be hated and disowned. This writer would use these definitions of 'the other' and 'the outsider' in an exploration of Bimal Roy's cinema interchangeably.

SECONDARY AIMS
The study aspires to fulfil the following aims:

1. Analyse the cinema of Bimal Roy, 'not' in chronological sequence of his directorial career but divided into categories ignoring the overlaps naturally present in the works of an 'auteur' filmmaker;
2. The concept and ideology of 'Bengaliness' that distinguished his school of filmmaking from *Udayer Pathey* to *Bandini*;
3. To explore the cinema of Bimal Roy through the elements of displacement present in almost all his directorial films over his career;
4. To elaborate on how his films, in some way or another, subtly or explicitly, pay tribute to the inner strength of a woman, even when a male is the protagonist such as in *Devdas*;
5. To focus on the significance of music and dance in his films even when dance is not the central theme/focus of the story;
6. To establish how the language and technique of cinema can be used with softness, genteelness and grace without losing out on strong social statements that emerge from the narrative texts of the films and from the technical strengths of cinema—script, dialogue, cinematography, music, choreography, sound, editing and acting.

---

[21] Robin Wood, 'An Introduction to the American Horror Film' in *Movies and Methods*, Bills Nichols, ed., vol. II, (Calcutta: Seagull Books, 1993), 199–200.

These divisions automatically bring out the limitation of this study that spans the directorial career of Bimal Roy from 1944 to 1963. The cinema of Bimal Roy is known for its powerful storylines, technical finesse and some subtle and not-so-subtle social messages that emerge from the very act of storytelling and the process of filmmaking. But we seem to have missed out on the essence of his cinema that reflects the impact of displacement on the emotions, actions and relationships on human lives. Bimal Roy was himself a 'displaced' person who migrated from what is now Bangladesh to a city like Kolkata, culturally, politically and historically distanced from Suapur where he grew up. He migrated before the Partition but the lines of division were invisible but sharp.

EXCLUSIONS

This work excludes the following because they do not lend themselves to this study in its aims and also due to logistics, as prints of most of these films are not available for viewing and, therefore, render content analysis impossible.

1. Content analysis of films which have no prints existing anywhere, such as *Pehla Aadmi*,[22] *Mantra Mugdha*[23] and *Anjangarh*,[24] are described in passing in terms of their content to get an idea of the mindset of a director whose choice of subject was almost always derived from literature, but in the absence of prints of the films, detailed critique is not possible.

2. Analytical study of films which Bimal Roy produced but 'did not direct' such as *Amaanat*,[25] *Usne Kaha Tha*,[26] *Kabuliwala*,[27] *Benazir*,[28] *Parivar*,[29] *Apradhi Kaun*,[30] and a few others. But these also reflect the mindset of a director who wished to fulfil the directorial aspirations of his assistant Asit Sen (Bombay) who directed *Parivar* (1956) and *Apradhi Kaun* (1957), while his

---

[22] *Pehla Aadmi*—The first man.

[23] *Mantra Mugdha*—Mesmerized.

[24] *Anjangarh*—Name of a fictitious place.

[25] *Amaanat*—Something one holds in trust on behalf of another person to be given to a third person. It could be land, jewellery, financial documents, even children.

[26] *Usne Kaha Tha*—She had said.

[27] *Kabuliwala*—Name of the film and the common name the protagonist is known by.

[28] *Benazir*—Title of the film meaning 'incomparable'.

[29] *Parivar*—Family.

[30] *Apradhi Kaun*—Who is the criminal?

old friend Aravind Sen directed *Amaanat* (1955) when Sen had fallen on bad days. *Benazir* (1964) was directed by S. Khalil while *Kabuliwala* (1961) was entrusted to Hemen Gupta who was without work after having made classic Bengali films such as *42* and *Bhuli Nai*.[31] He chose Moni Bhattacharjee to direct *Usne Kaha Tha* (1960) based on a story by Chandradhar Sharma Guleri to give a break to a new director who later directed *Mujhe Jeene Do*[32] (1963) followed by *Jaal*[33] (1967) and *Baazi*[34] (1968), all three films turning out to be commercial disasters.

3. *Yahudi*,[35] *Parakh*[36] and *Prem Patra*[37] have been excluded because *Yahudi* is a historical costume drama that marks an exception to the Bimal Roy school of cinema. *Parakh* is included briefly as a rare film that defines the value of honesty and integrity and *Prem Patra* is excluded because it is an adaptation from a very big Bengali box office hit *Sagarika*[38] starring Uttam Kumar and Suchitra Sen, so it may not permit a reading within his independent directorial space.

4. The documentaries made by Bimal Roy have been kept out of this work because they do not lend themselves to the subject of this study that focuses only on feature films.

The chapters in this work evolve from the following questions:

1. How 'Bengali' is the cinema of Bimal Roy when placed within the ambience of a globalized Bollywood cinema that is a highly glamourized blend of lavishly designed technology in colour, sound, costume, music, dance, characterization and depiction of love and big stars, foreign locations, item songs and so on?

2. What sets Bimal Roy apart as an 'auteur' with a distinguished body of work that identifies with his style, approach and treatment during a period when cinema was different in form, content and technique than it is today in the era of globalization?

---

[31] *Bhuli Nai*—Never forgotten.
[32] *Mujhe Jeena Do*—Let me live.
[33] *Jaal*—The net.
[34] *Baazi*—Wager/bet.
[35] *Yahudi*—The Jew.
[36] *Parakh*—The test.
[37] *Prem Patra*—Love letter(s).
[38] *Sagarika*—Proper noun that is the name of the leading character in the film and the name of the film.

3. Would it be in the fitness of things to define his cinema more as 'the cinema of displacement' than as 'the cinema of social commitment' that is a reflection of his own 'displaced' life that made him shift base from Suapur to Calcutta and then to Bombay where he settled down to a creatively productive life till his death?

4. In what way have some of the women characters in his cinema outlived their time and are considered universal though they are placed within a specific regional and/or national world?

REVIEW OF RELATED LITERATURE

The 'Absences'

One fact that emerged during researching this book is that no documents are available of an interview of Bimal Roy. He was known to be a man of very few words and, therefore, no interviews might have been possible. The other reason is that during the time he was a part of the film industry, directors were not the aggressive, media-friendly personalities they now are. Film journalism, per se, did not focus on interviews with directors though interviews of Guru Dutt, Mehboob and other contemporary directors are available in the archives. This is really sad considering that no account of the evolution of Indian cinema can be complete without an assessment of these films. They represent the pilgrimage of a true and dedicated artist. In them can be seen the maturing from poetry to philosophy, from emotion to music.

The second point to be noted is that even in edited collections of essays on Indian cinema and books devoted to Bombay cinema, scant recognition is given to the cinema of Bimal Roy.

In chapter 8, titled 'Affective Histories: Imagining Poverty in Popular Indian Cinema' by Esha Shah,[39] the author "looks at the affective narratives of poverty in Indian popular cinema in Hindi. It maps the way in which the 'poverty situations', as inter-subjective dramas, have been depicted in popular culture since independence."[40] Shah has picked some popular films made in Bombay since independence as an exemplary laboratory to map the historical shift in the depiction of poverty in the popular

---

[39] David Lewis, Dennis Rodgers, and Michael Woolcock, eds., *Popular Representations of Development: Insights from Novels, Films, Television and Social Media* (Abingdon, UK: Routledge, 2014).
[40] Ibid.

imagination. But in the section '1950s—Dignity of Labour', she covers only two films of the decade, namely *Naya Daur*[41] and *Mother India*, both made in 1957. How could the author leave out the classic *Do Bigha Zamin*? She clearly indicated that her analysis about "The 1950s to late 1960s, when the agrarian theme towards building a community—village and nation—dominated. This is when the conflicts between rural and urban, and rich and poor were popularly depicted in ways that morally privileged the rural and poor."[42] Does not *Do Bigha Zamin* fit into this classification of 'dignity of labour'?

The researcher Leda Ward in her paper 'Images of a Decolonizing India: Bollywood's Tawai'f and the Postcolonial Muslim'[43] has explored and analysed four of the most discussed courtesan films, namely *Devdas* (1955), *Sahib Bibi Aur Ghulam*[44] (1962), *Pakeezah*[45] (1972) and *Umrao Jaan*[46] (1981), exploring the identity of the courtesan as a dancer, and the social implications surrounding her dance allow Muslims to identify with her struggles and allow Indians of all religions to renegotiate the aftermath of the Partition.[47] Her thesis falls flat on its face because of the basic premise the character of the courtesan in *Devdas* is based on. Her first error is in misnaming the courtesan Chitralekha, while her real name, in the novel and in all its film remakes, is Chandramukhi. Second, though courtesans might have followed the practice of having their original names changed, nowhere in the novel or the film is Chandramukhi's communal origin expressed clearly. So, if one were to take her name as her identity, her religious root is Hindu and not Muslim. The third point that can evoke questions of authenticity and definition is about the deadline of 'After the Partition'. Sarat Chandra Chattopadhyay (1876–1938) wrote *Devdas* in 1901 at the tender age of 17. But he could not find a publisher for his manuscript till 1917. The rest is history. Bimal Roy's *Devdas* adhered to the original novel, barring one or two improvisations and the addition of song–dance numbers. This was during the colonial rule where 'Partition' does not enter into the time-frame or the story at all. Is this result of lack of proper research?

---

[41] *Naya Daur*—The new journey.

[42] Lewis, Rodgers, and Woolcock, *Popular Representations of Development*.

[43] Senior Seminar in Dance, Fall 2008, Thesis Director: Prof. L. Garafola.

[44] *Sahib Bibi aur Ghulam*—Name of the film—meaning 'the King, the Queen and the Jack in a pack of cards'.

[45] *Pakeezah*—means 'the pure one'.

[46] *Umrao Jaan*—Proper noun that is the name of the protagonist and also the title of the film.

[47] Lewis, Rodgers, and Woolcock, *Popular Representations of Development*.

Journal of the Moving Image (JMI), the journal of the Department of Film Studies, Jadavpur University, in its website,[48] states that it

> seeks to represent critical work on the state of contemporary screen cultures. There are many regions in our neighbourhood with large viewing populations, often with vast production infrastructures for film and televisions; but corresponding institutions or forums for critical engagement with such audio-visual regimes are still highly inadequate in South Asia.

Though in its introduction it insists that there is a special focus on India and South Asia and on issues of transnational media transactions, the journal offers a wide range of discussion on film and television from various parts of the world. JMI comes out in print and online.

However, a regular reader of this journal which works around a theme in every issue reveals that even a cursory study of Bimal Roy or any of his films is conspicuously absent in the journal. The themes vary from *Writing Histories for Indian Cinema* (MI9) through *Alternative Cinemas in India* (MI10) to the first issue released in 1999 which was a compilation of serious articles, book reviews and critical readings put together, each one equally informative, enriching and enlightening. The initial issues were focused on different aspects and features of the cinema of Satyajit Ray. The thematic perception came later. There was one issue dedicated to sound in cinema while a couple concentrated on different perspectives of television in India. It also publishes scholastic essays on international cinema and filmmakers. But for some reason or another, with the exception of 'Bollywood' or the South Indian mainstream, the annual journal has steered clear of Bimal Roy.

Deep Focus (recently went out of publication), which began as a film quarterly published from Bangalore by the Deep Focus Trust and edited by Georgekutty A.L., is a magazine on serious cinema covering Indian, Asian, South Asian, West Asian and international cinema in multiple ways: retrospective analyses, film theory, great masters—past and present—interviews, book reviews and so on. It was a magazine that went out of circulation and stopped publication several times between the late 1980s through 2014. It has stopped publication again. With an illustrious list of honorary editors, an editorial committee and an editorial advisory committee, *Deep Focus* was a much craved for film journal while it lasted. But as far as one can recollect from the archive, Bimal Roy has remained an absent entity.

---

[48] See http://www.jmionline.org/ (Accessed on 1 March 2017).

In its last avatar where the name was slightly changed to *Deep Focus Cinema*, the magazine sought to "explore the craftsmanship of all the professionals involved in the process of filmmaking to exhibition."[49] The mission statement went on to state that it would "provide a forum for deeper and dynamic engagement with the current debates on form, content, the grammar of cinema and censorship."[50] Its stress on different changes and innovations on regional cinema was commendable as was its underlining of new happenings in world cinema. But how Bimal Roy remained a persistent absence is a mystery. The sole exception I discovered in this magazine (March 2002, 76–79) was a very interesting article, *Bimal Roy—The Romantic Idealist*, by Maithili Rao that explored the romanticism in Bimal Roy's films that, contrary to common practice where the woman is presented through male eyes, places the woman at the heart of the romance through an exploration of films such as *Bandini, Madhumati,*[51] *Sujata* and *Devdas*.

The 'Presences'

All earlier books on different aspects of Indian cinema mentioned and described some of the early films of Bimal Roy, not as any exclusive analysis of his cinema but placed in perspective of other issues and features in Indian cinema belonging to a given period or filmmaking objectives, styles and approaches and so on. Among these, the ones that deserve mention are *The Moving Image—A Study of Indian Cinema* by Kishore Valicha,[52] *Seeing is Believing—Selected Writings of Cinema* by Chidananda Dasgupta,[53] *National Identity in Indian Popular Cinema (1947–1987)* by Sumita S. Chakravarty,[54] and *The Melodramatic Public—Film Form and Spectatorship in Indian Cinema* by Ravi Vasudevan.[55]

Dr Kishore Valicha, a professor of philosophy in Bombay's Khalsa College, won the National Award for the Best Book on Cinema for his book *The Moving Image*. He has explored Bimal Roy's *Devdas* (1955)

---

[49] See http://www.deepfocusonline.com/

[50] Ibid.; Masud, 'The Great Four of the Golden Fifties'.

[51] *Madhumati*—Name of the female protagonist and the title of the film.

[52] Kishore Valicha, *The Moving Image—A Study of Indian Cinema* (Hyderabad: Orient Longman, 1988).

[53] Chidananda Dasgupta, *Seeing is Believing—Selected Writings of Cinema* (Delhi: Penguin Books India, 2008).

[54] Sumita S. Chakravarty, *National Identity in Indian Popular Cinema, 1947–1987* (Delhi: Oxford University Press, 1996).

[55] Ravi Vasudevan, *The Melodramatic Public—Film Form and Spectatorship in Indian Cinema* (Delhi: Permanent Black, 2010).

by drawing parallels between the three characters in the story and the Radha–Krishna–Meera love triangle drawn from Indian mythology. "Devdas presented a deeply pessimistic view of human relations, of love and of life, an unmitigated philosophy of despair. It also typified an age that has almost departed."[56]

He has also discussed *Do Bigha Zamin* (1953) in view of the influence of neorealistic influence of Italian cinema on Bimal Roy. He states that this film

> revealed the early impact of neo-realist cinema in is simplicity of style and in its fairly authentic portrayal of the problems of the rural poor. The film tells of the struggle of a farmer to save his land from the clutches of a moneylender. One can see the genuineness that gives to the film a significant social purpose.[57]

Seeing is Believing, is a collection of previously published essays on Indian cinema. The essays are analytical, explorative and reveal the searching connections between our Indian cinema and society, literature, art, music and religion. Though this book has no exclusive chapter or even a segment dedicated to Bimal Roy, this senior film critic refers to Roy's milestone films such as *Do Bigha Zamin* and *Sujata* (1960), pointing out to Roy's beginning with a literature base, moving on to Italian neorealism with *Do Bigha Zamin* and again backtracking to literature with the latter film. Dasgupta states: "Roy brought a Bengali style of filmmaking to Bombay—gentle, relatively slow, free of crudities, concentrating on story development and other literary qualities without losing grip over film technique."[58] About *Sujata*, Dasgupta writes:

> The inhumanity of the caste system touched a chord in every heart and the film was an instant success. It was fully in tune with the optimist-reformist mood of the 1950s. Roy never quite gave up this course, despite changes in the country's situation and never played to the rising new gallery of the urban lumpen.[59]

National Identity in Indian Popular Cinema (1947–1987) by Sumita S. Chakravarty[60] is one of the very few serious works on Indian cinema that

---

[56] Valicha, *The Moving Image*, 49.

[57] Ibid., 80.

[58] Dasgupta, *Seeing is Believing*, 82.

[59] Ibid., 83.

[60] Chakravarty, *National Identity in Indian Popular Cinema*.

details an interesting and informative backgrounder on Bimal Roy's first independent directorial film *Udayer Pathey* (1944), later made into a Hindi version *Hamrahi*[61] (1945), and finds some common elements with Chetan Anand's *Neecha Nagar* (1946) and K.A. Abbas's *Dharti Ke Lal*,[62] pointing out that the Bengali version, *Udayer Pathey*, was a surprise hit, while the latter films did very badly in commercial terms. Chakravarty writes:

> Made at the height of the freedom movement, the film (*Udayer Pathey*) makes obvious use of symbols such as the national anthem, the Bengali literal and social reform tradition (photographs of Sri Aurobindo, Tagore, Vivekananda) as well as reference to an international socialist tradition (Bernard Shaw) to create the intellectual milieu of the protagonist Anup Lekhak (literally meaning Anup, the Writer).[63]

Chakravarty also goes on to discuss a rarely discussed Bimal Roy film *Parakh* (1960) which she curiously describes as 'social satire', which it is most certainly not. It is rather a precursor to the political campaigning based on a string of false promises made by contenders to a high seat which they have no intention of fulfilling if and after they win. This is beautifully explained through a village that stands as a metaphor for the nation.[64] *Sujata* occupies the maximum space in Chakarvarty's work who probes into, until then, unexplored areas of the film interpreted by her in new light.

Ravi Vasudevan devotes two pages to Bimal Roy's *Devdas*[65] where, under the sub-heading *Darshan*, he underscores the traditional end of deifying the male as an object of desire.

Poonam Arora in her paper 'Devdas: India's Emasculated Hero, Sado-Masochism and Colonialism'[66] concludes:

> In delineating the psycho-sexual dynamics of the *Devdas* narrative, this essay has tried to articulate the subjectivity of the colonial male subject. The enduring appeal of the *Devdas* narrative inheres not so much in its ability to represent the 'weak' hero of Indian cinema but in its subversive potential for indirectly opening up the space for a (tragic) resistance to imperialist gender ideology. It is through the latter that Devdas has become an ur-text of twentieth-century Indian culture.

---

[61] *Hamrahi*—Traveling companion.

[62] *Dharti Ke Lal*—Son of the earth.

[63] Chakravarty, *National Identity in Indian Popular Cinema*, 89–90.

[64] Ibid., 109–110.

[65] Vasudevan, *The Melodramatic Public*, 115–117.

[66] Arora, Poonam, *Devdas: India's Emasculated Hero, Sado-Masochism and Colonialism.*

She describes the character of Devdas as "[o]ne of the most enduring icons of the Indian film oeuvre is the aristocratic, lovelorn, sexually impotent, politically disengaged, and ultimately tragic hero." It may be pointed out that her paper deals with Sarat Chandra Chatterjee's novel *Devdas* and its various manifestations through Indian films and does not work exclusively on Bimal Roy's version of the film.

Rohit Phutela in a paper entitled 'Do Beegha Zameen: Textualizing Subalterns in Post-Independence Indian Cinema'[67] studies

> the important landmark in the Indian cinematic tradition adopting the neo-realism of the Italian cinema characterizing rebellion of the subalterns, which in this case, is by the migrant labourers studied as inland diaspora in the film *Do Beegha Zameen* directed by Bimal Roy, the architect of modern Indian cinema.

He adds that "the film tries to create a politically conscious milieu and an ethical awareness for social activism that are imperative to the proper functioning of a democratic nation. The melodrama and realism thus, accentuate the same national temperament."

Omar Ahmed in his essay 'Do Bigha Zamin' posted in *Senses of Cinema*[68] states:

> [T]hough it (*Do Bigha Zamin*) was intended as a melodrama aimed at a mainstream audience, the artists involved with the production of the film were not only inspired by a common ideological belief in socialism that defied the conservatism of Indian cinema they succeeded in demonstrating how genre could be subverted and adopted as a tool to address wider inequalities and afflictions.

Ahmed goes on to add that Ray's endorsement of Bimal Roy's introduction of 'realism' to mainstream Indian cinema suggests that the kind of cinema that went before was devoid of realism. However, according to Ahmed, who does not agree entirely with Ray's perspective,

> Roy was deeply moved by how film makers like De Sica and Rossellini had effectively rewritten the rules of cinema but the shattering realisation was that such an ideological breakthrough had occurred within the

---

[67] Rohit Phutela, '*Do Beegha Zameen*: Textualizing Subalterns in Post-Independence Indian Cinema', *Journal of Literature, Media and Cultural Studies* IV, no. 7&8 (January–December 2012); 195–204.

[68] Omar Ahmed, 'Do Bigha Zamin', *Senses of Cinema* (27 January 2009).

parameters of the mainstream. Roy understood how De Sica had made the seemingly impossible marriage of art and commerce a daring reality in the face of a bankrupt Italian society, and he had done so on his own personal terms.

Amir Ullah Khan and Bibek Debroy in their brilliant study, Indian Economic Transition Through Bollywood Eyes: Hindi Films and How They Have Reflected Changes in India's Political Economy,[69] use a chosen list of Hindi films and try and discover their connect with the country's economic policies. They argue that "Bollywood after all is not just a dream factory that belts out trashy material in the fashion of assembly line production." This list of films taken for discussion, analysis and exploration of how economic issues and policies intercut into the themes of these films includes Bimal Roy's Do Bigha Zamin, which according to Roy and Khan is one of the most realistic portraits of its times. "One of the issues that the film talks in the first half of the film is the issue of property, a shadow of the Requisition and Acquisition of Immovable Property Act, 1952. However, one wonders what made the writers exclude Bimal Roy's Naukri[70] (1954) from the study. The film dealt with the then-rare topic of the educated unemployed who migrate to the city with hope in their hearts but learn differently when they actually land in the big city."

The Man Who Spoke in Pictures: Bimal Roy by Rinki Roy Bhattacharya[71] is perhaps the first book exclusively focused on different aspects of the filmmaker's life, happenings and approach to cinema, contributed by a wide range of intellectuals, writers, journalists, film technicians and members of the cast and crew who worked with him.

This is the second book on Bimal Roy edited by Rinki Roy Bhattacharya. The earlier one was perhaps, in filmy parlance, a rough cut of this new one. This version has better production values and famous contributors and is comparatively better edited and proofread than the book that went before. Rinki Roy Bhattacharya happens to be the eldest child of the filmmaker's four children, three daughters and one son. She has been a journalist, documentary filmmaker and author and editor of books.

---

[69] Amir Ullah Khan and Bibek Debroy, Indian Economic Transition Through Bollywood Eyes: Hindi Films and How They Have Reflected Changes in India's Political Economy, (working paper 1, August 2002).

[70] Naukri—The job.

[71] Rinki Roy Bhattacharya, ed., The Man Who Spoke in Pictures—Bimal Roy (New Delhi: Penguin-Viking, 2009).

The Man Who Spoke in Pictures: Bimal Roy is divided into three sections in terms of the geographical roots of Bimal Roy's film landscape. The first features his work in 'Bengal' where contributors are drawn from his initial Bengal experience. The second moves chronologically to 'Bombay' where the filmmaker spent a major part of his life and passed away in 1966. The third deals with some brilliant inputs under the section 'Beyond Borders' where scholars from beyond Indians shores have contributed significantly to shed light on untouched areas of the filmmaker's genius, throwing up a world of information and education.

The book opens with some introductory essays comprised of a biographical sketch by Rinki Roy Bhattacharya, followed by a small nostalgic piece by her son Aditya Bhattacharya and Bimal Roy's very brief jury address, delivered by the filmmaker at the First International Film Festival in Moscow in July 1959. This is followed by an introduction in which the editor traces the uphill climb she had to make while working on the book, the obstacles she had to overcome and the hurdles that came her way, surprising the reader with an input from Nayantara Sahgal, a well-known author, who has not seen a single film of Bimal Roy! Bhattacharya requested Sahgal to watch some of Bimal Roy's films and the latter's reactions, set out in 'Discovering Bimal Roy'[72], and her reading of *Do Bigha Zamin* and *Devdas* give a perspective of a viewer who saw the films 50 years after their release.

Internationally renowned contributors to this valuable archival document, however, have invested the book with inconsistency because many of them seem to have been chosen to add to the celebrity value of this edited edition than for the content of their contribution. Amit Chaudhuri's input, 'A Quiet Man',[73] for instance, is a rather watered down repetition of the story of *Udayer Pathey* which he happened to catch at Kolkata's Chaplin theatre in 2002. Mahasweta Devi's 'Prelude'[74] is just one page of reminiscences that do not contribute to the content in any meaningful manner. 'Bimal Roy'[75] by Asit Baran, a celebrated singing-actor who played an important role in Roy's *Parineeta*, is quoted in a footnote as "from an informal chat with Rinki Roy Bhattacharya." One wonders how ethical or logical it is from a literary point

---

[72] Ibid., 54–58.

[73] Amit Chaudhuri, 'A Quiet Man', in *The Man Who Spoke in Pictures*, ed. Rinki Bhattacharya (New Delhi: Penguin-Viking, 2009), 5–8.

[74] Mahasweta Devi, 'Prelude', in *The Man Who Spoke in Pictures*, ed. Rinki Bhattacharya (New Delhi: Penguin-Viking, 2009), 1–2.

[75] Asit Baran, 'Bimal Roy', in *The Man Who Spoke in Pictures*, ed. Rinki Bhattacharya (New Delhi: Penguin-Viking, 2009), 18–19.

of view to include an 'informal chat' with the editor in a book that has high archival value. Ritwik Ghatak's 'My Memories of Bimal Roy'[76] is just a few paragraphs picked and translated from 1975 Bengali film journal. The piece says things that have been said a thousand times before and which Bimal Roy fans have known for ages.

Naseeruddin Shah's 'Actors in Bimal Roy's Films'[77] takes half the space to describe what acting is all about and prefacing his central topic but he has taken pains to do his homework well. A.K. Bir's 'The Visionary'[78] offers a very good insight into films from the perspective of a cinematographer. Bimal Roy's protégés such as Nabendu Ghosh and Gulzar recall their sweet associations with the great director, while Iqbal Masud in 'Discovering India' briefly recalls his experience of Bimal Roy through *Hamrahi*. Kishore Chatterjee's 'Mozart and Madhumati'[79] is a bit too obtuse for readers who are ignorant about Western classical composers.

The most outstanding section is 'Beyond Borders' that provides the 'outsider's view' on the filmmaker from different standpoints. Among the most illuminating are 'The Politics of Costumes in the Films of Bimal Roy' by Claire Wilkinson-Weber, 'Bringing Bengal Renaissance to Bollywood' by Manju Seal, 'Teaching Bimal Roy's Devdas in New Jersey' by Paula H. Mayhew and 'Bimal Roy—Master of the Erotic' by Soudhamini. Not that they are good because they have been authored by film scholars from beyond borders or that their writing style is particularly fluent, but because they offer a completely different take on the filmmaker in all his dimensions.

Not all the inputs have been properly edited and proofread. The most glaring example of bad editing is in Shyam Benegal's 'Bimal Roy: A Filmmaker's Perspective' that, says the editor in a footnote, was originally an interview that has obviously turned into an article that reads badly.

Bimal Roy's Madhumati—Untold Stories from Behind the Scenes by Rinki Roy[80] is authored by his eldest daughter Rinki who edited the earlier book. The book charts an unpredictable journey, not of a given film or a filmmaker per se, but about the story that actually created the film and

---

[76] Ritwik Ghatak, 'My Memories of Bimal Roy', in *The Man Who Spoke in Pictures*, ed. Rinki Bhattacharya (New Delhi: Penguin-Viking, 2009), 6.

[77] Naseeruddin Shah, 'Actors in Bimal Roy's Films', in *The Man Who Spoke in Pictures*, ed. Rinki Bhattacharya (New Delhi: Penguin-Viking, 2009), 92–101.

[78] A.K. Bir, 'The Visionary', in *The Man Who Spoke in Pictures*, ed. Rinki Bhattacharya (New Delhi: Penguin-Viking, 2009), 102–106.

[79] Kishore Chatterjee, 'Mozart and Madhumati', in *The Man Who Spoke in Pictures*, ed. Rinki Bhattacharya (New Delhi: Penguin-Viking, 2009), 84–87.

[80] Rinki Roy Bhattacharya, *Bimal Roy's Madhumati—Untold Stories from Behind the Scenes* (New Delhi: Rupa Publications, 2014).

the long journey across a span of time—57 years—and space, across roads and ways rarely stepped on before the film was shot in these hilly pastures, narrow rivulets and streams, difficult in those days to access much less shoot in.

Madhumati is Bimal Roy's most commercially successful film in his entire career. Though his admirers were taken aback by his sudden entry into a film that was spilling over with what appeared to be commercial elements with a compromising storyline, *Madhumati* went on to bag the National Award for the Best Feature Film in Hindi. It also won nine Filmfare Awards that included Best Film, Best Director, Best Music Director, Best Actor, Best Supporting Actor, Best Female Playback Singer, Best Dialogue, Best Editing and Best Cinematographer. Whew! Critically, *Madhumati* remains the least written about film by researchers and film scholars in India and beyond, perhaps because the mind of the discerning film scholars who mentally place the label of 'filmmaker of social relevance and literary adaptations' on Bimal Roy, find it difficult to place *Madhumati* within Roy's oeuvre and style.

Rinki Roy Bhattacharya's book, resulting from a long and arduous journey into the past and to faraway and rough terrains, offers a glimpse into the painstaking research—both field and reference-centric—Bimal Roy and his team were prepared to take just to shoot some segments of a given film whose fate at the box office no one knew. Over the three lengthy chapters of this 196-page book, we get to read some sad stories of people who felt marginalized by neglect, not because of the filmmaker they worked with but by someone else within the team.

In the section 'Backstage Workers' of Chapter 1—'Untold Stories'— we are introduced to one Sakharam Borsey of Dhule District who began working as a houseboy in editor Hrishikesh Mukherjee's large household and became assistant editor to Mukherjee in course of time. Borsey broke the reality behind the editing of *Madhumati* insisting that though Mukherjee won the Filmfare Award for Best Editing, it was another man named Das Dhaimade who had edited 60 per cent of *Madhumati*! Sakharam who had taught himself Bengali insisted that the editing of the film was handled by Das Dhaimade and that he (Sakharam) had assisted Das Dhaimade. Yet, the credits of Madhumati showed him as associate editor and not editor, a sad fact that "rankles him even after 55 years," writes Bhattacharya.[81]

Two other forgotten names the book mentions are of two sound engineers Essa M. Suratwalla and Dinshaw Billimoria. It was confirmed by a

---

[81] Ibid., 63.

very reliable source, Debu Sen, one of Bimal Roy's chief assistants, that though Essa *bhai* was in charge of the sound recording of *Madhumati*, his name did not feature as an audiographer in the *Madhumati* booklet![82]

The physical and geographical journey charts little-known terrains such as Bhowali, Gorakhal, Gethia, Navghar in Raigadh District, perhaps Haldwani and two places that are now famous tourist resorts—Ranikhet and Nainital—that begins in second part of the Chapter 1 called *The Start of a Long Journey*. Bhattacharya travelled the entire course with her journalist friend Maithili Rao who shares, other than friendship, her friend's respect for everything Bimal Roy and his cinema stood for. 'Recasting' is filled with anecdotal quotes from people associated with *Madhumati* such as Pran, Dilip Kumar and Vyjayanthimala. The author also embarks on different aspects of the actual filming of *Madhumati* gleaned from different sources she accessed through her focused attention to the responsibility she had undertaken to finish this difficult task.

The book also contains an archival review of the film written by the famous Baburao Patel in the magazine *Film India* published in October 1958. Anik Dutta, a filmmaker and related through family links to the Roy family, has written a brief but interesting afterword to the book. Sounak Chacraverti, a cinema and culture archivist, has orchestrated an interesting filmography of Bimal Roy by dividing his work 'before *Madhumati*' and 'after *Madhumati*'. Other interesting bonuses that the book offers are the complete lyrics of all the songs from the film printed phonetically in English for the Hindi original and the synopsis given in the original booklet when the film premiered in Bombay. The appendix that profiles the Filmfare Award winners is redundant because these are available across the Internet and did not need repetition. The details on the cast and credits of the technical crew are a necessity that a book on a single film cannot do without. A very good addition is Maithili Rao's 'Madhumati's Place in Film History' that places the ghost film and the gothic in perspective in relation to *Madhumati*. Amitabh Bachchan's brief tribute is an also-ran and has been added perhaps to raise the market value of this book, but in effect tends to dilute its real value. Repetition of quotes and passages from her earlier works on Bimal Roy, going back to the quotes from Anwesha Acharya and Dr Clare Wilkinson-Weber, dilutes the essence and value of the book to a small extent. The black-and-white illustrations enhance the written text. This book can be a valuable addition to film libraries across the world.

---

[82] Ibid., 66.

CHAPTER BREAKS

Introduction—This sets out the background, the questions, and the outline of this book and spells out the purpose of this study, its aims, and a review of related literature on Bimal Roy and his cinema, as well as chapter breaks and their elaboration.

Chapter I:—Bimal Roy, Life, Influences and the *Auteur* (1909–66).

Chapter II: Literary Adaptations—*Udayer Pathey*, *Do Bigha Zamin* and *Baap Beti*. Most of his films reveal the versatility of his choice in the literature he tended to explore through his films. *Udayer Pathey* is his first directorial and only Bengali language film in his entire career, though he made a Hindi version one year later; *Do Bigha Zamin* (1953) is a script created by Salil Chowdhury adapted from an emotionally moving long poem authored by Rabindranath Tagore that, contrary to intellectual impressions of Tagore, is conspicuously Marxist in message and theme; *Baap Beti* (1954) is his only film loosely adapted from a Western literary piece, namely, a Guy de Maupassant story called *Simon's Papa*.

Though these films cannot be termed 'literature' in its popularly accepted meaning, they scan different forms of literature that do not fall within the other chapters in this work which are all based on original, existing and noted Bengali literary works.

Chapter III: Sarat Chandra Chattopadhyay—*Parineeta*, *Biraj Bahu* and *Devdas*.

Chapter IV: The Woman Question—*Sujata* and *Bandini*.

Chapter V: The Role of Music, Song and Dance.

Summing Up: Was Bimal Roy a Displaced 'Outsider'?

CONCLUSION

The cinema of Bimal Roy was born and evolved in a world where the phrases 'parallel cinema', 'art house cinema' and 'mainstream' cinema were vaguely entering into discussions and debates on Indian cinema, especially following the release and very slow and steady rise of the turning point film *Pather Panchali* (1955) that released two years after Roy made his epoch-making *Do Bigha Zamin* (1953), steadily establishing his personal signature through his films. Read in perspective, Bimal Roy was a 'mainstream' filmmaker when these films were better known as commercial films. His cinema neatly fit into the groove of box office demands such as a solid storyline—a strong point of commercial cinema at that time—saleable actors, tightly knit script, melodious musical score and memorable lyrics, excellent dance numbers choreographed by renowned dance masters of the time and performed by dancer-actresses who knew their job, a bit of humour here and there and good technique in terms of sound, cinematography, editing and art direction. So, what is it that sets him apart more than five decades since he directed his last film *Bandini* that merits an entire book on his cinema? The answer to this significant question will emerge from an analysis of his films in the following chapters.

I. BIMAL ROY—LIFE, INFLUENCES AND THE AUTEUR (1909–1966)

Bimal Chandra Roy was born on 12 July 1909 in Suapur village of East Bengal, now in Bangladesh. The fourth of seven brothers, Bimal Roy belonged to a family of aristocratic zamindars.[1] The affluence of the family in those days placed leisure above hard work. Roy began his education at home, which continued till he went to Dacca (now called Dhaka), coming home to spend his holidays in the village. Ever since he was a boy, Roy was an avid photographer. He took up science as his stream after high school. A little-known fact about him is that he did female roles in plays like *Misar Kumari*.[2] These were pleasant boat journeys across rivers, offering an original audiovisual landscape that found their reflection in many of his films.[3] However, his father's demise was followed by economic disruption, which made everyone look out for a means of living. The estate manager is said to have thrown him and his family out of the estate upon his father's

---

[1] Zamindar formed an exploitative class of landlords—rich, powerful and oppressive—who ruled over the village community and extracted work from them without pay and tax from the proceeds of the sales of crops they grew on their own land.

[2] *Misar Kumari* is the name of a famous Bengali play that was translated into *The Princess of Egypt*.

[3] F. Rangoonwalla, *Life and Work—Bimal Roy: A Critical Study* (NFAI, 1991).

death. The family made its way to Calcutta, like the many migrants who, in the twentieth-century India, made a similar journey.

By the end of 1930, all the seven brothers had migrated to Calcutta. A business in transport set back the family into better days, some of the brothers joined British firms. Roy's interest in photography on the one hand and cinema on the other would often take him for long walks towards the film studios at Tollygunge. His pursuit of a career in films finally got him a job with New Theatres, first as an apprentice and then as an assistant cameraman. From assisting Nitin Bose as a cameraman, Bimal Roy graduated to a full-fledged cameraman for Pramathesh Chandra Barua's (henceforth, P.C. Barua) Hindi version of *Devdas*.

Bimal Roy started working as an assistant cameraman and a cameraman on documentaries in 1932–1933, but his foray into cinema effectively commenced when he was hired as a publicity photographer by P.C. Barua, whose *Devdas* (1935) would become a landmark film. At Calcutta's famous New Theatres, which helped to define cinema for a *bhadralok* (gentleman) audience, Roy was engaged as an assistant to cameraman Nitin Bose, where he soon won a reputation for his command over lighting and composition. He worked on close to 10 films as a cameraman before venturing forth as a director with his film, *Udayer Pathey* (1944, Bengali; remade in Hindi as *Hamrahi*, 1945), which in many ways echoes the aesthetic, moral and political sensibility so strongly on display in his films of the 1950s.

The collapse of New Theatres, the pressures of World War II upon Calcutta and the advent of Bombay cinema heralded a new phase in the life of Bimal Roy. His own migration to Bombay, one might say with a touch of exaggeration, precipitated his understanding of the migration from rural areas to urban centres as one of the great social phenomena of independent India. Bimal Roy's social sensibility and humanity, thus, are palpably on display in the superb film *Udayer Pathey*, which won him many international accolades.[4]

After more than three decades in films, Bimal Roy, a chain smoker, passed away in his Bandra bungalow in January 1966 of lung cancer. His banner, Bimal Roy Productions, was already teetering under a burden of heavy debts incurred during his illness, and following the fire at Mohan Studios that left almost everything in cinders it limped for a while and then stopped. *Do Dooni Char*[5] was completed and released after his death but flopped at the box office.

---

[4] Vinay Lal, *Bimal Roy* (2008). Available at https://www.sscnet.ucla.edu/southasia/Culture/Cinema/bimalroy.htm

[5] *Do Dooni Char* (Two into two is equal to four).

None of his four children have taken up their father's vocation. One of his daughters, Yashodhara, was an occasional costume designer for films and television. The eldest daughter Rinki, once married to Basu Bhattacharya and later estranged, did an occasional video documentary, toyed with journalism, edited some very archivally valuable books on her father, authored a very good book on *Madhumati* and founded and runs the Bimal Roy Memorial Trust to create an archive dedicated to her father's works. The Trust bestows awards annually on talented people in the film industry who belonged to the Bimal Roy era and thereafter for their contribution to Indian cinema. Joy, his only son, worked under Shyam Benegal for a while and then turned his attention to television and advertising. He made a documentary on his father, *Remembering Bimal Roy*, which brought back memories of another day, another man and another cinema. In short, none of his children have shown the brilliance of their father. Aparajita Sinha, the youngest of his three daughters, founded another Bimal Roy Foundation in Hyderabad where his films are screened from time to time alongside seminars and presentations on his cinema.

Manobina Roy, his wife, gave up what could have been a brilliant career in black-and-white photography to commit herself to her family. She also wrote a couple of books in Bengali and wrote in English for periodicals like *The Illustrated Weekly* for a brief while. She was a solid pillar of support for Roy right through his ups and downs. After Roy's demise, she tried her best to keep her children away from legal wrangling and to keep the Bimal Roy banner flying, but in vain. However, the money from his films keeps flowing in. His rented bungalow that stood on Hill Road in Bandra, an elitist Mumbai suburb, has now been converted into a multi-storeyed residential complex, destroying forever the dream of his widow to turn it into an archival museum dedicated to Roy. But the family has been given a small, self-complete bungalow that stands on one side of this complex where his two daughters and only son live together in harmony.

THE BIRTH OF THE 'AUTEUR' IN FILM THEORY

According to Dictionary.com, the word 'auteur' means "a filmmaker whose individual style and complete control over all elements of production give a film its personal and unique stamp." According to the *Random House Dictionary*, 'auteur' has been derived by the French from the original Latin and means 'originator'; in French, it literally means 'author' and has a wider connotation to include writers, poets, playwrights, artists etc. who are committed to creative forms of writing and expression. However, 'auteur' exclusively refers to a film director. Another meaning refers to 'a filmmaker', usually "a director who exercises creative control over his or her works and has a strong personal style," or "a director whose creative influence on the film is so great for him or her to be considered its 'author'."

The auteur theory draws on the work of a group of cinema enthusiasts who wrote for *Cahiers du Cinéma* and argued that films should reflect a director's personal vision. They offered examples of internationally renowned filmmakers such as Stanley Kubrick, Akira Kurosawa, Nicholas Ray, Erich von Stroheim, Alfred Hitchcock, Howard Hawks and Jean Renoir as absolute 'auteurs' of their films.[6] André Bazin, co-founder of the *Cahiers*, offered a forum for auteurism to flourish.[7] But he also warned against the danger of excesses that could possibly lead to a 'cult of personality'.

Another perspective from Alexandre Astruc expresses the notion of 'camera-stylo' or 'camera pen' which encourages directors to wield the camera as writers use pens to guard against the hindrances of traditional storytelling. Although François Truffaut and other members of the *Cahiers* accepted that making films required a technical and industrial infrastructure, it needed to work towards an ideal encouraging the director to use the technical and commercial apparatus at his or her disposal as the writer uses the pen and through what he called mise en scène, and place the stamp of his or her vision on the final film in effect, subordinating the role of a screenwriter.

The 'auteur critic' takes on the concomitant responsibility of honouring all films of a single director through a systematic reading of each. This helps in bringing out characteristic themes, structures and formal qualities.[8] In this light, the idea of 'auteur' does not solve all problems, nor does it provide answers to questions raised about the director's claims to authorship. It offers a way of looking at the films of a given director who has produced considerable work, quality being more important than quantity; not that any director actually comes forward to claim authorship. The critic decides whether a director lends his works to an 'auteur' critique or not. Since they recognized the difficulty of a director to reach a utopian ideal completely, because cinema was a fluid medium where the participation of many people was mandatory, they valued the works of those filmmakers who came close to the ideal they had created for the films they directed.[9]

The definition of an 'auteur' is a subject of debate since the 1940s. It almost coincides with the beginning of Bimal Roy's career as a director. Two major theorists of auteur criticism namely Bazin and Roger Leenhardt state that it is the director who injects and infuses life into his or her film(s) and uses the film to express his or her thoughts, beliefs, ideas and feelings about

---

[6] See https://en.wikipedia.org/wiki/Auteur_theory (Accessed on 1 November 2016).
[7] Andre Bazin, "La Politique Des Auteurs." *Cahiers du Cinema* 70 (1957).
[8] Alexander Astruc, 'Fire and Ice', *Cahiers du Cinema* 1, no. 1 (1966): 70–71.
[9] Ibid. See https://en.wikipedia.org/wiki/Auteur_theory

the subject he or she has chosen for his or her film(s), and the consolidation of his or her films offers a world view of the director as an auteur who uses lighting, cinematography, production design, music, editing and characterizations with actors to add to this vision.[10]

Peter Wollen and his contemporaries, however, held that filmmaking is a collective process and it is not a wise decision to look for the director's personality as embedded in a series of film texts. One should try and appreciate the director not as a meaning-maker but as a puller of several strings pertaining to a network of meaning which is produced by a larger system (Wollen 1981).[11] This group also took the 'auteur theory' as a 'reading strategy' (Staiger 2003: 45).[12]

Taking these views together, Edward Buscombe puts in his own view. According to Buscombe, cinema is an institution rooted in society. This presumes the consideration of exploring the effects of cinema on society, the effects of society on cinema and a film's effect on other films vis-à-vis ideology, economics and industrial logic. He insists on the finer codes originating in and outside of a film before venturing into auteur studies.[13] Stated simply, this theory believes that cinema does not exist in a vacuum and is a part of the society we live in. Therefore, any film reflects society in some way or the other depending on what the film deals with. Also, the film itself leaves its imprint on society which includes the director's world view, ideology and beliefs that get reflected in his or her film(s) some way or the other.

Another theorist Janet Staiger[14] argues that the author functions through a "repetitive citation of performative statement of authoring choice." So, according to her, it is this 'authoring choice' that produces the author. Does auteurship matter? According to Staiger, it indeed matters as shown by different official perspectives that have characterized or formulated the auteur as an 'origin', 'personality', 'sociology of production', 'signature', 'reading strategy' and, more recently, 'techniques of self' which allow for the foregrounding of minority expression.[15]

The common feature that emerges out of all these diverse auteur theories is that they are all based on the assumption that an 'auteur' must have

---

[10] Kristin Thompson and David Bordwell. *Film History: An Introduction*, 3rd ed. (New York: McGraw-Hill, 2010), 381–383.

[11] Wollen, 1981 cited in Sumit Dey.

[12] Sumit Dey, 'Authoring Space, Gender and the Past: A Film Called Shuvo Muhurat', *Journal of the Moving Image*, no. 10 (September 2012). Available at www.jmionline.org

[13] Edward Buscombe, *The Construction of Authorship—Textual Appreciation of Law and Literature*, eds. Martha Woodmansee and Peter Jaszee (Dublin, NC: Duke University Press, 1994).

[14] Staiger, 'Authorship Approaches', 27–60.

[15] Ibid.

a body of work in order to lend his or her works to an 'auteur' reading. This means that if a director has directed only one or two films during his or her career, irrespective of the archival and/or posterity value of these films, his or her work cannot become a subject for auteur study. The number of films a director has directed must be substantial enough to merit 'auteurship'.

Film authorship has shaped our understanding of many film cultures around the world and across different media beyond the cinema because the models of auteurism have evolved from France to the United States and through national cinemas from China and India to Iran and Denmark. What auteurism means in theory and in practice has changed significantly due to the pressures of post-structuralist theory, feminist interventions, cultural and racial distinctions and the challenges of new media, but it remains a central topic of debate in film and media studies.[16]

THE 'AUTEUR' IN INDIAN CINEMA

The term 'auteur theory' describes a basic principle and a method which, stated simply, is based on the idea of 'personal' authorship in the cinema. To simplify the concept further, one can cite the example of an 'author' in literature who, with his or her contribution in the form of a 'body' of significant work, can be recognized and identified easily through his or her language, style, plot-lines, approach, subject matter, content and, perhaps, resolution. Even when an author spans all categories of writing from short stories to novels through poetry, drama, lyrics and essays, he or she is recognized among his or her readers by his or her work per se. The best example of all times within Indian literature is Rabindranath Tagore. One line from his song carries his inimitable signature through lyrics, music, rhythm and beats across time and space, and language and culture.

This is easier done in cinema than in literature because cinema is an audiovisual medium embellished and enriched through other technical qualities such as editing, cinematography, music, dance, dialogue, song lyrics and so on. Although ever since the 1970s and the 1980s the term 'auteur' began to fade out within Indian cinema with the onslaught of Western cultural imports on the one hand and globalization of cinema on the other, this was not the case when cinema belonged to the black-and-white era. That was an era when the audience could identify the filmmaker from a single frame of a film, especially when it had seen other works by the same filmmaker. This one frame could be a small clip from a song picturization, a line of dialogue, the production design, the music, the cast and

---

[16] Timothy Corrigan, 'Auteurism'. Available at http://www.oxfordbibliographies.com/view/document/obo-9780199791286/obo-9780199791286-0009.xml (Accessed on 1 May 2015).

crew details or just anything. Some examples to this are films directed by P.C. Barua under the New Theatres banner which were not only critically acclaimed but also commercially successful. These belong to the archive of some of the best films within the history of Indian cinema. Raj Kapoor began a production house and kept away from directing his own films. But he lends himself to the title of 'auteur' even as a producer–actor because all films made under the RK banner, which itself had its distinct logo, have a common pattern in terms of storylines, music and song, dance numbers, characterization, narrative style and so on.

Before any Indian directors could qualify as an 'auteur', the studio system that preceded independent filmmaking evolved into something like what we know as 'auteur' within cinema. Each studio reflected its own genre of films and became known by that specific genre. This not only cut down the competition among the studios but also created and popularized different genres within cinema.

The birth of the studio system of production unwittingly took place with Phalke setting up his production house in his plot of land and house at Nashik. Many of these production studios achieved success in the 1930s. The big companies of the 1930s, like the Phalke Company before them, seemed to be extensions of the joint family system. Many of the companies had, in fact, clusters of relatives. Each studio had a wide range of personnel and almost never had to run to outsiders for help or services. Each had its own laboratory, studio or studios and preview theatre. Among these, the ones in Mumbai were The Imperial Films Company (*Alam Ara*[17]); Sagar Movietone (Chimanlal Desai—*Jagirdar*[18]); Wadia Movietone, founded by J.B.H. Wadia, specializing in stunt films and noted for its introduction of Nadia in the *Hunterwali*[19] series of films; Minerva Movietone, founded by Sohrab Modi, specializing in historical spectacles like *Sikander*;[20] Ranjit Movietone founded by Chandulal Shah with films like *Gunasundari* (Why Husbands Go Astray) and some others. During the 1930s, Ranjit Movietone maintained a payroll of about 300 artists, technicians and others. It produced Hindi, Punjabi and Gujarati films.

New Theatres, founded by B.N. Sircar, was a production banner that, with its two studios, changed the history of Bengali and Hindi cinema

---

[17] *Alam Ara*, an Urdu–Hindi feature film, was India's first talkie produced and directed by Ardeshir Irani. *Alam Ara*, released in 1931, means 'The ornament of the world'.

[18] *Jagirdar* means something similar to the landlord. It refers to a person who gives a *jagir*—a definite piece of land or a type of feudal land grant in South Asia bestowed by a monarch to a feudal superior in recognition of his administrative and/or military service.

[19] *Hunterwali*—the woman who wields a hunter as a weapon of attack, self-defence, etc.

[20] *Sikander*—Hindi equivalent for Alexander the Great, the Greek conqueror.

forever. Sircar, a foreign-trained engineer, drawn to filmmaking by sheer accident, produced 150 films under his production banner in Hindi, Bengali and even Tamil, making path-breaking films like *Devdas* and introducing the audience to some of the greatest talents of Indian cinema. P.C. Barua, R.C. Boral, Pankaj Mullick, Bimal Roy, K.L. Saigal and Nitin Bose are just a few names that found their feet and bloomed in New Theatres. B.N. Sircar founded the New Theatres studio and banner at a time when cinema in the country was going through its first paces. The studio is now a ghost of its former self, but the history it created through the benevolence of its founder can never be forgotten. Like the roaring lion of the Metro Goldwyn Mayer Studios Inc., the elephant on the New Theatres logo was a hallmark of quality films.

The unique selling point of a New Theatres production was (a) a solid storyline, (b) lilting songs and background music, (c) good sound technique and (d) good acting. Sircar never interfered with the making of any film. Afterwards, he would watch it at a morning screening at New Cinema in Calcutta. Among the 150 films under the New Theatres banner made in several languages over a span of 24 years (1931–1955), it would be difficult to sift the wheat from the chaff and say, 'These are the best'. From *Doctor* (1940) to *Pratisruti*[21] (1941) to *Udayer Pathey* (1944) to *Anjangarh* (1948), and from *Puran Bhagat*[22] (Hindi—1933) to *Vidyapati*[23] (Hindi—1937) to *Devdas* (Bengali—1935) to *Mukti*[24] (1937), every New Theatres' film marks a pillar in the architectural wonder of Indian cinema.

New interests and needs in the studios grew into new departments. Bombay Talkies maintained a school for children of staff members, which also became a school for child actors. Prized possessions of the costume department became a 'museum' of historic costumes. Books acquired for reference became a 'library' of 3,000 books and manuscripts. Prabhat Film Company also had its own 'zoo' including tigers, deer and birds. It also had a swimming pool for recreation as well as production needs. Bombay Talkies had its own physician who operated a clinic and also supervised the

---

[21] *Pratisruti*—Bengali equivalent of the English word 'promise'.

[22] *Puran Bhakt* or *Puran Bhagat* was the son of a king who became a saint when he grew up. Debaki Bose made a beautiful musical on this saint produced by New Theatres and released in 1933. It marked Debaki Bose's directorial debut and the screen appearance of the blind singer K.C. Dey who was an uncle to Manna Dey.

[23] *Vidyapati* is a 1937 film directed by Debaki Bose. The story is about the Maithili poet and Vaishnava saint Vidyapati.

[24] *Mukti* means 'freedom'.

sanitary practices of the canteen that served breakfast, lunch and dinner, and also midnight snacks for scene builders.

The scenario changed in the 1940s because it attracted new entrepreneurs and new capital. There was an influx of new producers. Most of them had no studio but could rent one. They had no laboratory but such services could be purchased. Similarly, they had no acting staff but this could be solved by hiring famous actors and actresses in exchange for paying them more than they were getting from the studio. Stars suddenly found that they could earn more in a one-picture contract than they earned as salary from the studio that employed them. They began to leave big studios and the practice of freelancing grew rapidly. Directors and songwriters were similarly lured by large fees in freelance assignments.

In the early years of World War II, the big studios began to find their self-sufficiency ebbing. They sometimes had to bargain competitively for hiring stars and then wait for their turn. By the end of 1941, various stars were found freelancing for three or four pictures simultaneously. As a result, production schedules slowed down and old companies could no longer afford to maintain large full-time staff. They began to divest themselves of overhead costs to evade box-office disasters. The emergence of the concept of independent filmmakers began to change the pattern of filmmaking and films, and the star system slowly replaced the studio system. But the studio system created its own distinct auteurs who, following the decline and collapse of the studio system, created their distinct signature through their films independent of their studio affiliation.

There are several directors in Indian cinema who are considered to be 'auteurs', and rightly so. Among them, the pioneer is Dadasaheb Phalke who made his mark with mythologicals in silent movies where, later, live music was performed by a live orchestra, sitting in the orchestra 'well' like in theatres. Himanshu Roy created city-based, modern plots for his films, and in *Karma* (1933) he also introduced a long kissing scene between the hero and the heroine. Other such pioneers are P.C. Barua, Mehboob Khan, V. Shantaram, Sohrab Modi, Guru Dutt, Bimal Roy, Raj Kapoor and so on. There was no distinction between 'art' and 'commercial' cinema, and if one looks back, one can define these films as a very happy mix of the commercial, a strong narrative and a social message interwoven with imaginative merging of form and content. They successfully expressed their personal vision through subjective expression.

Noted among them is V. Shantaram who began his career in Prabhat Film Company. A brilliant Indian director, social reformer and technical pioneer in film, and a studio mogul, V. Shantaram, travelled to Germany to process and print his (and India's) first colour film, *Sairandhri*[25] (1933), and was greatly impressed by German cinema. *Amrit Manthan* (1934),[26] which he made on his return, reflects that influence in both Shantaram's choice of subject (an action-packed tale of palace intrigue) and his effective use of expressionist visual techniques to heighten suspense. Shantaram's work with Prabhat Film Company included *Ayodhyecha Raja* (The King of Ayodhya, 1932) which was produced in both Marathi and Hindi versions. In 1936, his impressive spectacle *Amar Jyoti* (Eternal Light), made in Hindi, was shown at the Venice Film Festival.

But Shantaram's partners also shared in the rising glory of Prabhat. Though Prabhat films began with mythological themes and costume dramas, it soon graduated with films that had a strong social message embedded into the story and the structure of its later films. Among these are *Duniya Na Mane*[27] (Hindi) or *Kunku* (Marathi) released in 1937 and *Aadmi* (Life's for Living) released in 1939. In 1972, many years after he had made path-breaking films in Bombay under his banner Prabhat Talkies, Shantaram paid homage to his early influence of German expressionist filmmaking when he directed *Pinjra*,[28] a strongly Indianized, Marathi 'tamasha' dance version of *The Blue Angel* which, when compared to the original, makes for a fascinating study in cross-cultural adaptation. He became an established auteur with films on socially relevant subjects as the central focus, such as *Do Ankhen Barah Haath*[29] on rehabilitation of six dreaded criminal prisoners by a large-hearted jailor; *Dr. Kotnis Ki Amar Kahani*[30] about a doctor who sacrificed his life for furthering the cause of medical science towards the cure of infectious diseases like leprosy.

There are several directors across the Indian film industry who are thought of as 'auteurs', such as Dadasaheb Phalke, Himanshu Roy, P.C. Barua, Bimal Roy, Satyajit Ray, Guru Dutt, Adoor Gopalakrishnan, Govind Nihalani, Girish Kasaravalli, Mani Ratnam and several others,

---

[25] *Sairandhri* (1933) is a Marathi language film directed by V. Shantaram. The film revolved around an incident from the Mahabharata and told the story of Draupadi as Malini/ Sairandhari (female servant), the 13th identity she took in order to remain safe and hidden from the Kauravas.

[26] *Amrit Manthan* (Churning for nectar) is the name of a Hindi and Marathi film directed by V. Shantaram and produced under his banner of Prabhat Film Company in 1934. The story involves a reformist king who bans human and animal sacrifices and a fanatical head priest who is willing to cut off his own head for a perfect sacrifice.

[27] *Duniya Na Maane*—The world does not accept.

[28] *Pinjra*—The cage title of a film.

[29] *Do Ankhen Barah Haath*—Two eyes and 12 hands.

[30] *Dr. Kotnis Ki Amar Kahani*—The immortal story of Dr. Kotnis.

who have created different cinematic worlds though many of their films fall in the category of mainstream cinema, often relegated to secondary space for its commercial aims and objectives that are thought to somehow dictate the filmmaker's subject, style, approach and so on. Such writers do not believe in the artificial schism drawn between mainstream cinema and/or off-mainstream or art-house cinema within Indian cinema, because mainstream cinema offers more than enough directors whose works lend themselves to auteur readings of their works. There is an adequate body of works by authors and critics on auteur readings of mainstream Indian filmmakers.

The book *Sohrab Modi* in the series *Legends of Indian Cinema*[31] by Amrit Gangar spans the works of a filmmaker covering nearly 50 years of direction and production (1934–1983). Gangar, a well-known film historian and curator, takes the reader through a number of Modi's films that used lavish sets, were mounted grandly, spanned a huge canvas and ensured big-screen entertainment for the entire family sources often from historical stories. Though his name is immediately associated with *Jhansi Ki Rani*,[32] the film was a massive commercial flop. *Mirza Ghalib*,[33] on the other hand, won the President's Gold Medal, while *Pukar*[34] and *Sikandar* (1941) remain all-time historical classics. For *Jhansi Ki Rani*, he brought in technicians from abroad who had worked on *Gone with the Wind*. The author's painstaking research on Sohrab Modi who worked at a time for which documented material is hardly available, the journey comes out lucidly and makes for interesting reading with anecdotes but it does not go into content-analysis of his films that could have lent the book to an auteur critique.[35]

---

[31] Amrit Gangar, *Sohrab Modi*. Legends of Indian Cinema (New Delhi: Wisdom Tree, 2008).

[32] *Jhansi Ki Rani* is the name of a film directed by Sohrab Modi. It is a fictional biography produced under Modi's banner Minerva Movietone and released in 1953. It was a historical costume drama and the first made in Technicolor in Indian cinema. Set in the nineteenth century against the backdrop of the mutiny of 1857, the film is about the bravery of queen Lakshmibai, Rani of Jhansi, who took up arms and led her army against the British. She was one of the first Indians to do so.

[33] *Mirza Ghalib* (1954) was a Hindi–Urdu film directed by Sohrab Modi. It was based on the life of the well-known poet Mirza Ghalib. It won the Golden Lotus Award at the National Awards in 1955 for the Best Feature Film and Bharat Bhushan received accolades for his performance as Mirza Ghalib.

[34] *Pukar* means 'The call'. It was an Urdu–Hindi film released in 1939 and directed by Sohrab Modi under his Minerva Movietone banner. The film was a historical fiction. about Mughal emperor Jehangir's legendary justice and focuses on how Jehangir offers himself to be killed when a washerwoman accuses empress Noorjehan of killing her husband during a hunt.

[35] Edward Buscombe, 'Ideas of Authorship', in *Theories of Authorship*, ed. John Caughie, (London: Routledge and Kegan Paul Ltd, 1981), 22–34.

Similarly, *Mehboob Khan*, another book in the series *Legends of Indian Cinema*,[36] is authored by a veteran editor, journalist and film critic Rauf Ahmed. This book explores Mehboob Khan's transition from an actor—a junior artiste actually—to a director. He never came close to playing a lead role. Instead of complaining or losing heart, he decided to hold the camera and became one of India's leading filmmakers. Though his name is immediately associated with his biggest hit *Mother India*, a modernized and updated version of his earlier film *Aurat*,[37] this book sheds light on other path breakers in his directorial oeuvre—such as *Amar*,[38] *Aan*,[39] *Andaz*,[40] *Humayun*[41] and around 20 odd films he made between 1935 and 1962. This book is more about tracing and fleshing out of a man who rose from being a junior artiste to a legendary film director and producer and who does not delve into an analysis of his filmmaking choices, process, technique and so on. Although it would be a significant addition to the libraries of film studies and Indian cinema, it does not merit the label of a serious auteur critique on the director. One, however, would desist from criticizing this study, because within the limitations of a 100-page book, it is not possible to do a serious auteur reading of the filmmaker's works.

Rachel Dwyer's *Yash Chopra: Fifty Years in Indian Cinema*[42] is too adulatory of the filmmaker it explores to be objectively labelled as an honest auteur critique. This book is based on the many interviews Dwyer recorded with the filmmaker over the years. But as it has very little research that leads to an auteur critique and/or reading, there is little in the book that has historical value.

In the book *Guru Dutt: A Tragedy in Three Acts* by Arun Khopkar,[43] the author sheds new light on Dutt's genius through a close examination of

---

[36] Rauf Ahmed, *Mehboob Khan*. Legends of Indian Cinema (Wisdom Tree, 2008).

[37] *Aurat* means 'woman'. This movie was released in 1940.

[38] *Amar* means immortal. It is a black-and-white film, a love story produced and directed by Mehboob Khan in 1954. It is said to have been a delicately nuanced psychological drama.

[39] *Aan* (known as 'The Savage Princess' in the United States) was produced and directed by Mehboob in 1953. It was shot in 16 mm Gevacolour and was blown up in Technicolor.

[40] *Andaz*, meaning 'style', was an Urdu–Hindi film released in 1949, and was produced and directed by Mehboob Khan. At the time of its release, *Andaz* was the top grossing Hindi film ever.

[41] *Humayun* (1945) is a Hindi–Urdu historical fiction based on the life and good works of the Mughal Emperor Humayun, son of Babar, with Ashok Kumar playing the title role. It was the seventh highest grossing Indian film of 1945.

[42] Rachel Dwyer, *Yash Chopra: Fifty Years in Indian Cinema* (New Delhi: Roli Books, 2002).

[43] Arun Khopkar, *Guru Dutt: A Tragedy in Three Acts*, translated from the original Marathi book by Shanta Gokhale (New Delhi: Penguin Books India, 2012).

his three best-known films, namely *Pyaasa*,[44] *Kaagaz Ke Phool*[45] and *Sahib Bibi Aur Ghulam*.[46] This is auteur criticism done honestly and over time where the author, a film scholar and teacher, explores the historical context that influenced Dutt's deeply melancholic style while also analysing the intricacies of the medium such as acting, lighting, music, editing and rhythm that were carefully deployed to create a masterpiece. This book paints a layered portrait of a troubled genius for whom art was not merely a thing of beauty but a vial part of living itself. This is certainly not a biography and does not shed any light on Guru Dutt's personal life.

V. Shantaram—The Man Who Changed Indian Cinema[47] by Shantaram's daughter Madhura Pandit Jasraj is more an anecdotal and detailed, behind-the-scenes tribute by a daughter to his father. In a review on *Livemint*, Jai Arjun Singh writes:

> Twenty years before the international 'auteur' debates focused attention on a director as the principal creative talent, Shantaram occupied a rare, top-of-marquee position among Indian film-makers, comparable to that of Frank Capra and Ernst Lubitsch in the Hollywood of the same period. I have heard grandparents and their friends (all born in the 1910s or 1920s, a youthful audience for such celebrated films as *Ayodhya Ka Raja*[48] and *Amrit Manthan*) reminiscing about the special excitement of 'a Shantaram' movie. Jasraj treads the line between the personal, affectionate tone and the detached, descriptive one, usually referring to Shantaram by name, in the manner of a conventional biographer, but occasionally including a memory of 'Papa'.[49]

---

[44] *Pyaasa* means 'thirsty'. It is a cult classic directed by Guru Dutt who portrayed the title role. The film was released in 1957. In 2002, *Pyaasa* was ranked at number 160 on the Sight & Sound critics' and directors' poll of all-time greatest films.

[45] *Kaagaz Ke Phool* means 'Paper flower'. It is a 1959 classic produced and directed by Guru Dutt and shot in black and white. It is the first cinemascope film in Indian cinema. The film was a box-office disaster in its time but was later resurrected as a world cinema cult classic in the 1980s.

[46] *Saheb Bibi Aur Ghulam* is based on an original Bengali novel named *Saheb Bibi Golam* by noted post-Tagorean littérateur Bimal Mitra (1912–1991) who emerged as one of the foremost Bangla novelists of the post-World War II period. The film, released in 1962, has turned into a cult classic and is said to be the most outstanding performance of Meena Kumari in the role of a bahu in a landlord's feudal family who becomes an alcoholic while trying to wean away her husband from the courtesan he regularly visits.

[47] Madhura Pandit Jasraj, *V. Shantaram—The Man Who Changed Indian Cinema* (New Delhi: Hay House India, 2015).

[48] *Ayodhya Ka Raja*—The King of Ayodhya.

[49] Jai Arjun Singh, *Livemint* (5 September 2015). Available at http://www.livemint.com/Leisure/HSC7adYDI1WVtZJlKJzYqI/Book-Review-V-ShantaramThe-Man-Who-Changed-Indian-Cinema.html (Accessed on 1 March 2017).

In fact, Arjun Singh laments the lack of independently written auteur critiques on mainstream Indian filmmakers, because several of these are authored by people closely related to the director which could dilute the objectivity of the writer and keep critical analyses of the filmmaker's works beyond the purview of a book of this kind.

Slipping better into the Indian mould of auteur criticism is Jai Arjun Singh's *The World of Hrishikesh Mukherjee—The Filmmaker Everyone Loves.*[50] Singh looks closely at Mukherjee's oeuvre from well-known films such as *Satyakam,*[51] *Guddi,*[52] *Abhimaan*[53] and *Khubsoorat*[54] to lesser known but equally notable works such as *Mem-Didi,*[55] *Biwi Aur Makan*[56] and *Anuradha*[57] which won the President's Gold Medal at the National Film Awards. His writing is a finely nuanced blend of a fan's passion and a critique's objectivity though this is a tough demand to fulfil.

In an enriching and enlightening review of this book, critic Amitava Nag writes:

> Jai Arjun introduces us to Hrishikesh Mukherjee's '*makaan*'[58], his house, a seamless metaphor for the world of his films. There are brilliant insights like one from Gulzar—"Hrishida was very clear about not taking extra shots or extra angles." In today's world of digital filmmaking where saving the cost of reel is not something of a top priority in a filmmaker's mind, this seems irrelevant. But as we have seen in the works of major masters of world cinema, it is the preparation, the mental map that grounds the

---

[50] Jai Arjun Singh, *The World of Hrishikesh Mukherjee—The Filmmaker Everyone Loves* (New Delhi: Viking, 2015).

[51] *Satyakaam* (1969) is a film about a man who stands of honesty, integrity and principles at any cost and the title is a metaphor for this man portrayed by Dharmendra.

[52] *Guddi* (1971) is a family drama starring Jaya Bhaduri (Bachchan) in the title role.

[53] *Abhimaan* (Pride) was released in 1973 and starred Amitabh Bachchan and Jaya Bachchan as husband and wife.

[54] *Khubsoorat* (Beautiful) is the metaphorical title of this 1980 film that refers both to the family drama that forms the core of the story and to the protagonist played by Rekha who won awards for her brilliant performance in this film.

[55] *Mem-Didi* (1961) is a proper noun that stands for the common form of address and name of the leading character portrayed by Lalita Pawar.

[56] *Biwi Aur Makan* (Wife and House; 1966) is a rip-roaring comedy in which we discover, in a rare instance for that time, Biswajeet impersonating as a woman to get rental accommodation in Bombay.

[57] *Anuradha* (1960) is the name of the protagonist of the film that marks Leela Naidu's rare appearances in Hindi films. The film won the President's Gold Medal for the Best Hindi film at the National Awards in 1961 and had music by Pandit Ravi Shankar, while the writer Sachin Bhowmick said he was inspired by Madame Bovary to write the screenplay.

[58] *Makaan* is a Hindi word that means 'dwelling' or 'place of residence' or 'apartment'.

film in its cinematic reality—a platform where innovations can spring from. The author provokes us to ponder about some very interesting inferences—the use of the concept of house and framing that within the narrative of his multiple films, the pivotal use of *chai* (tea) as the drink of the middle-class people of and for whom he dedicated his cinema all throughout his career. As the author craftily conjectures, it is the choice of these rather unimportant aspects that stand in as recurrent motifs in Mukherjee's films—so sublime that you will not notice them as metaphors as well. Yet, if you dive deep, probably these are the brick and mortar of Hrishikesh Mukherjee's films where we have for years wanted to enter and live for a part of our lives.[59]

THE 'AUTEUR' IN BIMAL ROY

Bimal Roy's cinema is known for its powerful storylines, technical finesse and some subtle and not-so-subtle social messages that emerge from the very act of storytelling and the process of filmmaking. But what we seem to have missed out on is the core of displacement that defines his cinema almost from the beginning to the end. He was himself a displaced person who had to migrate from a village in Suapur, distanced from the noisy city of Kolkata and outstripped culturally, politically and historically from his roots. His displacement and migration happened in the 1930s when India was still under the British Rule and the political realities were different from what evolved later. He was an unwitting participant in this process of transition, though his cinema or his selection of stories and scripts for his films do not reflect any lament on this displacement, which also suggests that he perhaps accepted it as part of his life and coped with the changed circumstances of his life and work as they kept changing.

An unforgettable quality of Bimal Roy's range of films lies in its extracinematic perceptions. This was more or less seen in the works of other Indian directors of that time too, but a closer study offers an insight into his oeuvre that stands out distinctly for the films' extra-cinematic perceptions, no matter whether they were adaptations of literature or were developed from a created screenplay independent of any literary origin. In fact, it would truly be difficult to look into any film of Bimal Roy where an extra-cinematic perception is missing. His stylistic figurations partly stem from the social and political environment that shaped him, when he grew up in Dacca, shifted to Calcutta, joined New Theatres and looked at the world outside through the lens of his camera and also with his insightful eyes, both of which combined to create a third dimension which in turn

---

[59] Amitava Nag, 'Hrishikesh Mukherjee's Makaan', *The Statesman*, 31 October 2015.

spilled over into his films. All these elements came together when he arrived in Bombay to make Hindi films, having little knowledge or command over the language.

Placing the signature of an 'auteur' on Indian filmmakers is challenging because generally an Indian filmmaker, especially during the period when Bimal Roy, Guru Dutt and other contemporaries were known for their 'signature', often kept changing his or her stylistic figurations in keeping with the subject of the film. This flux in style and approach and treatment is so dominant in contemporary Indian filmmakers in the twenty-first century that it is impossible to label them with the tag of 'auteur'. In the case of Bimal Roy, it would be reasonable to conclude that he often permitted the content of the story to dictate his style and approach, and this was easier for him because he began his career as a cameraman. None of his films, except perhaps *Madhumati*, was placed in a social and environmental vacuum. His mindset was not structured to make films for his own sake, with the sole purpose of entertainment. Within his life and work as a filmmaker, he did not and could not wipe away his personal social context and history or the social context and history of the films he made. All his films exude an emotional aura that remains with the viewer long after he or she walks out of the theatre.

A strong reason why the 'auteur' in Bimal Roy is both acknowledged and recognized is that his films connote unity rather than diversity and conformity rather than non-conformity, and explore variations within symbiosis and harmony. To try and discover common elements of style, form, subject and so on is not a formidable challenge and yet there is no repetition; the films neither drag nor bore. Trying to discover the 'auteur' in Bimal Roy is no challenge for a discerning auteur critic. Studied individually, his directorial oeuvre might appear to differ from one film to the next, but when looked at closely, analysed in depth, placed in perspective and studied in retrospect, they bring out 'a pattern of performance' of a single director's vision that has stood the test of time.

The auteur theory, according to Andrew Sarris, is not so much a theory as it is an 'attitude', a table of values that converts film history into a directorial autobiography. A strong director imposes his or her own personality on a film. A weak director allows the personality of others to run rampant. This is precisely the criterion that picks out one director from a crowd of many others to place him or her under the 'auteur' microscope. Edward Buscombe proposes other ways of looking at cinema.[60] These are

---

[60] Stephen Heath, 'Comment on the "Idea of Authorship"', *Screen* 14, no. 3 (1973, Autumn): 88. This is a comment on Buscombe, *The Construction of Authorship*.

(a) the examination of the effects of cinema on society; (b) the effects of society on cinema (influence of ideology, economics, history, etc.); (c) a sub-division of the effects talked about in (b), that is, the effects of films on other films. Aparna Sen's directorial films offer an interesting blend of these two schools of thought—*Cahiers du Cinéma*'s theories of authorship and Buscombe's stress on extra-cinematic perceptions—although, since Buscombe is a critic of Sarris, this might seem to be a contradiction in terms of Indian cinema, including the cinema of Bimal Roy more in keeping with Bazin who attempted to combine the 'auteur' approach with an acknowledgement of the forces conditioning the individual artist.

In the Indian context, one can never totally agree with Sarris who says, "If directors and other artists cannot be wrenched from their historical environments, aesthetics is reduced to a subordinate branch of ethnography."[61] Noted critic Pauline Kael attacked Sarris' statement by saying, "[W]hen is Sarris going to discover that aesthetics is a branch of ethnography; what does he think it is—a sphere of its own, separate from the study of man and his environment?"[62]

It is interesting to note that though Bimal Roy began his career as an assistant cameraman who graduated to handle the camera independently, once he came to Bombay and founded Bimal Roy Films, he never handled the camera for his directorial films. But his command over the camera gave him the perspective of conceiving, orchestrating and choreographing the shot from the dual vision of a director and a cameraman. His principal cinematographer Dilip Dutta Gupta was a close friend and this overlapped their professional relationship as director–cinematographer, stripping it of a hierarchical relationship that might otherwise have sustained between them. Later, some of his films were cinematographed by Kamal Bose, and both cinematographers have left their footprints on the sands of time when black and white reigned supreme and wove its own magic.

Both Dilip Gupta (1911–1999) and Bimal Roy began as assistants in New Theatres in Calcutta, almost around the same time. While Gupta was retained for lab work, Roy assisted Bose who was a cinematographer. In 1943, Gupta migrated to Mumbai along with Bimal Roy during the Quit India Movement. This marked a turning point in Gupta's life and career. The three big milestones in his career as a cinematographer are *Street Singer* (1938), *Madhumati* (1958) and *Gautama the Buddha* (1967)

---

[61] Andrew Sarris, *Perspectives on the Study of Film*, ed. John Stuart Katz (Boston, MA: Little Brown & Company, 1971), 132–133.
[62] Pauline Kael, 'Circles and Squares: Joys and Sarris', in *Perspectives on the Study of Film*, ed. John Stuart Katz (Boston, MA: Little, Brown & Company 1971), 154.

a documentary by Bimal Roy. *Street Singer*,[63] a New Theatres' production, was directed by Phani Majumdar.

Madhumati is a milestone for several reasons. First, it bagged 11 Filmfare Awards, a record that remained unbroken for many years. Second, Filmfare introduced the Best Cinematography Award the same year. Dilip Gupta won it for his mind-blowing cinematography of the film. Third, it remains the biggest box-office hit under the Bimal Roy Films banner. Fourth, it is a film many students of cinematography consider to be a model lesson in black-and-white cinematography at its ideal best. In fact, K.K. Jaiswal, a faculty member of the FTII, Pune, saw *Madhumati* 14 times in a row when he was a student at the institute. "The two song picturisations 'Suhana safar' and 'Aja re pardesi' are next to impossible in terms of perfection," he says in a tributary note. It was impossible to say which shot was taken indoors and which outdoors, especially when the scene was supposed to be representing the exterior ambience.

Gautama the Buddha was one of the few documentaries Bimal Roy produced under the auspices of Films Division, while Rajbans Khanna directed it. It was a strikingly unusual documentary where the camera plays its magic on the murals, sculptures and art work narrating the life of Gautama Buddha without a single animated figure in the entire film. It was released by Government of India in 1957 as part of the Buddha's 2500th birthday celebration. It got an honourable mention on the Cannes Film Festival in 1957 because of its beauty and high morality. It is a black-and-white film comprising beautiful images of natural environments, archeological sites, reliefs and paintings, ancient and more contemporary ones. A voice-over narration by Partap Sharma revealed the story.

Although Gupta's main claim to fame is through some of the best films in the Bimal Roy camp beginning with *Biraj Bahu* (1954) and ending with *Do Dooni Char* (1966), his work is traced back to 1931 when he began his career as an assistant to Nitin Bose for Charu Roy's *Chorekanta*[64] (Bengali). He passed through the phases of the more or less 'ancient' techniques that heralded the birth of sound to make a smooth transition to more modern techniques when he came down to Mumbai and finally transcended black and white to step into colour cinematography. He spanned genres from

---

[63] *Street Singer* (1938) is the name of the film in Hindi but with an English title. It was produced by New Theatres and directed by Phani Majumdar and has become a classic for his wonderful songs rendered by K.L. Saigal and Kanan Devi who also played the romantic lead in the film.

[64] *Chor Kanta* means 'Hidden thorns'.

dramatic love stories (*President, Street Singer, Deedar*[65]) to family dramas (*Teen Bhai*[66]) through period pieces (*Yahudi*), literary classics (*Biraj Bahu, Kapal Kundala*[67] and *Usne Kaha Tha*[68]), surreal love stories (*Madhumati*), thrillers (*Jab Pyar Kisise Hota Hai*[69]) to comedies (*Do Dooni Char*). He was a cinematographer for films in Bengali, Hindi and Marathi.

Indian cinema, both mainstream and non-mainstream, offers innumerable examples where the director combines within himself the role of writing the story, the screenplay, sometimes, even the dialogue, and often acts in some important role in the film. Indian directors make films based on (a) their own story and screenplay, (b) a story written by someone else who may or may not also write the screenplay, (c) a story taken from some rich piece of literature in any of the Indian languages and (d) a story and screenplay written by the director himself.[70] Bimal Roy almost always relied on Bengali literature for the subject of his films. The few exceptions of films based directly on screenplays are *Parakh, Madhumati, Benazir* and a few others. For his film *Pehla Aadmi* (1950), he wrote the script himself. The story of this film that is said to be a tribute to Netaji Subhash Chandra Bose was written by an ex-INA member Nasir Hussain. His symbiotic relationship with his technicians and creative directors was so good and long-standing that for this man who spoke very little, the rapport was almost reflexive and automatic.

Take his association with his screenplay writer Nabendu Ghosh (1917–2007) as an example. The association began in 1947 and the two grew close during their years in New Theatres. Under Bimal Roy Productions, Ghosh wrote some of the best scripts ever in the history of Indian cinema. He began as assistant to Roy but got into script writing when Roy suggested

---

[65] *Deedar* (1951) means 'glance'. It is the name of the Hindi film that became a very big hit and had the unusual star-cast, that is, Dilip Kumar, Ashok Kumar, Nargis and Nimmi, was directed by Nitin Bose with unforgettable songs penned by Shakeel Badayuni and set to music by Naushad.

[66] *Teen Bhai* (1955) means 'Three brothers'. It is a rare film about which little is known except that it had some great songs sung by Geeta Dutt, Asha Bhonsale and a duet by Lakshmi Shankar and Manna Dey.

[67] *Kapal Kundala* (1939) is a proper name of a famous classic authored in Bengali by Bankim Chandra Chattopadhyay. There have been several film versions of this classic period piece and this one in Hindi was directed by Nitin Bose and Phani Majumdar starring Leela Desai and Sailen Choudhury.

[68] *Usne Kaha Tha* (1960) means 'She had said'. It is a Hindi film based on what is known as the first short story in Hindi authored by Chandradhar Sharma Guleri and marks the directorial debut of Moni Bhattacharya.

[69] *Jab Pyar Kisise Hota Hai* (1961) means 'When one falls in love'. Produced and directed by Nasir Hussain, it was a musical romance with a thriller twist and was a big box-office hit.

[70] Shoma A. Chatterji, *Parama and Other Outsiders—The Cinema of Aparna Sen* (Kolkata: Parumita Publication, 2002).

he do scripts. His first screenplay was for *Maa* directed by Bimal Roy, but the credits did not mention him. He wrote the story and screenplay of *Baap Beti* but still got no name in the credits. When he wrote the screenplay of *Parineeta*, the credits continued to elude him. His name began to appear in the credits withthe screenplays of *Biraj Bahu*, *Naukri* and *Amanat*, the last directed by Roy's friend Arabinda Sen. These films were a turning point for this great man called Nabendu Ghosh who remained unassuming and modest till the end of his days, belying the history he carved for Indian cinema. He wrote the screenplays of *Yahudi*, *Sujata*, *Devdas*, *Bandini* and the documentary on *Swami Vivekananda*. When Roy gave him permission to work with other filmmakers, Ghosh wrote the screenplay for Guru Dutt's *Aar Paar*[71], Hrishikesh Mukherjee's *Majhli Didi*[72] and *Abhimaan*. He wrote the script of Phani Majumdar's *Baadbaan*,[73] the first ever film in India to have been produced by a workers' cooperative. Ghosh wrote the screenplay of Raj Khosla's directorial debut film *Milap*,[74] starring Geeta Bali and Dev Anand. Much later, Manoj Kumar's first film *Kanch Ki Gudiya*[75] had its screenplay penned by Ghosh.

Ghosh's oeuvre bears the distinct stamp of his outlook on life. He viewed literature as an instrument for tackling all that is sordid and destructive in life, society or state. His literary efforts are like fingers pointing at the sufferings of humanity not caused by men alone but by the circumstances of history. His creative writing is characterized by a deep empathy for human emotions, mysterious layers of meaning that add to the depth of the spoken word, subtle symbolism and descriptions of unbearable life, yet not bound by worldly restrictions. Man, as portrayed by Ghosh, is at times empty and loathsome and at other times supernatural. He has authored 26 novels and 14 collections of short stories. His autobiography, *Eka Naukar Jatri*,[76] is about to be published. A notable theme of his comes out in *Aami O Aami*,[77] a piece of science fiction that explores the experience of twin life in outer space.

---

[71] *Aar Paar* (This or that) is a Hindi film of 1954 made under the Guru Dutt banner.

[72] *Majhli Didi* (1967) meaning 'The second sister' directed by Hrishikesh Mukherjee was adapted from a novel by Sarat Chandra Chattopadhyay. Though it did average business, it was claimed as one of the best films by Mukherjee.

[73] *Baadbaan* (1954) means 'A sail' probably springing from the backdrop of the story placed in a fishing village on the border of the sea.

[74] *Milap*—Union of two people or two parties or groups.

[75] *Kaanch Ki Gudiya*—The glass doll.

[76] *Eka Naukar Jatri* is the autobiography in Bengali by Nabendu Ghosh which means 'The lone boat sailer'.

[77] *Aami O Aami* means 'I and I'.

Through his long career, Ghosh penned about 60 scripts. The humane trait of his writing made him a natural choice for directors such as Satyen Bose, Guru Dutt, Sushil Majumdar, Hrishikesh Mukherjee, Raj Khosla, Asit Sen, Basu Bhattacharya and Shakti Samanta. He later teamed up with newer directors such as Dulal Guha, Prakash Mehra, Sultan Ahmed, Mohan Segal and Subhash Ghai. This offers a measure of the range and diversity of his screenwriting. Gyan Mukherjee's *Shatranj*, Satyen Bose's *Jyot Jale*,[78] Mohan Segal's *Raja Jani*,[79] Arabinda Sen's *Jaal Saaz*[80] and Ajay Kar's *Kaya Hiner Kahini*[81] (Bengali) were films based on his original stories. A shocking tragedy of his career is that though he penned the original story of Guru Dutt's *Kaagaz Ke Phool*,[82] the credits did not mention him at all.

The late Nutan said: "Two of my best roles were penned by Nabendu Ghosh for *Sujata* and *Bandini*. These films by my favourite director Bimal Roy brought out two unknown aspects of womanhood and fired an intensity not seen in any other film of mine. Nabendu-da and Bimal-da formed one of the greatest script-writer—director combination duos of Indian cinema."

On Nabendu Ghosh's 90th birthday celebrations, Amitabh Bachchan said, "I worked in three films scripted by Nabendu Ghosh, of which *Abhimaan* and *Do Anjaane*[83] could draw out of me the intensity the characters deserved. To this day, *Abhimaan* remains one of the films that are closest to my heart."

CONCLUSION

The concept of 'Bengaliness' in the cinema of Bimal Roy is almost like a given that does not raise any debate nor need to parry questions. This is nothing extraordinary for Bimal Roy who was a full-blooded Bengali who did not speak good Hindi even though he directed Hindi films. The extraordinary quality he invested Hindi cinema with lies in its innate 'Bengali-ness' even when his films were in Hindi; sometimes, the films such as *Madhumati* did not have a Bengali setting or Bengali characters nor did they narrate a Bengali story. There is something that is inherently

---

[78] *Jyot Jale* (1973) means 'The flame keeps burning'. It is a Hindi film directed by Satyen Bose.

[79] *Raja Jaani* (1972) is a proper noun, the nick name of the two protagonists of the film directed by Mohan Segal.

[80] *Jaal Saaz* (1959) is a Hindi film with Kishore Kumar and Mala Sinha in the lead. It is a Persian word that means 'the binder' or 'the one who binds things or people together'.

[81] *Kaya Hiner Kahini* (1973) is a Bengali film directed by Ajoy Kar. The title means 'The story of one without a body' because it is a ghost story with Aparna Sen in a double role—one as the ghost and the other as the real woman.

[82] *Kaagaz Ke Phool*—The paper flower.

[83] *Do Anjaane*—Two strangers.

'Bengali' in Bimal Roy's films that place him in an unique position in the history of Hindi cinema. The 'Bengaliness' in Bimal Roy's films cannot be compared with the hybrid, globalized 'Bengaliness' that sustains today among Bengalis, because post-liberalization and with modernization and globalization, the Bengali identity has metamorphosed and mutated so much that it would be difficult to discover a Devdas-like personality in the Bengali of the twenty-first century even in a small Bengali town or village in real life or in Bengali cinema. Devdas (*Devdas*) or Shekhar (*Parineeta*) or Biraj (*Biraj Bahu*) represent the Bengali identity we find in Bimal Roy's films and not the globalized Bengali of today.

According to Sumanta Banerjee,[84] the Bengalis had to reconstitute their identity in the eighteenth and nineteenth centuries in the face of British colonization. He also said:

> At that time, after several phases of internal conflicts, the Bengali Hindu middle class managed to formulate a code of conduct that helped them reconstruct themselves as an identifiable distinct community, called bhadraloks. This was done by reconciling their past tradition with the contemporary colonial rule. It was a minced pie, consisting of vegetarian slices from Hindu customs and rituals and pieces of meat from western society and culture. The Bengali Muslim gentry underwent a similar crisis of identity during the same period, swinging between a desire to associate themselves with pan-Arabic Islamism on the one hand and the need to accept English education and still retain their Bengali characteristics on the other. Over the years, both the educated Hindu and Muslim middle classes merged into a Bengali intellectual identity, sharing common concerns of social reforms, and writing in a Bengali which has by now become the standardized form.[85]

When we talk about the Bengali identity in Bimal Roy's cinema, we are referring to the cultural identity of the Bengali who is a composite of his social background, his financial status that might define him as a farmer or a bhadralok,[86] his language of communication, his education and cultural leanings and his lifestyle. But in essence, 'Bengaliness' is an internal and abstract value. It goes deeper than clothes, language or eating habits. It is

---

[84] Sumanta Banerjee, *Paradoxes in Inventing Bengali Identity*. (May 2013). Available at http://www.india-seminar.com/2013/645/645_sumanta_banerjee.htm

[85] Ibid.

[86] Bhadralok is the Bengali equivalent that roughly translates to 'gentleman' in English. Literally, '*badhra*' means 'decent' and '*lok*' means 'person'.

that mental unity where differences melt. It is in the filmmaker's blood and mind. It is a matter of inner compulsion. It is something that can neither be crushed nor suppressed by an Indian filmmaker even if he wishes to crush or suppress it. It is a birthright of an Indian filmmaker. It is the native-ness that marks him different from others. It is a connecting link between generations. This abstract value has been successfully given a concrete form in the audiovisual art and craft of cinema by Bimal Roy which itself could have been an uphill task but was not as this Bengaliness was a part of his genes, his bloodstream and his system, and he could not let go of it even if he had wanted to.

His technical crew was almost entirely Bengali by birth. Those who were not born Bengali, such as his veteran make-up artiste Babu, or one of his editors Das Dhaimade, and his dialogue writer Paul Mahendra, picked up Bengali so well that even those who could not speak Bengali fluently could understand what was being said. Choosing Bengalis to work with him was not a conscious decision because he had migrated to Bombay from Calcutta and had to pick up local technicians too. What aided him was that some of his technical crew came almost along with him when he came to Bombay and they stuck to him for good till they went out on their own such as Hrishikesh Mukherjee, who began to direct his own films, and Gulzar.

Lighting, an extremely important element in his works, acquired greater vibrancy in *Parineeta*, *Parakh*, *Sujata* and *Bandini*. Whenever the narration grew nostalgic or throbbed with inner crisis, whether in anguish or in ecstasy, the mood was captured in delicate chiaroscuro patterns of black, grey and dove white. In *Parineeta*, there is a shot of Lalita hiding under a dark staircase, moving her fingers along the now-withered garland of flowers, tears streaming down her cheeks, which offers a classic example of how personal pain can be handled with great restraint. His language was painted in every possible shade of grey, white and black. One never thought of colour even in a pastoral romance like *Madhumati* nor did anyone miss it.

He chose his actors with care and their knowledge or closeness to Bengali as a language, a lifestyle or a culture did not come in the way of this choice. Thus, it is amazing to discover how much 'Bengaliness' these actors could imbibe to be able to invest their Bengali characters with the right touch of authenticity and conviction. Kamini Kaushal, who played the title role of Biraj in *Biraj Bahu*, is one example and Meena Kumari as Lalita in *Parineeta* is another. Dilip Kumar's role in *Devdas* is another classic example. The 'Bengali' identity of Upendra Choudhury is not stressed in *Sujata* nor is Adhir's identity portrayed by Sunil Dutt, but the suggestions are clear.

What is outstanding about his cinema is that one cannot mark his work with the slightest sign of a conflict of interest between honesty and aesthetics, between ideology and reward, and between commitment and fame. His choice was clear as evinced in his oeuvre—it was honest aesthetics, ideology overshadowed all thoughts of reward, fame followed commitment and not the other way round. The beginnings of the negative impact of industrialization on the rural poor came to the surface in *Do Bigha Zamin* which offers a different slice of Kolkata where Bihar and UP migrants live shoulder-to-shoulder with local Bengali urban poor. This clearly goes on to show that his views on industrialization and modernization made his realization of the exploitation of the marginal and the oppressed more acute than ever before.

In this, we discover that in terms of social commitment as an honest and gifted filmmaker, the issues that impacted negatively on the marginal and the periphery people—be it a woman imprisoned for murder, an untouchable girl not included within the mainstream family or a poor peasant forced to leave his homestead for the city—the 'Bengaliness' loses out to humaneness. And that is what makes Bimal Roy the sole champion of his time of a collective and universal cause—the cause of the displaced outsider.

II. LITERARY ADAPTATIONS —
UDAYER PATHEY, DO BIGHA
ZAMIN AND *BAAP BETI*

INTRODUCTION

Literary classics have been an inspiration for filmmakers in India and Indian filmmakers across borders. Gurinder Chadha's *Bride & Prejudice* is a contemporized adaptation of Jane Austen's *Pride and Prejudice*. Vidhu Vinod Chopra made a modernized adaptation of Sarat Chandra Chatterjee's *Parineeta* with Vidya Balan as Lalita, the character played by Meena Kumari in the earlier film version of the same Sarat Chandra classic directed by Bimal Roy many years ago.

Rohinton Mistry, a contemporary Indian novelist, provided inspiration to Rahul Bose for *Everybody Says I'm Fine!*. Although it was a brilliantly original story put across with rare insight, it did not find favour with the Indian audience. Bengal has been instrumental in this revival. Rituparno Ghose made his version of Agatha Christie's *The Mirror Crack'd from Side to Side* as *Shubho Mahurat*[1] in Bengali. Goutam Ghose made a sequel to Satyajit Ray's *Aranyer Din Ratri*[2] based on Sunil Gangopadhyay's novel of

---

[1] *Shubha Mahurat*—The auspicious moment.
[2] *Aranyer Din Ratri*—Days and nights in the forest.

the same name. For *Dekha*,[3] Gangopadhyay collaborated with Ghose on the story and the script. Aparna Sen made *The Japanese Wife* in English based on a very unique novel by Kunal Basu, and a complicated ghost story based on Shirshendu Mukhopadhyay's *Goynar Baksho*.[4] Anjan Das made *Bansiwalla*,[5] adapted from Shirshendu Mukhopadhyay's novel.

Noted poet Gieve Patel says:

> Works of literature can be adapted for the screen with a greater or lesser degree of success depending on the depth and perception of the screenplay writer and director of the film. For instance, Charles Dickens' *Great Expectations* was made by David Lean in his early career. You do lose out on a lot of the novel, yet it was a very authentic and rewarding attempt. It was delightful to see all the characters present before you visually. Bresson's adaptation of Fyodor Dostoevsky's *A Meek Woman* (*Une Femme Douce*) is a different kind of adaptation where both time and place are changed from the original story and some of the ideological emphasis was also changed. It needs a person of Bresson's genius to measure up to the greatness of the literary work. Satyajit Ray's adaptation of *Charulata*[6] and *Teen Kanya*[7] are also exquisitely successful works. Sidney Lumet's film on Eugene O'Neill's *A long Day's Journey into the Night* preserved the original play's script almost entirely and is also a successful film. You need a special kind of talent and sensitivity to make a film which preserves the script and is cinematically fulfilling at the same time.[8]

The link between cinema and literature was established from the very inception of cinema as a medium to interpret literature in a language of its own. The immense potential offered by this medium to transfer a tale in print into a living visual experience has long tempted filmmakers and authors alike. The prospect of reaching a much wider audience with cinema as the most popular mass medium inspired many literary figures to seek a full-fledged career as a writer for cinema. The Bengali film industry of earlier times stands testimony. This is particularly true of the 1940s and the 1950s when many writers and poets entered the Bombay and Madras film worlds in a big way. But so far as Hindi cinema is concerned, Urdu writers,

---

[3] *Dekha*—Seeing.

[4] *Goynar Baksho*—The jewel box.

[5] *Bansiwalla*—The flautist.

[6] *Charulata*—Name of the protagonist and title of the film.

[7] *Teen Kanya*—Three daughters.

[8] The interviews with the authors were in an article on cinema and literature published in *Cinemas of India*, the erstwhile monthly publication of the National Film Development Corporation of India which does not come out any more.

however, led the group coming forward in large numbers to join the film industry, while Hindi writers were not as eager as history shows.[9]

Period films attempt to recreate the authentic culture of the past. The success or failure of the attempt is controlled by manipulation of the text, recreation of the script and the attitude of the audience. While a film and its literary source both have the common aim of expressing concrete situations involved in the development of a plot and the exposition of character and environment, the media through which they seek to accomplish these ends are entirely different. Films depict concrete situations involving plot development and characterization, the setting and the environment, emotional reactions, philosophic attitudes and concepts by means of a series of plastic images and visual representations projected onto a screen in a darkened room before an audience. It is, thus, seen and heard by its audience and secures its characteristic form and rhythm by a purely filmic process of editing. The medium of literature, however, is words. A novelist originally creates words or sentences in order to achieve the maximum literary power and to stir the thoughts and emotions of the readers. In spite of such basic differences of form and style, it is a well-accepted fact that right from the birth of this new art form in the twentieth-century, filmmakers had to turn to literature, and especially novels, to obtain the essential ingredient upon which their narration is based, namely the story.

BIMAL ROY AND THE LITERARY LINK

Bimal Roy's cinema reveals his fondness for literature as his source. His films are based on literature—both classic and contemporary. *Sujata* was from a Subodh Ghosh novella. *Usne Kaha Tha* was based on a short story by Chandradhar Sharma 'Guleri' (1883–1922). There is an ongoing debate that *Usne Kaha Tha* (1915) is the first short story in Hindi. *Kabuliwala* based on Tagore's short story was directed by Hemen Gupta. *Bandini* was a faithful adaptation of Jarasandha's Bengali novel *Tamasi*.[10] *Biraj Bahu, Devdas* and *Parineeta* were based on Sarat Chandra's novels. Nabendu Ghosh, who wrote the screenplay of the three Sarat Chandra classics, said:

> These novels had the basic dramatic premise essential for any film. *Parineeta* is about a girl who seems to be unmarried but is married in spirit, and how she finally manages to establish her rightful status.

---

[9] Ashok Raj, *The Pen and the Camera: The Influence of Literature on Cinema*, vol. 1 *Hero* (Carlsbad, CA: Hay House, 2009).
[10] *Tamasi*—Girl of darkness.

Devdas is a tragic love story in the manner of *Romeo and Juliet*. *Biraj Bahu* is a psychologically rich story about a tragic misunderstanding between a husband and his wife. All three films carry a message and deal with human values.

Nabendu chose Sarat Chandra's stories because he liked them, found something in them that he wished to adapt in his films and something that he wanted to communicate to his audience through his chosen language— cinema. His films have no truck with interpreting a piece of literature, questioning its arguments and taking a time leap to make it contemporary or to challenge its thesis through cinema, question it or confront it. He picked his stories selectively without any intention of twisting or tweaking them for the sake of cinema except when the audiovisual cinema as an entertainment demanded some additions and enhancements through song, music, dance and, perhaps, a few tweaks that did not disturb the essence of the story in any way.

His first directorial venture, *Udayer Pathey* (the Hindi version was called *Hamrahi*) was based on an unpublished story by Jyotirmoy Roy. *Anjangarh* in Bengali and Hindi, his second film under the New Theatres banner, was based on *Fossil*, a short story by Subodh Ghosh. *Mantramugdhu* (1949) was based on a story by the famous writer Bonophul, the pen name of Balai Chand Mukhopadhyay. It was a topical satire on the fall out of excessive religious rituals and superstition that is a part of Hindu practice. When a devoted wife oppresses her husband by placing him next to the Gods, he decides to teach her a lesson. On a parallel track, there is a lively romantic tale full of fun and laughter.

Bimal Roy's choice of stories from original literary works was not based solely on the merits of the story but also on its social relevance. Bimal Roy's films had some humanism structured into them seamlessly as an integral part of the story even if they did not originate in literature. *Naukri, Do Bigha Zamin, Parineeta, Devdas, Biraj Bahu, Sujata, Parakh* and *Bandini* had some message that carried a strong social significance timeless in the Indian context. However, they also sprung from his fondness for undiluted, refreshing and simple love stories narrated in a straightforward manner. *Sujata* remains one of the most humanistic films made on untouchability. *Sujata* saw Bimal Roy returning to more realistic imperatives after the comparatively lightweight *Madhumati* and *Yahudi*. Both films were big successes at the box office.

Not a single print of *Anjangarh* is available today. Based on Subodh Ghosh's short story *Fossil*, it was a political drama about the collusion of the pre-independence aristocracy and bourgeois business interests against the common man. The film shows that when a local mining company has the audacity to provide its workers a fair wage for a fair day's work, and lets its workers unionize, the kingdom's villainous potentate is less than pleased. After considerable pressure, the company agrees to blame unrest in the region on a blameless workers' collective. The film is a bold statement on the gradual encroachment of the powerful political lobby into the tribal belt of Bihar, with a view to dispossess the Adivasis, the original occupants of the land. A direct conflict arises between the ruling class and the tribal minority. Made the year after India's independence, one cannot ignore the adroit references to India's colonial masters who had usurped power.

Bimal Roy's films are replete with innumerable instances of screen performances and technical achievements never known to have been attained earlier. Although his background is traced back to the days when screen acting was directly influenced by the melodramatic exaggeration that marked theatrical performances, Bimal Roy was noted for his marked restraint. He evolved a subtle, normal mode, contributing to the richness of the tapestry of the realistic theme of his films.

The camera was his brush and his unfailing grip over it made him manoeuvre it with gentle strokes, sweeping into his canvas the rich poetry and the powers of human beauty, the intensity and the variety of human emotions. His narrative was unhurried and lingering, yet it never tended to drag like slow-paced films usually do. The editing was marked by his characteristic spontaneity, while his dialogues were always delivered in low-key and soft tones. Loudness, in other words, was conspicuous by its absence. Bimal Roy, perhaps, is the only filmmaker of the post-Barua–Debaki Bose era who towered over the Indian cinema scenario with such consistent command over the medium. His work is a fine blend of the sophistication of P.C. Barua, the emotional lyricism of Debaki Bose and the skilled craftsmanship of Nitin Bose.

In this chapter, the author has taken a very broad view of literature to reach beyond conventional literary sources Bimal Roy dipped his directorial wand into a treasury of stories to pick three very diverse pieces of literature adapted by Bimal Roy. The writer takes the word 'literature' beyond what it is commonly understood in relation to its film adaptation, because the more rigid adaptations from renowned works of literature have been studied extensively within film studies and analyses. Therefore, this author felt that the choice should veer away from films that are already analysed and studied in depth in other chapters of this work.

The names of the films and the criteria of choice are as follows:

(a) *Udayer Pathey* (1944) has been chosen because it is the only film Bimal Roy made in two versions, that is, in Bengali and in Hindi (as *Hamrahi,* a year later). Second, it also marks Bimal Roy's debut as an independent director. Third, it was produced under the New Theatres banner where Bimal Roy was a full-fledged cameraman. Fourth, it is the only film within the Bimal Roy oeuvre to have been made during the British Rule before India attained independence in 1947 and consequently became a sovereign, democratic republic in 1950. Last, but never the least, the Bengali version turned out to become a big box-office hit that prompted the Hindi version which, however, failed to recreate the magic of the original. *Udayer Pathey* has been chosen also because it offers perhaps the first example in the history of Hindi cinema of a novel being published after the film was released, and like the film, the novel became a bestseller and turned writer Jyotirmoy Roy into an overnight literary star. Jyotirmoy Roy was an active member of the Indian People's Theatre Association.

(b) *Do Bigha Zamin* (1953) was based on a story written in Bengali by music director Salil Chowdhury under the title *Rickshawala,* but a Tagore poem of the same title *Dui Bigha Jomi* was the inspiration for the story. Bimal Roy had asked Chowdhury to write the story and he also scored the music for this film. This film has been chosen because it has a Tagore source fleshed out by Salil Chowdhury who was also a lyricist, poet and writer apart from being a talented music director. This blend of Tagore and Chowdhury, who was a proclaimed Marxist, turned into a film by Bimal Roy made for a unique choice for a literary source for one of the most memorable films in post-colonial India that was said to be influenced by Italian New-Realism in a big way, and introduced the relatively unknown theatre actor Balraj Sahni in his first big film role. After *Do Bigha Zamin*, Salil-da composed music for over 75 Hindi films, around 26 Malayalam films and several Bengali, Tamil, Telugu, Kannada, Gujarati and Assamese films. He became famous as the most non-conformist composer in Indian cinema of the time.

(c) *Baap Beti* (1954) is not a single celluloid print or DVD copy is available anywhere in India including the Bimal Roy family. Yet, this writer has chosen this film because she is perhaps one of the few surviving Indians who had the good fortune to have watched the film, though memories are dim and blurred. The film has been chosen because it is the only film within Bimal Roy's cinema that was loosely adapted from a famous short story by French author Guy de Maupassant and also because it is perhaps the only film in which the director took the maximum liberties with the original story.

Udayer Pathey (1944)

Roy made his directorial debut with *Udayer Pathey*, a sensational success about an author's fight against exploitation. It proved a benchmark in social realism in Indian cinema. It released in Calcutta's Chitra Talkies on 1 September 1944. He turned out to become a big box-office hit. The story later turned into a play and the entire dialogue was transferred onto eight discs that sold very well, creating a new way of marketing dialogue. *Udayer Pathey* introduced a new era of post-World War II romantic–realist melodrama that was to pioneer the integration of the Bengal School style with that of Vittorio De Sica.

The screenplay of the Bengali film was jointly authored by Bimal Roy, who also cinematographed the film, and Nirmal Dey. Dey assisted Roy when the latter was a cinematographer with New Theatres. He later ventured into direction with the milestone film *Sharey Chuattar* and is still labelled the first genuine purveyor of Bengali social comedies. This film also launched the romantic pairing of Suchitra Sen and Uttam Kumar. Nirmal Dey, who was formally trained in visual arts, literature and photography, is said to have produced a skilful merging of witty dialogues, inventive acting and a fluid narrative style that mastered the art of using the comic without needing to resort to superfluous sentimentalism or melodrama.

Many years later, Pramod Chakravorty made a Hindi version of the story and called it *Naya Zamana*[11] (1971) but did not mention the source in the credits of the film. It was entirely a commercially packaged film starring Hema Malini, Dharmendra, Aruna Irani and Ashok Kumar in stellar roles filled with songs, dance numbers and the heightened melodrama Hindi cinema was famous for at the time. For the contemporary non-Bengali audience that did not know of *Udayer Pathey* or *Hamrahi*, *Naya Zamana* was a thorough entertainer with a Leftist touch but nothing more. The title of the Bengali film was borrowed from a Tagore poem

---

[11] *Naya Zamana*—The new era.

which fits neatly into the political context of the film that was pro-labour and anti-feudalism. The Bengali title *Udayer Pathey* that translates into *Towards the Light* reflects the hope for the workers vis-à-vis the darkness that is a metaphor for capitalist exploitation that sustained even when India was under the British Rule and remains unchanged today, nearly seven decades after Independence.

The story revolves round the life, love and struggles of Anup (Radhamohan Bhattacharya), a poor novelist who, in order to keep his body and soul together, is compelled to work as a speechwriter for Rajendranath (Biswanath Bhaduri), who is a millionaire owning a factory and has a beautiful sister Gopa (Binata Basu). But Anup quits his job in disgust when at a party where his sister Sumitra is falsely accused of theft in front of the entire crowd gathered at the party. But Gopa, who has fallen in love with Anup and is a close friend of Sumitra, has empathy for the friend and for Anup who has a bigger cause to live for—to get justice and fair play for the disgruntled, underpaid and overworked workers of Rajendranath's mill. His commitment to the workers' movement increases and in the meantime, he also writes a novel. Rajendranath's evil and corrupt son plagiarizes the book which becomes famous. This man also gets Anup bashed up badly during a union rally because Anup's dedication to the movement invests it with enough strength to threaten the business interests of Rajendranath. The end finds Rajendranath standing on the balcony to watch Anup and Gopa leave the house and walk towards the rising sun.

Arabinda Mukherjee, a noted director, says that his career in films was triggered off by Bimal Roy's *Udayer Pathey*.

> I assisted him for *Anjangarh*. In those days, we were put through a hard, grilling process. I was already employed as editing assistant. Here, I had to train for three months in the laboratory, three months on editing and three months in sound. In the meantime, I had to learn to work under Bimal Roy. He asked me to rewrite scene number 176 from the script of the film he was then making. I was told that he had asked many people to write out the same scene but remained dissatisfied with the results. So, I approached playwright Bidhayak Bhattacharjee and he helped me out by suggesting the 'drama' element needed for the scene. I was on.[12]

Udayer Pathey soon had a Hindi version called *Hamrahi*, completely re-shot on new sets with the same artistes. However, *Hamrahi* did not repeat the success of the Bengali original. His leanings towards the poor and the

---

[12] Lecture delivered at Seminar on Bimal Roy at Nehru Auditorium, Calcutta, organized by Bimal Roy Memorial Trust, in a weeklong programme in January 2002.

downtrodden perhaps came from his basic humanism rather than from purely Leftist leanings as some critics opined. His Leftist leanings, if any, stemmed from conviction and not from active association because he never held any party ticket.

The film refers to Anup as a journalist who led a precarious existence in financial terms. But he does not seem to bother him much. His sympathetic editor offers him the possibility of an opening as publicity officer at Modern Industries Limited. His personality impresses the boss's son Shouren Banerjee (Devi Mukherjee) who offers him the job. Anup does not care this way or that but accepts the position all the same because of his family responsibilities. He is a bit miffed for having to give up the kind of writing he loved best—creative writing that does not brook dictation compared to the conditioned writing for publicity of a given firm and/or the employer(s).

Some of his political ideologies are reflected in the way *Udayer Pathey's* hero Anup's room is made to look. The walls of his room are covered with his own drawings of Rabindranath Tagore, Bernard Shaw, Swami Vivekananda, Sri Aurobindo, Mahatma Gandhi and Karl Marx that stand in complete contrast to Rajendranath's lavishly decorated, spacious home that has a limousine driving out of the parking lot. His portraits are far from perfect but he believes that photographic reproductions do not bring out the spirit of the person and so he draws them himself. Anup also has inscribed the lines of a Tagore poem on the wall which has the words *Udayer Pathey* in it, which is the source for the film's title. Bimal Roy's command over suggestion comes across as the camera pans across these images of leaders and thinkers before Anup appears on screen, therefore, effectively foreshadowing his appearance with his character traced through his intellectual leanings. This is the inscription that attracts Gopa to Anup after she reads the line of poetry on the entrance.

The difference between Gopa and Sumitra lies in the saris they wear and their body language. Gopa is confident while Sumitra is uncertain of the response she will get from the elite and snobbish crowd gathered for the party, and when she sings at Gopa's request, she does so unwillingly. Her singing is cheered only by Gopa, while others are silent in response. There are other suggestive frames fleshing out the class and status distinctions between Gopa and her friend Sumitra who is Anup's sister. In one shot, we find Gopa dropping off her friend Sumitra from her chauffeur-driven limousine in a poorer neighbourhood of the city where Sumitra lives. Sumitra's mother does not know where to ask Gopa to sit in their sparingly furnished little apartment when Gopa comes to invite her friend to her niece's birthday party.

Gopa's spacious home also has a fabulous home library. Her brother Shouren prides in owning an original Jamini Roy painting and brags about it to Anup who comes to their home to ghostwrite a speech for Shouren at his request. There are differences between the personas, behaviour and body language of Shouren and Anup also and this comes across in a scene that shows an argument between the two of them as they each try to rationalize the difference between the industrialists and the workers, the rich and the poor, the haves and the have-nots where Shouren is dressed in a Western suit and Anup is dressed in the Bengali garb of kurta-dhoti. Shouren walks with a swagger, while Anup's walk is dignified.

The birthday party at Rajendranath's lavish home reinforces the class distinctions that sustain between Gopa and Sumitra. At Gopa's niece's birthday party, the guests are dressed in expensive clothes and jewellery, while Sumitra's personality pales in comparison by its very earthiness. Drinks are served by liveried servants and Sumitra shies away from placing the frock that she has stitched for the birthday girl on the table where gifts are laid out. She hides it within the folds of her sari because she feels embarrassed to place it there. Much of the party conversation is peppered with descriptions of the price of each gift and the identity of the one who gave it to qualify the financial status of the people in the party. There is also a dance number performed to a famous Tagore song by a danseuse at the party. Sumitra is suddenly accused by Gopa's sister-in-law, who is the mother of the birthday girl, of stealing from the gift table. Hearing this, Gopa is shocked and Sumitra is horrified. When Sumitra faints of shock, Gopa discovers the frock Sumitra brought from the folds of her sari. Gopa escorts Sumitra home. But a very angry Anup, who finds his sister in tears, refuses to accept Gopa's apology on her family's behalf. After Gopa leaves, Anup tells his sister that, for him and his ideology, her insult at Gopa's party is tantamount to a grievous insult to all the poor by all the rich.

Though *Udayer Pathey* had the rich-girl–poor-boy cliché of romance which became a stereotype for mainstream cinema over the years, it had a socially and politically relevant storyline that marks Anup, the protagonist, at the centre of the conflict between the petty bourgeoisie that Rajendranath and his son represent and the workers who symbolize the proletariat. Anup is an intellectual, well-read and a writer himself influenced by icons like Rabindranath Tagore. He uses his intellect to better a wrong done to the poor and the deprived workers instead of using it to make money by continuing to write speeches for Rajendranath and Shouren which takes him back to his impoverished background.

Anup was portrayed by Radhamohan Bhattacharya in a stylized performance dominant in Indian cinema till P.C. Barua in Bengal and Ashok

Kumar in Bombay brought in the style of natural acting without theatrical flourishes. Bhattacharya was one of the best educated actors in Bengali cinema of the time. He was a renowned film critic and the regular critic for *The Statesman* for many years. He was the automatic choice for directors when they were looking for an actor to portray characters that defined class, dignity and an upbringing that reflected high educational levels. He later role-played in Tapan Sinha's *Kabuliwala*, *Kshudhita Pashan*[13] and *Jhinder Bandi*[14] which are examples of the class he brought into the characters he played.

Anup, an intrepid writer–intellectual, upholds the cause of the proletariat in a system where the balance of power is skewed towards the moneyed class. Just the previous year, in 1943, Bimal Roy had made a documentary for New Theatres on the subject of the moment, the Bengal famine. Thus, *Udayer Pathey* came about when the rich–poor divide was in plain view, and inescapably so. The famine, the inflation of the war years and the economic hardships that were the exclusive lot of the poor had irredeemably polarized the haves and the have-nots into incompatible camps.[15] Anup learns that his landlord and Gopa's brother Shouren are hoarding rice in huge quantities. He also learns that they are not doing it because there is a deficit in their own stock but because their aim is to sell the same rice at black market prices "four times more than the price I paid for it," says Shouren at one point. The landlord urges Anup to follow suit, but he not only refuses to hoard but also suggests the landlord to give up hoarding for the cause of the masses.

Udayer Pathey carried seeds of the fiery zeal that chartered the earlier directorial career of Bimal Roy and later metamorphosed into a social concern in a more subtle way than it did in this film as well as in *Anjangarh*, *Pehla Aadmi* and *Do Bigha Zamin*, where it is quite pronounced and more clearly articulated. Yet, his total restraint in keeping away from any kind of political propaganda or pamphleteering in his films makes the films stand apart and gives them the auteur character they define. Satyajit Ray is quoted to have said about the filmmaker:

> With his very first film Udayer Pathe (Hamrahi in Hindi), Bimal Roy was able to sweep aside the cobwebs of the old tradition and introduce a realism and subtly that was wholly suited to the cinema. He was undoubtedly a pioneer. He reached his peak with a film that still reverberates in

---

[13] *Kshudhita Pashan*—Hungry stones.
[14] *Jhinder Bandi*—The prisoner of Zenda.
[15] Nivedita Ramakrishnan, *Udayer Pathey (1944), Bimal Roy's Realistic Inference of Socialism*. Available at *Dear Cinema.com*. http://www.imdb.com/name/nm0149831/news (Accessed on 1 March 2017).

the minds of those who saw it when it was first made. I refer to Do Bigha Zamin, which remains one of the landmarks of Indian Cinema.[16]

Is Anup an 'Outsider'? Redefining the Bhadralok in Bengali Cinema and Culture

Anup is an 'outsider' in *Udayer Pathey* because he redefines the term bhadralok and brings it within the mainstream of the petty bourgeoisie or the working class. His 'displacement' from the bhadralok gentry is not forced on him, socially or economically, but is purely out of choice. He is an 'outsider' in Gopa's family and is also an 'outsider' crusading for the working class which he certainly does not belong to. That does not strip off the 'bhadralok' stature but gives the very status of 'the bhadralok' a new definition in keeping with the birth of a new dawn as the name of the film suggests.

According to the definition given in Wikipedia,[17] the bhadralok in Bengali means the new class of 'gentlemen' (*bhadra* meaning decent and *lok* meaning man) who rose during British colonial times that is roughly defined as falling between 1757 and 1947 in Bengal. Giving the bhadralok tag, in formal terms, was subject to certain 'unwritten qualities', such as the person had to be born of an upper caste, had to belong to a family with class or directly into aristocracy that includes extended feudal families keeping their present financial status aside, educated and preferably well-read, articulate and decent in manners.

However, it may be noted that many bhadralok in the nineteenth century came from an underprivileged Brahmin or Priest caste or middle-level merchant class. On the other hand, it was also established that anyone who could show considerable amount of wealth and standing in society was a member of the bhadralok community. The word bhadralok acquired a dignity of its own among the Bengali mass and evolved into a 'class' as distinguished from the 'mass'. All members of the professional classes, that is, those belonging to the newly emerging professions, such as doctors, lawyers, engineers, university professors and higher civil servants, were members of the bhadralok community. However, an individual bearing the title *Esquire* at the end of the name, denoting a rank just below a knight, was also considered to be higher than a bhadralok.

Historically, the bhadralok class was a group of tax-collectors and clerics who occupied some of the highest positions in colonial hierarchy.[18]

---

[16] Omar Ahmed, '*Do Bigha Zamin*/Two Acres of Land', *Senses of Cinema* (27 January 2009).

[17] See https://en.wikipedia.org/wiki/Bhadralokry (Accessed on 14 January 2017).

[18] Indira Chowdhury, *The Frail Hero and Virile History: Gender and the Politics of Culture in Colonial Bengal* (New Delhi: Oxford University Press, 1998).

The bhadralok class, thus, comprised of social elites created by land reforms and trade policies of the East India Company, particularly the Permanent Settlement of 1793. To ensure the highest revenue collections from land, the Company gave 'ownership' rights to zamindars who were responsible for extracting levies from the peasantry. The bhadralok class benefited from these colonial privileges but was ultimately powerless under colonial rule. Heterogeneous in its caste membership, it comprised of new and old elites in equal measure.[19] Nirad Chaudhuri writes[20] that the bhadralok class comprises people of a wide range of economic means, from those in acute poverty to those with access to a great quantum of wealth.[21] In his informed paper, Romit Chowdury lays bare how masculinities, "far from being natural, are made in particular socio-cultural contexts." His paper has "drawn on literature in the field of masculinity studies to highlight the interactional dynamics through which ideas of *bhadralok* masculinity are produced in a particular form of sociality in contemporary Kolkata."

The consolidation and growth of the bhadralok class in the nineteenth century was closely connected to the Bengal renaissance. It was with the Bengal Renaissance and the introduction of Western education (available for the most part to urban middle-class Hindu males only) that the bhadralok—a new class of secularized intelligentsia, clerks and bureaucrats—emerged at the confluence of colonial trade and educational institutions like the Hindu College in Calcutta.[22] Sumanta Banerjee[23] has pointed out that the babus of the latter part of the nineteenth century seemed to be of two types—first, decadent scions of the eighteenth century *baniyas*, who squandered away their inherited wealth on entertainment, and a second retinue class comprising of barristers, doctors, teachers, and so on.[24]

Anup, who is perhaps the first left-of-centre bhadralok in Bengali cinema, uses the title *lekhak* meaning 'writer' after his first name which is the first departure of the bhadralok from his conventional practice of using

---

[19] Lata Mani, 'Abstract Disquisitions: Bhadralok and the Normative Violence of Sati', in *Contentious Traditions: The Debate on Sati in Colonial India* (London: University of California Press, 1998).

[20] Nirad C. Chaudhuri, 'From The Autobiography of an Unknown Indian', in *Memory's Gold: Writings on Calcutta*, ed. Amit Chaudhuri (New Delhi: Penguin, 2008).

[21] Romit Chowdhury, 'Bengalis but not Men? Bhadralok Masculinities in Adda', *Journal of Emerging Research in Media and Cultural Studies, School of Media and Cultural Studies* 1, no. 1 (2013): 146–170.

[22] Chaudhuri, Sukanta. *Calcutta—The Living City: Volume II: The Present and Future*, 1 January 2000, (New Delhi: Oxford University Press, 2010).

[23] Sumanta Banerjee. "The 'Beshya' and the 'Babu': Prostitute and Her Clientele in 19th Century Bengal." *Economic and Political Weekly* 28 no. 45 (1993): 2,461–2,472.

[24] Ibid.; Chowdhury, 'Bengalis but not Men?' 152.

his family name proudly after his first. He refuses to use his last name. When called for an interview, he says his name is Anup Lekhak. When asked "why," he simply replies, "Why not? If you can accept 'Ghatak' or 'Pathak', why not Lekhak?" 'Ghatak' in Bengali is a family name that originally attached itself to the occupation of marriage fixers called 'Ghatak' in Bengali. 'Pathak' was originally the family name of those engaged as professional readers. So, he extended the argument to attach 'Lekhak' which means 'writer'. When read from a different angle, the use of 'Lekhak', by Anup marks out his stand against caste, class and creed distinctions of any kind, his secular mindset and his confrontational approach towards the ruling class be it the British in power or the industrialist Rajendranath and his son Shouren. Anup became an iconic hero of all time with this film and the success of the film consolidated his position as a strong man whose strength is derived from the power of his pen and from his belief in his out-of-the-box ideologies, and is empathy for the exploited, the oppressed and the marginalized.

Anup is educated, well-read, articulate and rational, but poor. Rajendranath and his son Shouren are also bhadraloks according to the common understanding of the term, but they are 'mainstream' bhadraloks with rather Westernized lifestyles and stick to their class and status within their social networking worlds, while Anup with his agenda for the workers in Rajendranath's factory is an 'out-of-the-box' bhadralok or more appropriately, he redefines the term bhadralok in his own way. This redefinition is accepted by the masses because the film was a big box-office hit which it would not have been had the audience rejected the film. He is a writer and influenced by the works of Rabindranath Tagore which defines him as an intellectual but not a snob. He is a social rebel and a non-conformist which is not in keeping with the 'colonial construct' that the Bengali babu was sharp of intellect but frail of limbs, a configuration that was internalized to a great degree by the bhadralok himself.[25]

Anup is not 'frail of limbs', though he is stoned by Shouren's man when Shouren feels threatened by Anup's leadership of the workers and by what he feels is instigation of the workers to rise against their employers. But in looks, body language and manner of speech, dented a little by Radhamohan Bhattacharya's somewhat stiffened manner of acting and slightly stilted dialogue delivery, Anup does not reveal the 'softness' and the rather 'effete' demeanour of the historically defined bhadralok. At no point of the narrative does he 'become' a worker. Even in the end as he is making his way to Asansol leaving Gopa behind on her father's desperate request,

---

[25] Chowdhury, *The Frail Hero and Virile History*.

his destination to another similar industrial unit with the same social agenda—to secure justice for the workers—suggests that his agenda defines an ongoing journey for the people he considers exploited, overworked and underpaid by the capitalist class, and what began with Rajendranath and his son Shouren marks the beginning of the journey, not the end.

Anup at the same time adheres to the bhadralok identity when he ghostwrites a speech for Shouren and then writes a novel called *Purbachal* (The Eastern Space) which in sharp and incisive terms depicts the lives of the working class. How does he know so much about the pains and struggles and about the injustice heaped on the working class? This makes him an exception to conventional bhadralok who takes pride in remaining complacently cushioned by their bhadralok identity, yet it is not as though he lives with the working class or even works alongside in the factory with them. The film is silent about Anup's source of information about the workers, but his action proves it all when even in spite of being hit with a stone, he refuses to give up his agenda. In other words, by redefining the conventional interpretation and understanding of the term bhadralok as defined by social and cultural studies, Anup sort of uproots the term bhadralok from its original place and plants it differently in a different space to give it a different persona within the history and culture of Bengali cinema, later reinforced by his successors Uttam Kumar and Soumitra Chatterjee.

This 'mainstreaming' of the bhadralok identity redefined by Anup in *Udayer Pathey* turned into a pattern among the top heroes of Bengali cinema which had begun, in a manner of speaking, with P.C. Barua before Anup appeared in the scene and later with Uttam Kumar and Soumitra Chatterjee, the two stellar actors, became an established, recognized and accepted trend in Bengali cinema.

Uttam Kumar redefined the concept of 'masculinity' that, placed in a perspective, merges into the Bengali bhadralok identity that found favour with his audience—male and female—with equal appeal. Soumitra Chatterjee entered the cinema scenario to tinge the history of Bengali cinema with his unique brand of masculinity distanced from his predecessor and rival Uttam Kumar. His screen masculinity is more appropriately placed within post-colonial, independent India, though it was 'born' in Satyajit Ray's *Apur Sansar*[26] related to an earlier time in Bengal's history. He still represented the Bengali Bhadralok but in a more refined, subtle, understated and sophisticated form. The screen bhadralok, in fact, had metamorphosed from P.C. Barua's *Devdas* to Uttam Kumar's *Harano Sur*[27]

---

[26] *Apur Sansar*—The world of Apu.
[27] *Harano Sur*—The lost note.

to Soumitra Chatterjee's *Saat Pake Bandha*.[28] Within this scenario, Anup stands out as different. None of these heroes bared their bodies to show off their six abs or eight abs, did not perform action scenes, fight much, use swear words and abusive language or indulge in aggressive sport activities. They spouted poetry and sang songs. They, therefore, neatly fit into the conventional Bengali bhadralok persona that led to their massive popularity among and identification with the Bengali audience. These heroes corresponded to the concept of hegemonic masculinity because they turned into live icons to imitate, be fascinated by and to worship.

The Transformation of Gopa

The most amazing feature of *Udayer Pathey* is how Gopa becomes an 'outsider', first, by befriending Sumitra who is from a poor family; second, by falling in love with her brother Anup slowly without quite realizing it; third, after reading the manuscript of his novel and being influenced by its ideology and its thesis and, finally, by the way he solidly first initiates and then backs the workers' movement. She is a class apart within the family she belongs to, which means that she is probably a bit off-mainstream despite the affluence she is brought up in and lives within. A girl like Gopa who wears expensive saris, rides a limousine to college and drinks tea from China cups cannot be expected to befriend a 'commoner' like Sumitra or fall in love with her brother Anup. But she does! Later, Anup convinces her with the argument that the very fact that she learns about the pitiable situation of the working class from his manuscript points out to the ignorance of the classes about the situation the masses live in. The transformation from 'mainstream' to 'outsider' comes across when she comes dressed in a simple sari to Anup's frugal home and cheerfully accepts tea from a cup with a broken handle. She accompanies him to the huts of the workers too.

Purbachal (The Eastern Space) is published later by Shouren under his own name when he realizes the literary and social value of the manuscript. This heightens the negativity of Shouren's character and is part of the melodramatic twist that places Anup on a higher platform in terms of values. This is prioritized by the metamorphosis the manuscript brings in Gopa who, almost literally, crosses over to the 'other' side from her original one. These are dramatic incidents intelligently woven into the script to unfold, layer by layer, the change taking place in Gopa. When the published book becomes famous, a celebration party is organized by his crowd

[28] *Saat Paake Bandha*—This is the name of a mandatory ritual in a Bengali (Hindu) marriage where the groom and bride take seven rounds about the holy fire and swear to be together through seven obstacles.

of friends with a lavish dinner laid out on the table. But in her manner of protest, Gopa does not attend the party and goes along with Anup to attend the meeting of the workers' union in a hut. There are contrast scenes inter-cut to juxtapose the wonderful food at the party table accompanied by loud laughter against the hut where the air is filled with tension, and suddenly, Gopa discovers a little child who has not been fed for two whole days.

Gopa's displacement from her roots—her father, her brother, her sister-in-law, and the affluence she is brought up in is voluntary, brought about not only because she has fallen in love with Anup but also because she has first been initiated into his ideology, then is convinced by it and then joins him in his crusade. She walks out of her parental home only to find that Anup has already left for Asansol on the request of her father. Not one to turn around and go back, she goes chasing him in the family car for one last time, catches up with him and the two set off together in partnership born of love and a commonly shared agenda for the masses. Gopa perhaps is the first *bhadramahila*[29] rebel in the history of Bengali cinema.

The story goes that a noted recording company of the time brought out the complete dialogue track of *Hamrahi* following the thumping box-office success of the film. The record was also very popular among the masses.

Do Bigha Zamin (1953)

Background

Do Bigha Zamin was one of the first mainstream Indian films to receive international acclaim; it was awarded the Prix International at the 1954 Cannes Film Festival. Though it clearly was intended as a melodrama aimed at a mainstream audience, the artists involved with the production of the film were not only inspired by a common ideological belief in socialism that defied the conservatism of Indian cinema but they also succeeded in dem-onstrating how genre could be subverted and adopted as a tool to address wider inequalities and afflictions.[30]

Do Bigha Zamin is said to be the first-ever Indian film to express the deep influence of Italian neorealism in cinema. Neorealism is a movement that arose in Italy after World War II, dominated the Italian cinema in the late 1940s and influenced filmmakers all around the world. At a time when musicals and light comedies were allowing moviegoers to escape from the grim facts of war, the neorealists presented an authentic treatment of the

---

[29] *Bhadramahila*—It is the feminine of the word *bhadralok* meaning 'gentleman' so *bhadrama-hila* means 'lady' suggesting respect for the woman of high birth and decent demeanour.
[30] Ibid. Ahmed.

wartime experience and grappled with the social problems of post-war Italy. Mainly Marxists and liberal Catholics, neorealists advocated Leftist ideas and were strongly influenced by the Soviet cinema.

Ironically, the development of neorealism owes a great deal to the Fascists. Like the German Nazis and the Russian Communists, the Italian Fascists realized the power of cinema as a medium of propaganda, and when they came to power, they took over the film industry. Although this meant that those who opposed fascism could not make films and that foreign films were censored, the Fascists helped established the essential requirements for a flourishing film industry. In 1935, they founded the Centro Sperimentale in Rome, a film school headed by Luigi Chiarini, which taught all aspects of film production. Many important neorealist directors attended this school, including Roberto Rossellini, Antonioni, Zampa, Germi and DeSantis. It also produced cameramen, editors and technicians. Chiarini was allowed to publish *Bianco e nero*, the film journal that later became the official voice of neorealism. In 1937, the Fascists opened Cinecittà, the largest, the best-equipped movie studio in all of Europe. Once Mussolini fell from power, the stage was set for a strong, left-wing cinema. Film historian Amrit Gangar says:

> One of the earliest artistic/cinematic renderings of peasant displacement and their subsequent migration to metropolitan cores of post-colonial India was Bimal Roy's *Do Bigha Zamin* (1952), a film about the peasants of Bengal and their losing battle for survival against avaricious land-lords.[31] Shambhu, the protagonist in the movie, sets out to get his land released from local landlord landing in Calcutta as a migrant labourer. The travails of Shambhu and his son along with a host of such subalterns and marginalized subjectivities critiques the implications of such an existence. The film offers a microcosm of the ability of cinema to render the human experiences in a unique way through its technocratic quotient and imagistic jugglery which enthralls the audience like literature.[32]

Though Bimal Roy embraced the aesthetics and ideological principles of neorealism, he was constrained by the reality of having to work within a set of limitations, for example, *Do Bigha Zamin* for all its socialist ideals was nevertheless a studio film. Working within the conventions of social/family

---

[31] Amrit Gangar, 'Do Bigha Zamin/Two Acres of Land and Migration in Indian Cinematography', *Café Dissensus* (1 August 2014).

[32] Rohit Phutela, 'Do Beegha Zamin—Textualizing Subalterns in Post Independence Indian Cinema', *Journal of Literature, Culture and Media Studies* IV, nos. 7&8 (January–December, 2012).

melodrama genre, Bimal Roy integrated songs into the narrative which in the eyes of purists went against the stylization and escapist nature of what neorealism was trying to oppose. However, apart from this musical compromise, *Do Bigha Zamin* is closer to the work of Vittorio De Sica than it is to many other neorealism films, especially when you compare the humanist depiction of the relationship between father/Sambhu and son/Kanhaiya. The parallels are striking when compared to *Bicycle Thieves*, the most significantly perhaps in the idea of the son having to work tirelessly so that he can support his father's desire to reclaim the ancestral land which rightfully belongs to him. Bimal Roy's success in being able to integrate neorealist influences with the traditional trappings of the Hindi melodrama. Ideologically, the pessimistic ending illustrates that social oppression is something monolithic, inevitable and a hegemonic extension of industrial change and capitalist triumph.[33]

The Story

The long poem, like a ballad that narrates a story, was written in the first person, as if it is a narration by the subject to the reader, the subject being a victim of feudal dominance and power. The narrator does not have a name or a specific identity which is common in poetry. Salil Chowdhury while transforming the long poem into a story and a script turned the narrator into the third-person subject of the film, gave him a name and an identity, though farming remained his occupation. The ethnic identity of Shambhu Mahato is never clearly defined in the film, but as the story unfolds, we learn that he is not Bengali. The film also gave him a family and a social and professional backdrop necessary to convert an abstract narrative poem into a concrete shape of a film in a way that the story acquired an identity of its own independent of the poem Tagore wrote. The original poem was like an elegy in terms of content, a painful song sung by the narrator where the reader is told the story and not called upon to be judgemental or questioning because there is no scope for the reader to comment. But the film version creates its own large ambience by inviting the audience to participate in Shambhu's story as a listener, a viewer and audience. The viewer draws his own conclusions and carries the film with him outside the precincts of the theatre. The very idea mooted by Bimal Roy to ask Chowdhury to write a story from the original poem with his own inputs as a writer underscores the director's richness of vision as a filmmaker, a storyteller and a social commentator on the New India that is making its presence felt after Independence.

---

[33] Ahmed, 'Do Bigha Zamin/Two Acres of Land'.

The story is about Shambhu Mahato (Balraj Sahni), a poor peasant who owns a small plot of land that measures two acres and for which he owes the landlord in Gopipur, a small village near Kolkata. The village does not have electricity but the zamindar lives in a spacious home lit with chandeliers. Shambhu lives in a small home with his old and asthmatic father (Nana Palsikar), wife Paro (Nirupa Roy) and growing son Kanhaiya (Ratan Kumar). The zamindar, Thakur Harnam Singh (Sapru), lands in his car with two prospectors from the city at the land where the peasants are tilling the land. He says he wants to build a factory on the land, a huge tract of fertile land. The problem is, Shambhu's two acres stand right in the middle of the tract earmarked for the factory tentatively named "The Great Janata Mills Ltd." When Shambu refuses to part with his land for a factory, the landlord says that he was willing to surrender the debt Shambhu owes him if Shambhu agreed to the exchange.

"Zameen to kisan ke maa hoti hai huzoor, maa ko bech doon?" (A shocked Shambhu asks the zamindar how he can sell off the land that he looks up to as his mother.) "Maa baap ban jayegi," says the landlord (meaning, 'It will become the father') in response. Shambhu is adamant and asks the landlord for four days to repay the loan.

The camera cuts to Shambhu Mahato's humble home where his father and son are planting a mango sapling that, the old man says, will bear fruits after five years. This suggests hope for the future for the family which, however, remains a dream as the story unfolds. With the help of his son, Ratan, who goes to school, Shambhu calculates the money he owes to the landlord. Ratan says it amounts to a total of ₹65 which includes ₹5 as interest.

He begins to collect utensils from his wife for selling in order to make a total of ₹65. Paro adds to this by pooling the gold earrings she got from her father. But when Shambhu comes back after four days to repay the loan in full, the accountant tells him that the amount is ₹235.50 and shows the document that carries Shambhu's thumb impression as proof. Shambhu goes to court where he is told that there three years of land tax has fallen due in Shambhu's name. Shambhu keeps insisting that he has paid two years' land tax and only of one year is due. Shambhu refuses to give away his land to the zamindar in lieu of the loan and the land tax. The court gives Shambhu three months' time to repay the loan failing which his land will be auctioned away to the landlord. The court case leads to Shambhu's losing the entire sum he had collected against the sold utensils and Paro's earrings. The family is now deeply in debt and is also threatened by the loss of its sole source of livelihood, the two acres of land.

After about half an hour of screening time, we find Shambhu walking towards the station to catch the train and the soundtrack plays the famous Manna De number 'Mausam beeta jaaye' (seasons pass by) with men and women engaged in different chores in the fields as if they are bidding a fond farewell to Shambhu. The camera cuts to the train compartment filled with a debate on village versus city while a hawker hawks a mosquito killing agent suggesting the proliferation of mosquitoes in the city. Shambhu suddenly discovers his son Kanhaiya hiding in the compartment. He has followed him secretly because he has never travelled in a train and wants to be with his father.

The scene now shifts to a Calcutta we do not get to see anymore. The father and son look puzzled and wonder in surprise as they walk below the Howrah Bridge with big cars moving by. Kanhaiya laughs at a man wearing a bush shirt with a newspaper print on it because the boy thinks the man is wearing a newspaper. A hungry Kanhaiya is captured smelling jalebis[34] near a sweetmeat shop and laughs at a two-storey house that has wheels—his interpretation of a double-decker bus. The ruthlessness of the city comes across when no one answers Shambhu's questions and we see the Monument (Shaheed Minar) standing in the backdrop. Bimal Roy throws up a very vivid perspective of the city looked at through the eyes of a villager and his son who have never been to a city ever before. Father and son are forced to sleep on the pavement, but a thief comes and does away with their bundle and the bowl and only Shambhu's stick is left behind. They finally find shelter in a slum called Lalababu's *basti*[35] with its own collage of colours offering a microcosm of the downtrodden in the city. Most of the people there are from other states and are Hindi-speaking, except the landlady and her daughter. The Bengali landlady (Rajlakshmi Devi) of the room that is let out to Shambhu and his son has a rude and loud tone, but she is kind at heart.

Small vignettes of the city capturing the downtrodden, the marginalized and the poor living in a slum, mostly from outside the city and the state, show the regular quarrels around the public tap. The sound track fills with screams in the night, for which we are told that the man has lost his leg and still has nightmares of his leg being amputated. Another group that has landed in the city in search of a livelihood sings 'O meri Rama Gajab teri duniya' (Oh my rama your world is really strange) which spells out the

---

[34] *Jalebis*—Name of an Indian sweet that is made of refined flour, fried in deep oil in circles and dipped in sugar syrup.
[35] *Basti*—Slum.

merciless behaviour of city people. Yet, not everyone can be measured by the same measuring rod of ruthlessness. Shambhu begins to work as a porter carrying baggage and burdens he is too underfed to carry. Then one day he gets to draw a hand-pulled rickshaw by a twist of fate when a rickshaw puller, who is his friend, falls sick.

The Bengali landlady (Rajlakshmi Devi) of the room she lets out to Shambhu and his son is rude-talking and loud but she is kind at heart. A rickshaw puller falls sick and Shambhu takes his rickshaw to ride it one day. The old and sick rickshaw puller teaches him to draw the rickshaw properly. Shots of streets being washed early in the morning with municipal workers using a hosepipe and streets lamps lit with a long stick in the evenings are scenes from a Calcutta that does not exist anymore. In this sense, the film offers a social and cultural historiography of the city. Shambhu is overjoyed when a passenger pays him an eight-anna coin. Among the cameos other than the fat but straight-talking landlady and her young daughter is a hawker who lives there and likes the young girl. This is Mehmood who acquired great fame in later days. Lalloo Ustad (Jagdeep in his debut performance) befriends Kanhaiya and initiates him to become a shoeshiner. Lalloo is a teenager but street smart and helpful; he loves movies in general and Raj Kapoor's *Awaara* in particular. Kanhaiya also befriends a pickpocket with oiled down short hair who teaches him to pick pockets, which Kanhaiya wants to learn so that his father can accumulate enough money to repay the loan. But he is caught while stealing, and when his honest father gets to know this, he tells the boy, "A peasant's son never steals." Shambhu bashes his son up till the landlady comes and rebukes him.

One of the most unforgettable scenes in the city is the one that features a rickshaw race. A passenger promises a very good fare to Shambhu if he can race the other rickshaw in which the passenger's girlfriend is seated. Shambhu is egged on by the man's hiking up the fare, but he is unaware that he is getting exhausted by the minute, is running out of breath and, most importantly, one of the wheels of his rickshaw has turned loose till the rickshaw begins to roll and then topples taking Shambhu along with it. The race is beautifully shot and edited with fast intercutting shots of the man and the lady and though one can anticipate the tragedy about to happen, the suspense is accelerated by design to reach a high pitch only to fall suddenly. This brings across the coarse insensitivity of the relatively affluent towards the very poor as the respective looks and costumes of the couple and Shambhu reveal, the man busy showing off some non-existent bravado to his girlfriend and the lure of more money to Shambhu at the cost of the latter getting into a big accident that might have taken his life. That it does not is another 'accident' of destiny, but it deprives him of his daily earnings for some weeks and demands medication plus nourishment.

Back in the village, Paro and Shambhu's father are worried because there is no letter from him for 20 days. The juxtaposition of two mothers—the one from the upper middle class (Meena Kumari in a brief role) and Paro who comes to request her to write a postcard to her husband—throws up the contradictions in the lives of two women, both mothers. While Paro's son is away in the city slogging his way as a shoeshiner instead of going to school, this beautiful mother is singing a lovely lullaby to her infant sleeping in a cradle. Paro's tattered sari is for all to see. This scene of interaction between the two women is superimposed with flashbacks of Paro holding the baby Kanhaiya in her lap.

There are some interesting intercuts of the city and village—Kanhaiya polishing shoes, Paro engaged in some work, Shambhu pulling the rickshaw that ends in a bad accident, the pickpocket who sells racing tickets and also plays the harmonica, Paro at the post office asking if any letter has arrived at the Chandanpur Post Office and so on. She finds she is pregnant but is almost on a forced fast since only ₹50 is left in the family kitty. She begins to work at the construction site which pays her ₹2 per day. The badly injured Shambhu cannot shave so he grows a beard. The landlady gives money to Kanhaiya to get fruits for his father who needs nutrition. One day, his shoeshine box is taken away and broken. He is beaten up by his father when he brings a big sum of money.

Paro is forced to leave for Calcutta in search of her husband who is still sick. From this point on, the film suddenly becomes melodramatic filled with incredible coincidences that partly strip the film off its beautiful rhythm in story, script and pace, plus editing. The bad man's attempt to molest and rape Paro, Paro falling under a car as she tries to flee the man and Shambhu approaching the crowd gathered around the accident site to discover with shock that the victim is none else than Paro all bring down the film several notches from its earlier plank. But it picks up again in the climactic sequences.

Shambhu comes back to the village with Paro and Kanhaiya only to find a wired fencing built around the land that was once his with the factory under construction. He pushes his hand inside the wire fencing to pick up a fistful of the earth. When the watchman comes chasing him and asks him what he has in his hand, he opens his fist to allow the earth to pour away.

The story goes that for the Calcutta screenings of the film, Bimal Roy shot a different ending in which Paro, Shambhu's pregnant wife, comes in search of her husband and son and dies in a road accident. But the audience could not take the morbid end where the man loses everything. He had to replace this end with another in which Shambhu loses his land, but is left to struggle with his wife and son. This is the one we have all seen and still get to see.

Of Forced Migration and Permanent Displacement

Shambhu had gone to the city with the sole intention of coming back one day, with enough money to release the land from the grasp of the landlord. But on his return he sees the fertile land fit for agriculture has already been turned over to an industry. This spells out the beginnings of industrialization at the cost of agricultural land, not really for the benefit of the peasants but in the name of development, for cushioning the pockets of those whose pockets are already cushioned with money and land by ulterior means from the poor, the oppressed and the marginalized. The film defines a powerful and scathing but restrained social comment on the destiny of the forced migrant farmers and small landowners who create the capital but are deprived of their rightful share in the contribution. The film tries to create a politically conscious milieu and an ethical awareness for social activism that are imperative to the proper functioning of a democratic nation. The melodrama and realism, thus, accentuate the same national temperament.[36]

For Balraj Sahani, who rose to fame for the first time with his performance in *Do Bigha Zamin*, it was a long arduous journey into acting in films because he remained extremely nervous in front of the camera for years together. On the other hand, his wife Damayanti became a famous star of Hindi films in Bombay and he confesses that he was jealous of her success countered by his persistent failure to make it in films. He realized the true worth of Damayanti when she passed away quite young, leaving behind their two children Parikshit and Shabnam.[37]

In his autobiography,[38] Sahani says that for the role of Shambhu Mahato in Bimal Roy's *Do Bigha Zamin*, he visited a colony monopolized by *bhaiyas*[39] of Bihar and Uttar Pradesh in Jogeshwari, Bombay, to learn about their way of working, the way they walked, squatted on the ground to eat, their accent, their dress and the way they wrapped the turban around their heads. But when the unit went to Calcutta for location shooting, he

---

[36] Ibid.

[37] Balraj Sahani. *Balraj Sahani: An Autobiography* (Hind Pocket Books, 1979).

[38] Ibid.

[39] *Bhaiyas*—Bhaiya is a colloquial term that refers to men mainly from Bihar and UP in India who are clubbed together under this term. The word means 'brother'. Sometimes, the term is used as a joke, sometimes as a sign of kinship and sometimes, just as a way of establishing the regional identification.

visited the office of the rickshawallah's union. One member taught him to ride a hand-pulled rickshaw which was much more difficult than riding a cycle rickshaw. An old rickshaw puller walked up to him and asked him about the story of *Do Bigha Zamin*. After Sahani had finished narrating it to him, he sighed deeply and as he walked away, said, "Yeh to meri kahani hai babu, yeh to meri kahani hai!"[40] (This is my story Babu, this is my story!).

All the script and the humanist acting styles, including a hard but kind landlady in the Calcutta slum and the happy-go-lucky shoeshine boy (Jagdeep) who takes Kanhaiya under his wing while humming Raj Kapoor's 'Awara hoon'[41] number, find their ancestry in Nitin Bose's ruralist socials at New Theatres, such as *Desher Mati*[42] in 1938, enhanced by IPTA overtones in Salil Chowdhury's music. The film's neorealist reputation is almost solely based on Balraj Sahni's extraordinary performance in his best-known film role. Also remarkable is Hrishikesh Mukherjee's editing, virtually eliminating dissolves in favour of unusually hard cuts from the falling wheel of the film's famous rickshaw race sequence to Kanhaiya coming to the bedside of his injured father.

Mukherjee claims that such a cut from day to night was unprecedented in Indian cinema. Sahni, however, is reported to have given a similar performance along neorealist lines in K.A. Abbas's first film *Dharti Ke Lal* (1946). Some earlier films of K.A. Abbas (1914–1987), such as *Dharti Ke Lal*, made under the IPTA banner and drawing on Bijon Bhattacharya's famous classics *Nabanna*[43] (1944) dealing with the Bengal famine of 1943, followed much later by *Munna* (1954) made without songs and dances, and *Shaher Aur Sapna*[44] (1963) cheaply made on location in slums, were described as being influenced by neorealism other than Satyajit Ray's milestone, all-time classic *Pather Panchali* which came after *Do Bigha Zamin*.

The opening frame focuses on a close-up of a parched, cracked land because there has been no rain for two years. This crack is a metaphor both for the drought-stricken village and its people as well as a foreseeing of the 'cracked' future of the villagers whose land and livelihood is placed at stake by the landlord who wants to build a factory in the village. Then there is rain and this is heralded by the beautiful song 'Hariayala saval dhol bajata aaya'[45] sung and danced in chorus reflecting the happiness they are suddenly

---

[40] Sahani, *Balraj Sahani: An Autobiography*.

[41] 'Awara hoon'—(I am a vagabond). This is the title song of the film *Awaara*.

[42] *Desher Mati*—The earth of the homeland.

[43] *Nabanna*—The new crop. This is a Bengali harvest celebration usually celebrated with food, dance and music.

[44] *Shaher Aur Sapna*—The city and the dream.

[45] *Hariyala Saawan Dhol Bajata Aaya*—The green monsoon has arrived playing on the drums.

made a part of. This is soon followed by another song, 'Dharti kahe pukar ke' with visuals showing villagers happily tilling the soil after having victimized by drought for two years. This crack also stands of the homeland that threatens the very survival of the inhabitants and owners of the land forcing some of them to migrate. This migration suggests permanent displacement for those who went away with the hope of returning home and is a form of displacement that can never be remedied.

Life in the city for people like Shambhu does not offer the succour he seeks nor is he able to collect the money he has to pay back to reclaim his possession of his land. It is a migration from known roots to unknown and uncertain dangers of temptation for making quick money through pick pocketing, committing petty thefts, living in bad conditions in a slum-like environment, making a living out of an uncertain occupation that can go away without warning or posing a threat to life, molestation of village women not wise to the ways of city people and so on. Shambhu, his son Kanhaiya, Lalloo (the pickpocket), the old and sick rickshaw puller, the *kulfiwallah*[46] and the hawker are cogs in the wheel of exploitation by the system that gives the capitalist structure of the economy its power and renders the Shambus of India weaker in every sense than they were before. If Shambhu migrated to come back home one day, when he really comes back—also through force of circumstances—he is still a migrant, rootless and displaced.

Bimal Roy does away with the then-dominant cinematic mode of idealizing the village against critiquing the city or, romanticizing either. Through Shambhu's journey, *Do Bigha Zamin* shows that for people like him, migration does not solve problems but creates other problems without taking care of the earlier ones. Going back to the village is even more problematic because that means you have left behind the faintest ray of hope—if it was there at all—to step into a world filled with hopelessness and defeat. This is not a war between the city and the village but a depiction that for people like Shambhu and his family, there is just no escape, thanks to people like the zamindar, his deceitful accountant, the realtors who live in the city but are eager to confiscate space and land in the village without letting go of their city properties. Other people who live a precarious existence in Lal Babu's basti are also migrants, but some of them, like Lalloo Ustad, have adjusted to the migrant state in their own way. *Do Bigha Zamin* is an allegory of the persistence of feudal structures in post-colonial India. Law does not protect the poor peasants nor could the oppressed peasantry

---

[46] *kulfiwallas*—'Kulfi' is an indigenously prepared ice-cream, a hybrid Indian version that is made of milk condensed and thickened and frozen in chunks of ice inside an earthen pot and taking out in small cones for serving. The ones who sell these 'kulfis' are known as *kulfiwallas*.

fight injustice and exploitation in solidarity. "Shambhu and his family are the norm in this sense," writes Amrit Gangar.[47]

Gangar goes on to state that *Do Bigha Zamin* is a complex combination of what a post-colonial, post-independence, pro-development nation building milieu moulded into the framework of neorealist cinema could achieve. In its powerful rendering of the asymmetrical relations of power between the spatialities that we call urban and rural, and the haves and the have-nots, and its underlining of the political nature of spaces, *Do Bigha Zamin* belongs to the oeuvre of Chetan Anand's *Neecha Nagar* (World down below, 1946), and K.A. Abbas's *Dharti Ke Lal* (Children of the Earth, 1946), based on a play on the Bengal famine of 1943. It also anticipates what we are witnessing in post-liberalization India at a catastrophic scale, that is, an ever-deepening agrarian crisis and unprecedented migration of rural poor to the urban core.[48]

Shambhu went to the city to free himself from the oppression of the zamindar symbolized by the fictitious amount of the loan and the imaginary addition of two years to the tax burden. But the spatial and human configurations he has to negotiate with in the city environment, steeps him in deeper debt of a different kind that appears to be graver and more threatening than what he faced back in the village. From one tunnel of hopelessness he has migrated to another longer and darker tunnel of defeat, and as he tries to return, he finds that the tunnel is open only at one end and there is no exit at the other. Despite the presence of regular commercial ingredients of lots of songs—beautifully written, composed and sung—an attempted rape scene and melodramatic twists and unrealistic coincidences, *Do Bigha Zamin* found favour with an intelligent audience because behind the shining glimmer of these commercial twists was a genuine concern for the marginalized 'outsider' whose struggle for survival cuts across spatial barriers of the rural and the urban treated equally with empathy and a certain cinematic distance. The characterizations came across very naturally, with actors shorn completely of make-up and ornamentation of any kind which stripped them off the plasticity of screen glamour. Chidananda Dasgupta[49] writes:

> Among others who shared in this post-Independence zeal for social reform was Bimal Roy.... Roy brought a Bengali style of filmmaking to Bombay—gentle, relatively slow, free of crudities, concentrating on story development and other literary qualities without losing grip over film

---

[47] Gangar, 'Do Bigha Zamin'.

[48] Ibid.

[49] Chidananda Dasgupta, 'Precursors of Unpopular Cinema', in *Seeing is Believing: Selected Writings on Cinema* (New Delhi: Penguin-Viking 2008), 82.

technique…. The film broke many conventions and heralded a new language of cinema that Satyajit Ray was to fashion from *Pather Panchali* onwards.

It would be in context to remind readers that in 1952 this initiated India's first International Film Festival. Outside the confines of film clubs, this was the first large-scale exposure of Indian audiences to some of the best products of world cinema. Its immediate effect was seen in Bimal Roy's *Do Bigha Zamin* and Raj Kapoor's *Boot Polish* (1954) and many other lesser attempts at creating an Indian equivalent to Italian new-realism.[50]

Do Bigha Zamin is one of the most realistic portraits of its times. One of the issues the film talks of in its first half is the issue of property, a shadow of the Requisition and Acquisition of the Immovable Property Act, 1952.[51] The village landlord wants the two *bighas* of land Shambhu to make it a part of his upcoming mill. The parallel theme of the film is the element of rural–urban migration when Shambhu migrates to Calcutta to earn enough money and pay back the loan to free his land and reclaim it from the landlord. We are made witness to the dehumanized face of the city within its industrial and materialistic environment where things are no better for Shambhu than they were back in his village. Perhaps, they are worse because he is a peasant and is neither a city dweller nor a rickshaw puller. This forced shift from his traditional occupation to a completely new and urbanized one brings along with it associated changes that in no way improve his life or his livelihood.

Do Bigha Zamin was the turning point for Bimal Roy as a filmmaker 'par excellence'. The film continues to remain the most significant film that bears the distinct stamp of the Italian neorealism school from Bimal Roy's films. The influence of Bimal Roy was far-reaching, both within and beyond Indian shores extending both to mainstream commercial Hindi cinema and the then-emerging parallel cinema. His *Do Bigha Zamin* was the first Indian film to perfect the balancing act between mainstream and off-mainstream cinema. The film's critical success across the world paved the way for the Indian New Wave. *Madhumati*, his first and only collaboration with Ritwik Ghatak who had written the story and screenplay of the film, is one of the earliest films on reincarnation. It became

---

[50] Ibid.

[51] Amir Ullah Khan and Bibek Debroy, *Indian Economic Transition through Bollywood Eyes: Hindi Films and How They Have Reflected Changes in India's Political Economy*, Multimedia Presentation by the authors at the April 2002 seminar on India's Political Economy held at the Rajiv Gandhi Institute for Contemporary Studies (working paper no. 2, August 2002).

an inspiration for many Indian filmmakers to make films on the reincarnation theme over the years.

Baap Beti (1954)

Background

This is one film that few have had the opportunity to watch for two reasons—one, the film is perhaps the greatest commercial disaster in Bimal Roy's career and, two, not a single print, review or write-up or trailer of the film is available even as a frame of reference much less for viewing purposes. Why then take up a film few have seen and few even know about? Because it is the only film Roy picked from an original short story by French author Guy de Maupassant. It is also the only literary adaptation in which Roy, besides 'Indianizing' and 'contemporizing' the story, changed the gender of the chief protagonist who is a boy in the original story to a girl in his celluloid version. This is also a film that reverses the basic argument of this book—Bimal Roy's cinema dealing with migration and displacement in its varied manifestations looked at from different perspectives. This is a story of wanting to belong, to get rooted to a person, to get a socially acknowledged 'identity' in order to be accepted by the mainstream that considers the girl Meena, an 'outsider' from their point of view for whom the 'insider' is (a) one who uses a second name after his or her first name and (b) has two parents (c) with the balance tilted in favour of the father who gives the child his family name.

This writer saw the film only once at the now-extinct Rivoli cinema in Bombay near Mahim at the age of nine. So, though the film was inspiring and impressive, memories of scenes are rather blurred over time and age and hundreds of films viewed since 1954. The analysis, therefore, in the absence of any reference material, review or critique of this film, is based on slices of memories of the film captured from childhood. Although the essence of the story sustains because of its literary source, the detailing at best is an approximation and not precise and the summing rooted in the childhood memories of a film with children as the main characters presented from a child's perspective seen also as a senior adult today.

Guy de Maupassant

Henri René Albert Guy de Maupassant (5 August 1850 to 6 July 1893) was a French writer, remembered as a master of the short story form and as a representative of the naturalist school of writers, who depicted human lives and destinies and social forces in disillusioned and often pessimistic terms. He wrote some 300 short stories, six novels, three travel books and one volume of verse. His first published story, *Boule de Suif* ('Ball of Fat', 1880), is often considered his masterpiece.[52] His stories are universal because though they were written more than a century ago, they still have universal relevance across time, space, language, culture and geography.

This is backed by the fact that many of his stories have been adapted for the stage, television and cinema and have reportedly done well both artistically and commercially. *Necklace*, for instance, has been adapted by different filmmakers at different times and one was even done in Bengali, though it did not do too well. In an insightful introduction to *Works by Guy de Maupassant*, Arthur Symons writes:

> He wanted to tell stories just for the pleasure of telling them; he wanted to concern himself with his story simply as a story; incidents interested him, not ideas, nor even characters, and he wanted every incident to be immediately effective. Now cynicism, in France, supplies a sufficient basis for all these requirements; it is the equivalent, for popular purposes, of that appeal to the average which in England is sentimentality.[53]

Usually, they were built around simple episodes from everyday life, which revealed the hidden sides of people. Among Maupassant's best-known books are *Une Vie* (*A Woman's Life*, 1883), about the frustrating existence of a Norman wife, and *Bel-Ami* (1885), which depicts an unscrupulous journalist. *Pierre Et Jean* (1888) was a psychological study of two brothers. Maupassant's most upsetting horror story, *Le Horla* (1887), was about madness and suicide.[54]

By the second half of the twentieth century, it was generally recognized that Maupassant's popularity as a short-story writer had declined and that he was more widely read in the English-speaking countries than in France. This does not detract from his genuine achievement—the invention of a new, high-quality, commercial short story that has something to offer to all classes of readers.[55]

Maupassant's stories are very popular among filmmakers who have dipped into his works from 1909 to 2012. In 1909, D.W. Griffith made *Necklace* based on a story of the same name. Some of the world's most outstanding filmmakers have made films based on Maupassant's stories.

---

[52] See https://en.wikipedia.org/wiki/Guy_de_Maupassant (Accessed on 15 February 2017).

[53] Arthur Symons. 'The Works of Guy de Maupassant'. University of Adelaide, Australia, ebook updated on January 2015. (eBooks@Adelaide, 2016).

[54] See http://www.online-literature.com/maupassant/ (Accessed on 28 February 2017).

[55] See http://www.britannica.com/biography/Guy-de-Maupassant (Accessed on 14 August 2007).

Examples to these are Jean-Luc Godard who made *Masculin Féminin* in 1966 and also made four short films based on Maupassant's works beginning with *A Flirtatious Woman* in 1955; Max Ophüls adapted three short stories to make *House of Pleasure* in 1952; Luis Bunuel made a Mexican film called *A Woman Without Love* based on *Pierre et Jean* in 1952 and the latest addition to this list is *Bel Ami* (2012) directed by Declan Donnellan and Nick Ormerod based on Maupassant's novel of the same name penned in 1885.

For a writer who lived a very brief life of 43 years, Maupassant's literary contribution, in terms of quality, quantity, style, plot, treatment and characterization remains without dispute among the best the world has ever produced. Sadly, the Internet lists only one Indian film and that is *Baap Beti*. One wonders why Indian filmmakers did not pick his short stories for their films.

Simon's Papa vis-à-vis *Baap Beti*

The story of *Baap Beti* revolves around a small school girl's search for a 'father' who, for all practical purposes, does not exist. Meena is admitted to a girl's residential school because her mother, a working woman who is a stage actress without a husband, has little time to look after her. Meena's experience with her new friends is two-pronged—some, such as Maya and Radha, are warm and friendly, while others do not seem to accept her. This leads to the usual girl quarrels in school and in the residential campus.

The drama builds up when Meena sees the girls excited when letters from their parents arrive from home. Most of the girls get letters from both mother and father. But Meena gets no letters from her father. The girls corner her to ask her why she gets no letters from her father. Meena has no answer because she has no clue who her father is, but she bluffs that her father's letter will certainly come one day. She had never seen her father and does not know his name. The father figure so to say does not exist within her experience. Her mother has always told her that he lived far away and could not come to see them. Meena asks her mother for her father's postal address so that she could write to him. Her mother gives her an address, but Meena does not get any response. The girls who do not like her keep poking her and make fun of her accusing her of not having a father at all, and she feels sad, forlorn and alone. As she sits weeping quietly in a corner, the school clerk Biswanath Babu hears her sad story and promises to help her. He writes letters to her pretending to be her father and Meena happily reads these out to her school friends. But this cannot go on forever as the girls demand to see her father in person. Meena chances upon a man, catches him and says, "You are my father."

From this point on, the story changes tracks. The man (Ranjan), apparently of affluent background, is taken aback and is very reluctant to take on the role of the 'father' of a girl he hardly knows. He is a man of dubious record and dispels all attempts to 'belong' to anyone or any family. There is a constant cat-and-mouse game between the older man and the little girl where the man is constantly trying to evade the girl and the girl is determined to catch him and make him agree to be her father. Once, she even goes and hides herself in his house when he is asleep and he is surprised to wake up and find her hiding behind his bed. The girl introduces this man to her friends as her 'father' and peace seems to have been restored because Meena has lost her mother in a car crash and is now, for all practical purposes, an orphan. The adoptive father and his daughter evolve an unwritten bond unsanctioned by biology, law or all common understandings of human relationships. But, when the girl holds him by the hand, she feels she 'belongs', and the man is no longer emotionally or morally able to disown the relationship or the girl who is finally accepted as a girl who indeed has a father who can be seen and heard.

Maupassant's story *Simon's Papa* is set in the countryside and instead of exploring a girl's search for her non-existent father, it is a boy of eight named Simon from which the story gets its name. Simon goes to a regular school, while Meena went to a residential school. The boys who study with him are from a poor slum neighbourhood and not like the girls in the residential school who are uniformed and placed in better circumstances. Simon in the original story is the illegitimate boy of a beautiful lady who lives alone and lives constantly in guilt for being an unwed mother. Meena's mother works in a theatre and is ostracized by the neighbourhood because they know she has no husband and always wears a very sad and martyred expression on her face. Phillip who pretends to be Simon's father is an ironsmith, while the acting father in *Baap Beti* is a tall and handsome man apparently from an affluent background dressed in Western suits outdoors and satin dressing gowns at home. *Simon's Papa* ends with Smith proposing marriage to La Blonchette, Simon's mother, because his friends insisted that Phillip cannot be Simon's father as he is not married to his mother like their fathers are. This happy ending is changed in *Baap Beti* because the mother dies in an accident and Meena is orphaned to depend on this man she has come to love and look upon almost like her own father. The film has an open end that suggests that this man and the little girl finally find each other and accept their evolved relationship as a father and a daughter, though they are not connected either by blood ties or through family relationship or friends and acquaintances or class.

Questions That Remain

This film raises more questions than it can afford to answer because there is no DVD or screen version of the film and one has no knowledge whether it exists in the private collection of any film archivist. Bimal Roy himself maintained complete silence about this film. Whether his silence was due to the massive commercial disaster this film turned out to be or whether it was due to the feelings of guilt for having failed the producer S.H. Munshi who came forward to produce a Bimal Roy film for the first and understandably the last time, one has no way of knowing.

The few traces of writing on the film that remain labels *Baap Beti* will not feature among Bimal Roy's better films. Since there is no film left to offer a framework of reference, one tends to question this contention because it marks several 'firsts' in his career. First, it is his only adaptation of a French short story by an internationally renowned author, Maupassant. Second, it is his first and only film featuring children in a big way and he gave breaks to several child artists among who was Tabassum who played Meena and was an already known name through her roles in *Deedar* as the child Nargis and *Baiju Bawra*[56] as the child Meena Kumari. Her fame as a child actor was consolidated with this film. Asha Parekh, who was featured as one of the school friends, later went on to become a top star in Hindi cinema. Lesser known actors were chosen for other roles such as Mridula who was typed in syrupy and weepy mother roles all through her career. The film also featured Baby Naaz who rose to fame with Raj Kapoor's *Boot Polish* being released the same year. Nalini Jaywant, already a famous star through the thumping success of *Sangram*[57] opposite Ashok Kumar and several more films like *Samadhi*[58] was in the film besides Nazir Hussain and Nana Palsikar who played important cameos.

The biggest casting coup the director made was by choosing the southern actor Ranjan to play the man who is forced to play-act as Meena's father. Till date, Ranjan remains the most versatile and multitalented actor Indian cinema has produced. He portrayed the father with the charm and charisma it demanded, but since his was not a known face in Hindi cinema, the audience did not take to him positively.

Gemini Studio gave Ranjan his first big break in 1949 with a negative role as the villain Shashank in the path-breaking film *Chandralekha*. His

---

[56] *Baiju Bawra*—This is the name of a big musical hit based on the life of Baiju, a noted classical singer who was 'crazy' with his music and whose love for his childhood mate ends in tragedy.

[57] *Sangram*—Revolt.

[58] *Samaadhi*—Tomb.

action scenes and flashy style of the swashbuckling villain is said to have set a high watermark for villains in Indian cinema. He turned into a living icon and is said to be responsible for the brilliant box-office success of this ₹39 lakh-budget film acclaimed the highest budget film in India till then. It was dubbed in Hindi and released all over India.

Ranjan was an accomplished Bharatanatyam dancer well-versed in its history and theory. He had studied music. He was an artist par excellence with several canvases and portraits in his collection. He was a pilot and had clocked over thousand hours of flying. He was a linguist, globe-trotter and a writer who had a collection of short stories to his credit. He had quietly done many acts of charity and encouraged young talent. Ranjan sponsored Zora, a brilliant young singer from Trinidad to study at Kalakshetra (Chennai). He had written scripts for films and several of his stories had been made into successful films, but other writers claimed them as their own and cheated him of both remuneration and credit. His bungalow was coveted by other filmy personalities. Ranjan was an ocean of talent but without adequate opportunities to channelize it. And he was the owner and editor of the magazine *Natyam*. He acted in a few Hindi films such as *Bullet, Saazish*,[59] *Rajdhani Express* and *Professor X* but none of them got the box-office success his Tamil roles brought him. One has no idea what made Bimal Roy pick him to play perhaps the most against-the-grain of the mould he was usually typecast in and he made a good job of it. But it did nothing to add to the box-office fate of the film.

Another unusual feature of *Baap Beti* was the camaraderie and fights among the girls in the residential school not seen till then in Indian cinema that emphasized the element of the impact peer pressure can play on the psyche of a child. Roy underplayed the illegitimate child issue to focus on the unconventional relationship issue and did not articulate the marital status of Meena's mother at any point in the film except by suggestion since it is not as if her father is dead and her mother is a widow but as she does not have a father and has never had one. The importance of the physical presence of the father in a child's life came to Meena only when her friends demanded her to show them her father in flesh and blood. They refused to be satisfied with letters.

What made Bimal Roy switch the gender of the protagonist to a girl from a boy is not known, but it could be due to his desire to project a growing girl group's point of view. This also is unusual in the scheme of Hindi cinema where friendship and peer relationships among boys were portrayed more than in girl groups during the time this film was made. A few

---

[59] *Saazish*—Conspiracy.

examples to these are *Jagriti* released the same year which takes an insightful look into the goings on in a boy's residential school and the hostel campus, *Dosti* [60](1964) and *Hum Panchi Ek Daal Ke* [61] (1957) among others. Talking of peer relationships in residential schools, looking back, no film comes to mind that tackles girls except perhaps for Hrishikesh Mukherjee's *Guddi* [62] (1971) which featured girls in a day school and not a residential school. If one were to undertake a study on girls in residential schools as portrayed in Hindi cinema, one would perhaps have to fall only on *Baap Beti*.

The humane angle Bimal Roy is so famous for comes across in a tiny sub-plot which shows the school clerk offering to write letters for Meena pretending to be as her non-existent father. The entire film is, therefore, an exploration into humane angles in different kinds of interrelationships between and among individuals as single people, in pairs and in groups. It is sad that no one will ever get to watch this film. The music for the songs was by Roshan, while the lyrics were penned by Pradeep.

CONCLUSION

Cinema has often been compared to literature by Eugène Clément Cocteau who was a French writer, designer, playwright, artist and film-maker. His work is the best example that explores how much the art of cinematography inherited from other artistic expressions, especially from literature. There have been studies that provide new and interdisciplinary insights into precisely the ways in which a film, as an artistic expression, is intimately related to literature. Studies have also been done showing how cinema can be directly related to different ideologies, philosophies and culture that are already manifested in literary works. A film inspired by, adapted from or just transliterated from an original source of literature by a single filmmaker makes for a singular representation of the very notion of artistic intuition and the role of the artist. The artistic expression Bimal Roy invented through the means of the cinematic image that includes sound, music, silence, editing and so on is also a way to attract timeless public attention to a literary work that might otherwise remain beyond the domain of those who do not know the language of the literary work or those who are unlettered or do not read. This applies to all filmmakers committed to literary adaptations at one time or another, but it especially applies to Bimal Roy because it is rare in his oeuvre to discover a film not rooted in literature.

---

[60] *Dosti*—Friendship.
[61] *Hum Panchi Ek Daal Ke*—We are birds of the same branch (of a tree).
[62] *Guddi*—Name of the protagonist of the film and also the title of the film.

Alexandre Astruc, a French filmmaker, was a journalist, a novelist and a film critic before he turned to directing films. He likened the camera to a pen and the structure of a film with the grammar of writing. The main difference between the two aspects that literature uses abstract symbols while films consist of concrete images is well known. Both film and literature can deal very freely with time and space, much more freely than can theatre make possible. Both have forms such as essay in literature and documentary in cinema, or textbook in literature and technical film in cinema where time is largely irrelevant. Initially, cinema was divided into a continuous part more like theatre, but with the invention and innovation in editing techniques, cinema developed the flexibility of the novel.

There, however, is a permanent difference: writing has more exact and readier means of pin-pointing and of describing time relationships. The immediacy of what film shows surpasses everything in other art forms and can have terseness and pace that literature cannot match.

It would be in context to quote a film scholar to conclude this chapter:

> The ambiguity about the role of the author, or rather, about his real location will be paralleled by heterogeneity of both the text and its reception. Elements in the body of the film would resist full 'rationalization'; they would often remain detachable, so to speak. Like the star, the spectacle and the song, now the story and sometimes the dialogue would become separable to an extent from the film for independent circulation. I would remind you of what happened to the writer Jyotirmoy Roy's dialogues in Bimal Roy's *Udayer Pathey* (1944).[63]

---

[63] Moinak Biswas, 'Bengali Film Debates: The Literary Liaison Revisited', *Journal of the Moving Image* 1, no. 1. (1999).

III. SARAT CHANDRA CHATTOPADHYAY — *PARINEETA, BIRAJ BAHU* AND *DEVDAS*

BACKGROUND

The love–hate relationship between literature and cinema is not new. But among all Indian authors, Sarat Chandra Chattopadhyay's works have remained a hot favourite with filmmakers in India, apart from perhaps Munshi Premchand and Sadat Hasan Manto, mainly in Hindi and Bengali. What is it that makes him so popular decades after his novels were first published, and later translated in all the major Indian languages? Is he different from other Indian writers in some ways? Or, does his fiction lend itself better to the language of cinema than do those of other Indian writers? What makes his fiction attractive equally to both Indian filmmakers and to the Indian audience? These were some questions explored at a seminar, 'The Influence of Sarat Chandra Chattopadhyay on Cinema', held at Panitrash village at Bagnan in Howrah District in January 2004. The village is situated some miles away from Calcutta, where the author breathed his last on January 16, 1938. The venue of the seminar was the playground of Panitrash High School that holds a very good library filled with Sarat Chandra's works and research papers about him and his writing. Not many are aware of its existence however, as it stands forlorn in one corner till the annual day comes to celebrate Sarat Chandra's birth or death anniversary.

SARAT CHANDRA CHATTOPADHYAY

Sarat Chandra wrote novels, novellas and stories. His maturity coincided with the growing momentum of the national movement together with a social awakening about the ills that plague society, mainly rural and also urban. Much of his writing bears the mark of social turbulence. Sensitive and daring, his novels captured the hearts and minds of hundreds of readers both in Bengal and in the rest of India. His best-known novels include *Palli Samaj*[1] (1916), *Choritrohin*[2] (1917), *Devdas* (1917), *Nishkriti*[3] (1917), *Srikanta* (an autobiographical novel in four parts), *Griha Daha*[4] (1920), *Sesh Prasna*[5] (1929) and *Sesher Parichay*[6] published posthumously (1939).

Sarat Chandra Chattopadhyay's (1876–1938) earliest writings show the striking influence of Bankim Chandra Chatterji. In *Devdas*, written in 1901 (published in 1917), *Parineeta* (1914), *Biraj Bou* (1914) and *Palli Samaj* (1916), the themes and their treatment are not very much different from Bankim Chandra's. But they are presented in a modernistic setting and in an easier and more matter-of-fact language. Tagore's influence, especially of his short stories and his novels *Chokher Bali*[7] and *Gora*,[8] is revealed in some of Sarat Chandra's stories and novels. Sarat Chandra was sympathetic to the woman—repressed at home and tortured outside. He was partial to those who, for no fault of theirs, incurred the disapproval or displeasure of the family or community. The social and domestic ambience of Sarat Chandra's writings has ceased to exist. But the story interest still keeps the reader hooked, irrespective of the plausibility or otherwise of the narrative. He was a critique of contemporary society when it did not agree with his own ideas. But not once did he flout the accepted morals of Hindu society. No wonder then, that till this day, his literary outpourings remain the most attractive for Indian filmmakers across the country.

---

[1] *Palli Samaj*—The village society.
[2] *Chairtraheen*—One without 'character' (meaning man of loose morals).
[3] *Nishkriti*—Deliverance.
[4] *Griha Daha*—Home fires: a metaphorical title for a Sarat Chandra novel.
[5] *Shesh Prasna*—The last question.
[6] *Shesher Porichoy*—The final identity.
[7] *Chokher Bali*—Sand in the eye.
[8] *Gora*—The white one.

Dilip Roy sums it up:

Sarat Chandra's stories are tinged with the smell of earth. So are the works of writers like Bibhuti Bhushan and Tarasankar. But the difference lies in his simple and straightforward manner of storytelling that can easily be translated into the language of cinema while one has to wait for a man like Satyajit Ray to make a film out of Bibhuti Bhushan's *Pather Panchali*. Sarat Chandra's description of an Indian village is not time-bound. Nor does it seem backward or very different from life in the city so far as human relationships, family politics, love and betrayal are concerned. We find our lives reflected in some way or another, in his works. When we see his characters come alive on the screen, watch them laugh and cry, love and hate, shout or remain silent, we somehow get lost in their happiness and in their woes, in their love and in their despair, and there is this sense of identification, even if we have never lived in a village.[9]

In the acceptance speech in a meeting organized in his honour to celebrate his 57th birthday at the Calcutta Town Hall on 15 September 1933, Sarat Chandra said:

My literary debt is not limited to my predecessors only. I'm forever indebted to the deprived, ordinary people who give this world everything they have and yet receive nothing in return, to the weak and oppressed people whose tears nobody bothers to notice and to the endlessly hassled, distressed (weighed down by life) and helpless people who don't even have a moment to think that: despite having everything, they have right to nothing. They made me start to speak. They inspired me to take up their case and plead for them. I have witnessed endless injustice to these people, unfair intolerable indiscriminate justice. It's true that springs do come to this world for some—full of beauty and wealth—with its sweet smelling breeze perfumed with newly bloomed flowers and spiced with cuckoo's song, but such good things remained well outside the sphere where my sight remained imprisoned. This poverty abounds in my writings.[10]

According to Dr Sukumar Sen,[11] Sarat Chandra (arguably) did not appreciate poetry much and, hence, deprived his work a little of the vast wealth of the Tagore literary ocean which could well have enhanced the texture and depth of his masterpieces. In spite of being flanked by the two pillars

---

[9] Dilip Roy, *The Influence of Sarat Chandra Chattopadhyay on Cinema* (seminar; Panitrash village, Bagnan in Howrah District, West Bengal, January 2004).

[10] See http://bengalonline.sitemarvel.com/saratchandra.html (Accessed on 12 January 2017).

[11] Sen, *History of Bengali Literature*.

of Bengali creative writing, Rabindranath Tagore and Bankim Chandra Chattopadhyay, Sarat Chandra was the most popular among the masses who loved his short stories and novels because they were narrated in simple, straightforward Bengali that did not make the readers rush to grasp a dictionary, and also because they could identify with either the characters, or the interactions, or the incidents and events in his writings or all of these put together. Unlike Tagore and Bankim Chandra, Sarat Chandra was born into a poverty stricken family and had experienced poverty first-hand. Perhaps this is one of the reasons that drove him to write stories and novels that subtly brought forth some kind of marginalization of the downtrodden, the oppressed and the poor in mainstream society, mainly rural.

In his carefully crafted, if not frighteningly real, characters and events, he captured the late nineteenth to early twentieth century Bengali society. But he did not get his materials from history because he did not need to. The rawness of life he had experienced within his private life, and his schooling from boyhood to youth, shaped in him the inspiration to write about grassroots men, women and children who became the ingredients for his writing.

> He plucked characters for his stories and novels from his life experience and created them in his own inimitable style. The distinctive features and the essence of purpose that he added to them made them more attractive and perhaps larger than life. This is why his stories had such universal appeal—a reason which may explain why such a large number of them were translated to other languages.[12]

At one point, writing about his life, Sarat Chandra states:

> My childhood and youth were passed in great poverty. I received almost no education for want of means. From my father I inherited nothing except, as I believe, his restless spirit and his keen interest in literature. The first made me a tramp and sent me out tramping the whole of India quite early, and the second made me a dreamer all my life.[13]

Writing in the pre-Independence era, he was a part of the Bengal Renaissance that, along with many turbulent political insurgencies/movements, shook—both culturally and socially—the British Bengal violently. But it was not shaking enough either to weed out the deep-seated 'castigated' practices or to set the mind of the people (including both the privileged and the

---

[12] See http://bengalonline.sitemarvel.com/saratchandra.html (Accessed on 12 January 2017).
[13] Theodosia Thompson, introduction to Srikanto Part I (London: Oxford University Press, 1922), as quoted in the *Sarat Sahitya Samagra*.

unprivileged) ablaze in the process of bringing out the man inherent.[14] Jana, in his well-researched and analytical paper writes that 'Mahesh' centres around a more empathetic than sympathetic bond between Mahesh, the bull, and Gafur, its owner, and a Muslim vassal in the stratified 'zamindari' (the locale is identified as Kashipur) of a caste Hindu landlord, Shibu Babu; it also projects the 'consequences' that overtake them in an arid, draught-struck circumstance. Throughout the story, the narratives expose, question and undermine issues related to both the Dalit subject and the conventions/practices of a lop-sided society.[15]

The most marked feature in Sarat Chandra's work was his concern for the inner life of his characters. Most of his novels are explorations of personal relationships, uncomfortable relations between judgement and compassion, torturing conflict between instinct and ideals, and problems of finding space between social consciousness and half-awakened personal instincts.[16] Dilip Kumar Roy, the noted poet, singer and philosopher, recounts Sarat Chandra saying:

> There are, in each of us, two ever-warring elements—judgment and com-passion. They represent two opposing viewpoints; hence, they cannot but clash.... Man drifts away in diverse directions in the cross-currents of life—how and why, nobody knows for certain.... I have witnessed even among fallen women strange nobility or unthinkable generosity. On the other hand, I have come across instances of abominable meanness and incredible small mindedness among members of polished circles. I have often shuddered, but, believe me; I have not succeeded till now in describing the real nature of man.[17]

His writings did not demand social change, but it pointed out in different degrees of sharpness that social and economic life was not the same for everyone and the discrimination worked against the have-nots and for the haves. Conservative Hindu social leaders did not like his works such as *Palli Samaj* or *Mahesh*, while the imperial establishment did not like his *Pather Dabi*.[18]

---

[14] Soumen Jana, 'The Problematics of "Dalit Space" in Sarat Chandra Chattopadhyay's "Mahesh" and Mahasweta Devi's "Shikar"', *The Criterion: An International Journal in English* 4, no. VI (December 2013).

[15] Ibid.

[16] See http://sreenivasaraos.com/2012/10/09/tagore-and-sarat-chandra/ (Accessed on 12 January 2017).

[17] Ibid.

[18] *Pather Dabi*—The right of way.

Pather Dabi (the right of way) was different from the usual Sarat Chandra creations. Set in British India, the story has a passionate freedom fighter and charismatic leader of a revolutionary group as its protagonist. The introduction to the book mentions the thrilling story behind its release. All its 5,000-odd first prints were apparently sold out in a week. But it caused an enormous furore and a ban was imposed soon after. The government proscribed *Pather Dabi* under 99 (A) of IPC and was about to book Sarat Chandra for sedition under Section 124 (a) of IPC. The ban lasted for 12 long years from 1927 to 1939 but was re-imposed in 1940 under the Dramatic Performance Act after Sarat Chandra had passed away.

Pather Dabi is the name of a secret society that aims to free India of colonial rule. The leader of this group is Sabyasachi, a true patriot with hero-like qualities that draws his followers to him. The story touches upon several social issues, beginning with untouchability, orthodoxy, the Hindu–Muslim divide and the status of women in society. It is a scathing critique of the policies adopted and implemented by the British in India, focusing also on India's traditional customs relating to religion and social structure.[19] Sarat Chandra was actively involved in the Indian freedom movement, became the president of the Howrah District Congress at the request of C.R. Das and wrote regularly in *Narayan*, edited by the latter.

Many years later, Calcutta University honoured him with the *Jagattarini Gold Medal* in 1923 and Romain Rolland recognized him as one of the best novelists of the world in 1925. Dacca (now Dhaka) University bestowed on him the honorary DLit degree in 1936. He passed away two years later of liver cancer. But he lives on through his writings and, more importantly, Indian films in different languages adapted from his works. He is one of the most translated authors in India.

He poured into his novels and stories the varied experience he had gathered in different parts of India and Burma (now Myanmar). The most remarkable qualities of Sarat Chandra's writing are (a) directness in approach, style and language; (b) narrating stories of ordinary people one can identify with; and (c) a sense of intimacy. His descriptions of rural life and of human joy and suffering are drawn from first-hand knowledge. He excelled in the depiction of the plight of the downtrodden and the intricate feelings and emotions of women. His literary style is lucid and direct. He was a critic of contemporary society when it did not agree with his own ideas.

---

[19] See http://indianexpress.com/article/india/remembering-sarat-chandra-chattopadhyay-the-awara-masiha-on-his-139th-birth-anniversary (Accessed on 12 January 2017).

INDIAN CINEMA AND SARAT CHANDRA CHATTOPADHYAY

Sarat Chandra's works have a sense of timelessness, a universality that makes them both cinema-friendly and topical for filmmakers. The director's fascination for this author never seems to cease. The audience never fails to be trapped by its transient hypnosis. The social and domestic ambience in his novels may belong to days long past, but the story interest, the romance of his characters, and the fluid and dramatic changes in their inter-relationships hold the reader and the audience in a trance, never mind any question of credibility or logic they might raise. Among the novels drawn from his personal experience are *Srikanta* in four parts (1917, 1918, 1927 and 1933), *Charitraheen* (1917), *Biraj Bou* (1914) and *Palli Samaj* (1916.) Every single one of these novels has been made into films, some of them more than once and in more than one Indian language.

Sarat Chandra Chattopadhyay remains the most cinema-friendly writer from Bengal for all filmmakers in India across time, language and geography. The first (silent) film *Andhare Alo*[20] based on his story was screened at the Rasa (Purna) Theatre and was directed by Nata Samrat Sisir Bhaduri jointly with another pillar of theatre, Naresh Mitra. Mitra also made a film on the author's much-debated *Palli Samaj* in 1932. Kamallata, a novel by Chattopadhyay with Kamallata as the female protagonist in one of the four parts of Srikanto that was made into a silent film by Kanjibhai Rathod in 1925.

The first sound film based on his story *Dena Paona*[21] was directed by Premankur Atorthy (1931). Dhirendra Nath Ganguly directed *Charitraheen* (1931). In 1936, Prafulla Roy made *Pujarin*[22] (Hindi) based on *Dena Paona*, which featured K.L. Saigal, Chandrabati Devi, Pahari Sanyal and the great blind singer Krishna Chandra Dey. P.C. Barua directed two versions of *Grihadah* (1936), where noted Urdu writer Arzoo Lucknowi wrote the script for the Hindi version with Prithviraj Kapoor playing the villainous Suresh and Jamuna portrayed Achala opposite P.C. Barua as Mahim, the wronged hero. The Hindi version was named *Destination*. In 1967, Subodh Mitra directed a new version of *Grihadah* with Suchitra Sen, Uttam Kumar and Pradeep Kumar playing the pivotal roles in this twist-filled triangular love story filled with ingredients for a film melodrama. In 1939, Amar Mullick directed two versions—Hindi and Bengali—of *Bardidi*[23] (1939) and *Basri Didi*, and the Hindi script was done by Kedar Sharma who later became a famous filmmaker in Bombay.

---

[20] *Andhare Alo*—Light in the darkness.
[21] *Dena Paona*—Debts and dues.
[22] *Pujarin*—The worshiper (female).
[23] *Bardidi*—Elder sister.

The biggest trigger that drove filmmakers to pick Sarat Chandra's stories for films was New Theatres' *Devdas*. Hindi cinema's tribute to Sarat Chandra began years before Bimal Roy made three celluloid versions of his works in the 1950s with *Parineeta, Biraj Bahu* and *Devdas*. This is traced back to New Theatres' Hindi version of *Devdas* directed by P.C. Barua who introduced two new actors, K.L. Saigal to play the title role and Jamuna to portray Parvati. This was released one year after the Bengali version and became a big box office hit, mainly due to the beautiful songs and their rendering by Saigal who was a much better singer than an actor. This perhaps could be said to lead to the popularity of Sarat Chandra Chattopadhyay's literary works among filmmakers, crossing barriers of language, space and time across India. Hrishikesh Mukherjee made *Majhli Didi*[24] with Meena Kumari while Gulzar made *Khushboo*[25] based on *Pondit Moshai*,[26] giving Jeetendra the most off-beat role of his career. Gulzar took a lot of liberties with the original story, but his characterizations were fleshed out so lucidly that it turned out to be one of his best films, though commercially it was a flop. Basu Chatterjee did two film versions of two different Sarat Chandra works. But of the two, *Swami*, with Shabana Azmi and Girish Karnad, was the better-made one with a memorable musical score. *Apne Paraye*[27] (1987) was also made on Sarat Chandra's *Nishkriti*, but this film did not do well at all.

Sarat Chandra Chattopadhyay's stories were favoured by producers of television software and many serials were made on his stories specially in Hindi and Bengali. *Sreekant*, with Farooq Sheikh in the lead, turned out to be a very popular serial. *Charitraheen* did not do that well since it was not well made and was not promoted and marketed properly and was telecast on Doordarshan. *Bijoya* was made as a telefilm which few could get to see because of the wrong timing of the telecast and no marketing. The Bengali channels are spilling over with nearly the entire works of Sarat Chandra. Debasree Roy did the title role in *Biraj Bahu* that was aired on Alpha Bangla. Akash Bangla has completed telecasting *Swami* in its five-episode slot at prime-time and the response is so good that the programmes are repeated on demand. The latest is Bollywood filmmaker Sudhir Mishra who announced in November 2015 that he would make a completely different version of *Devdas*, would call it *Dasdev* and would merge it with some work of Shakespeare. Anurag Kashyap already set the trend for a completely reversed and post-modern celluloid interpretation of Devdas in *Dev. D* (2009).

---

[24] *Majhli Didi*—The middle sister.
[25] *Khushboo*—Fragrance.
[26] *Pandit Moshai*—The pundit (meaning teacher).
[27] *Apne Paraye*—Ours and not ours.

Another unique feature of this novelist is that his stories find strong repeat value across generations of filmmakers of all genres because films on his novels have not only been made in different languages but also in the same language several times. Pradeep Sarkar surprised everyone with his version of *Parineeta* (2005) which was a remake of the original story with too many twists and turns. The Sarat Chandra charisma for Indian filmmakers goes on.

BIMAL ROY AND THE SARAT CHANDRA TRILOGY

Parineeta (1953)

Parineeta belongs to the three Sarat Chandra classics Bimal Roy placed on celluloid. The other two are *Devdas* and *Biraj Bahu*. It unfolds the sweet love story between Lalita (Meena Kumari) and Shekhar (Ashok Kumar) and the twists and turns the relationship takes as there is an economic and social metamorphosis in the two families as the story moves on, finally leading to a happy closure. All three films are defined by strong and powerful characterizations of women, though *Devdas* is named after the hero of the novel.

Sarat Chandra wrote *Parineeta* in 1914. The backdrop is the city of Calcutta during the early part of the twentieth century. It is a tender love story that weaves in social issues regarding marriage, an orphan being brought up in her maternal uncle's house and finally, the issue of the displaced Lalita who symbolizes the title of the story which, when translated, means 'the wedded woman'.

The story centers around a poor 13-year-old orphan girl, Lalita, who lives with the family of Gurucharan, her uncle. Gurucharan, who is a bank clerk, has five daughters and the expense of paying for each dowry has impoverished him. He is forced to take a loan from his neighbour, the wealthy Nabin Roy, for his eldest daughter's marriage and this makes the diabolic Nabin Roy hold him to ransom because he eyes Gurucharan's small house next door to his big one. Roy is a very rich man who has earned his wealth by dubious means.

Roy's younger son Sekhar is a 25-year-old successful lawyer who coaches Lalita and, though there is an age gap between them, takes care of her and grows to become both fond of her and possessive of her without realizing it. Lalita slowly realizes that she is in love with Shekhar and likes being scolded by him and ordered by him, who depends on her for every small need such as fetching his clothes or getting him a paan and so on. Shekhar has an elder brother who is married and the extended family lives a contented life. But Nabin Roy is an arrogant man who looks down on Gurucharan because he is impoverished and is also unable to repay his loan. The differences in wealth and class which translate into difference in status preclude any thought of marriage between Shekhar and Lalita.[28] Bhuvaneshwari, Shekhar's mother, is very fond of Lalita and is liberal enough to suggest Shekhar marry the girl of his personal choice instead of bowing to the family's dictates.

One fine day, Girin Babu, who is an uncle of Lalita's friend Charubala, arrives to stay with his niece and her family and befriends Gurucharan's family, often dropping in to play a game of cards. Girin belongs to a Brahmo[29] family and is progressive in his outlook. Though Lalita keeps a distance when he comes to play cards, Girin seems to develop a liking for her. He is not only an affluent man but is also generous hearted. He helps Gurucharan repay the money he owes to Nabin Chandra which hurts the latter's pride. Shekhar, who is fiercely possessive of Lalita, does not care for the frequent visits of Girin to Gurucharan's home and he often lets off steam to express his anger by venting it out on Lalita who is mystified by his mood swings because she is committed to him and is subtly aware of her feelings for him.

Girin influences Gurucharan to convert from Hinduism to the Brahmo cult because he explains that it is a very progressive belief and does not believe or demand dowry in marriage from girls' families which will help Gurucharan to free himself from the burden of debt with every marriage. This triggers a quarrel between Gurucharan and Nabin Roy who builds a wall between the two houses, angry about the former wanting to change his religion from being a Hindu to becoming a Brahmo. Lalita is devastated and so is Gurucharan's entire family. Sekhar, who had taken his

---

[28] '[C]hild marriages were the norm during much of Sarat Chandra Chattopadhyay's lifetime s life time…and did not attract any penalties from the law at the time of *Parineeta*'s publication in 1914.' See Swagato Ganguly, introduction to the 2005 English translation of *Parineeta, translated by Malobika Chaudhuri, with an introduction by Swagato Ganguly*. Delhi: Penguin, v–vi.

[29] Founded in 1828 by Raja Rammohan Roy in Calcutta, the Brahmo Samaj is a religious movement. At its centre is the belief that there is one God, who is omnipresent and omniscient. It initially evolved in India where it differed from existing practice, as it did not believe in idol-worship or the caste system. The Brahmo religion is now practised in many parts of the world. The Brahmo Samaj has played a significant role in the renaissance of India, and the roots of much of the modern thinking in India can be traced back to the Brahmo movement. Rabindranath Tagore, the Nobel laureate, was one of the luminaries of the Brahmo Samaj. As British Rule consolidated in India during the eighteenth century, two factors contributed to the formation of the Brahmo Samaj in the following century. Firstly the Hindu social system had begun to stagnate and placed too much emphasis on traditional rituals. Second, an English educated class of Indians began to emerge to fulfil the administrative and economic needs of British Rule. Raja Rammohan Roy, a Bengali, was a product of the latter trend. See Supriyo Chanda, http://www.chanda.freeserve.co.uk/brahmoframe.htm (Accessed on 12 January 2017).

mother on a holiday to Madhupur, is shocked when he comes back to find a brick wall blocking the common passage between the two houses. Nabin Roy decides to socially ostracize Gurucharan's family, but Gurucharan for once stands up to this insult and gives it back to Nabin word for word. The warm relationship between the two families is destroyed forever. Girin takes the entire family of Gurucharan to his home in Munpher where Lalita again takes control of things. Nabin Roy passes away while they are in Mungher and Gurucharan also falls seriously ill and then passes away.

In the end, however, after several twists and turns and misunderstandings and coincidences, Lalita and Sekhar are united and everything ends on a happy note, barring the fact that Gurucharan passes away sometime along the story. Girin marries Annakali, Laltha's cousin, and takes the responsibility of Gurucharan's surviving family.

Bimal Roy remains almost completely loyal to the original story except some liberties he had to take because of the demands of a different medium, film. The first change is Lalita's age which jumps from 13 in the original story to around 18 in the film because Meena Kumari was chosen to play Lalita and it was not possible to make her look like a 13-year-old. Besides, the audience would not have been able to accept a love story where the girl is only 13 and the boy is 25. Ashok Kumar who played Sekhar was also much older than 25, but for the film they suited each other very well. Asit Baran, who was picked to play Girin, was also much older than the character in the original story.

The most striking element of Bimal Roy's films, including *Parineeta*, was his ability to project the Bengali family in a language like Hindi without losing out on the essence and spirit of the ethnic ethos that the story and the characters belong to. Meena Kumari's Lalita is like Sarat Chandra's Lalita coming alive on screen, albeit older in age but coy yet firm, apparently timid yet in command of herself when the situation so demands. Her strong conviction in the Hindu ritual of exchanging garlands as a sign of being married to the one the garland is exchanged with, even if this has been done as a light-hearted joke, underscores the strength of her character vis-à-vis Shekhar who is too weak to articulate his wish to marry her to his dictatorial father. Yet, she is prepared to surrender her love for what she feels is her duty towards the uncle who brought her up when she was orphaned in childhood.

The other characters—Lalita's uncle played by Nazir Hussain, the affluent guest who drops in (played by Bengal's Asit Baran) and the young girl who portrayed Lalita's cousin—gave solid support to the principal characters. The film has multiple perspectives that essay the importance of the joint family, the significance of values such as faith, responsibility and friendship, hidden between layers that alternate between light camaraderie such as a simple strategy like a game of cards or Lalita taking out money from Shekhar's cupboard whenever she needs some underscoring the richness of human relationships during the time-setting of the film.

Bimal Roy did not believe in straying from the original literary source, except through the use of songs in these films. Manna Dey's rendering of 'Chale Radhe rani ankhiyon mein paani apne Mohan se mukhda mode ke' (meaning: Radha Rani turns her back to her Mohan and walks on with moist eyes) in *Parineeta*, lip-synched on screen by a beggar, remains one of the best situational songs in Hindi cinema till today. The other song, 'Gore gore haathon mein mehdi lagaake' (meaning: having decorated fair palms with henna dye), sung by the girls during the dolls' marriage ceremony, is also a memorable number. The dolls' marriage is more metaphorical than literary. It has more than a purely surface role to enact in the film's narrative. Looked at in retrospect, it raises questions about the institution of arranged marriage within the Hindu family where girls are reduced to dolls when the issue about their marriage comes in.

The questions that get raised about *Parineeta* are Is Lalita a lover or is she the wife, unwittingly married clandestinely to the man she loves, Shekhar, on the very minute of the ritual hour as the large clock in the distance strikes the hour of eight, which is the precise *shuvo lagna*[30] for Hindu marriage on that day and that time? Had Bimal Roy wished to draw parallels between Anna's doll's wedding and Lalita's and Sekhar's exchange of garlands to reinforce the value of rituals in marriage or had he used it as a critique against arranged marriages? One has no way of knowing if Lalita's marriage negotiations with Girin as the possible groom was already suggested. What comes across is that for the simple, naïve and uneducated Lalita, that precise moment when the garlands are exchanged became the centre of her life from then on. She held on to that garland, hiding it from other's views, caressing it almost in secret, as if her entire life depended on the garland, till it had wilted and withered and might have fallen to pieces any minute. It was the precise moment when Lalita decides that she is married to Shekhar and is his wife forever. In fact, she was never his lover and there were no amorous exchanges between them. Shekhar was a

---

[30] *Shuvo lagna* is the precise hour and minute already declared in the Bengali almanac that lists the celestial hours for religious ceremonies such as marriage, thread ceremonies, *annaprashan* for a newly born and even the post-cremation pooja hours. Shuvo means 'holy' and lagna means 'precise hour/minute'. In *Parineeta*, Lalita's cousin has decided on the wedding of her doll, a girl doll, and the boy doll, having asked her father to look into the almanac for the right time for her doll's wedding, and it is exactly at this hour that Lalita throws the garland around Shekhar's neck.

control freak as far as Lalita was concerned. *Parineeta*, in fact, translates as 'the married woman'.

Sekhar remains oblivious to the impact this incident had made on Lalita because he was too engrossed in suspecting a liaison between Lalita and Girin, which was playing tricks in his mind. The doll's wedding plays a catalyst in the garland exchange between Sekhar and Lalita, on the one hand, and draws attention to little Lalita's cousin whose focus is completely on everything that goes on in a girl's marriage, on the other. This is a pointer to the significance of marriage among little girls in Bengali families at the time who were, like this little cousin, conditioned to 'rehearse' or fantasize about their own marriages using dolls as substitutes. It is not clear whether they went to school or played any other games. The garland in all its manifestations functions as agency in the love and suggested marriage of Sekhar and Lalita. With Sekhar's father having passed away and his mother being very fond of Lalita, the way to a happy ending is rendered seamless and smooth.

Who is the Displaced Person and Who is the Outsider?

Lalita in one sense is displaced because she lives with her maternal uncle and his family since her parents died when she was a child. The uncle loves the niece and, as far as one can see, there is no discrimination between his own children and Lalita. Yet, through Lalita's low-key, quiet demeanour, her eagerness to please, obey, serve and nurse without help from her cousins who are also close to her, somehow point out to the fact that she is very conscious of her position in her uncle's family. In order to absolve herself of the guilt of being a burden on an increasingly impoverished family doddering under heavy debt, she keeps herself busy all her waking hours, helping her aunt who is not healthy because she has given birth to several children without proper nourishment and rest. The love she gets from Sekhar's mother and the dependence on her that grows in Sekhar give her a kind of moral support strengthened by the love she has for Sekhar.

But Lalita is not an 'outsider' in her uncle Gurucharan's family. They look upon her as one of their own. In fact, when Girin arrives in their lives, Gurucharan thinks of making a match of him with Lalita and not with his growing daughter. The fact that Girin subsequently marries one of Gurucharan's daughters is precisely because Lalita has confided in him about her married status. Girin is an 'outsider' who becomes an 'insider' within Gurucharan's family of his own volition. He probably is happy that he has been able to convert the family from Hinduism to the Brahmo sect. On the other hand, he might have felt guilty too for having triggered a kind of permanent schism between Gurucharan's family and Sekhar's family, symbolized by the wall that comes up in the narrow gulley between the two houses. He firmly establishes his position as an insider by marrying into the family and by taking full responsibility for Gurucharan's family after he passes away. He accepts Lalita's rejection of him as a possible groom with his natural poise and quiet acceptance. Placed in perspective, Girin comes across as a stronger, confident and genuinely better human being than the suspicious, possessive and control-freak Sekhar. One is left to wonder whether Girin would have made a better husband for Lalita than Sekhar would turn out to be. But that is where love triumphs above everything else, and since Lalita and Sekhar have grown to love each other over time, their love cannot be shrugged away as a momentary weakness or infatuation that will pass with age, maturity and time. Lalita is almost the diametric opposite of the woman's role that Sarat Chandra questioned in his famous essay *Narir Mulya*.[31] Lalita failed to emerge as a role model unlike the other women Sarat Chandra projected in his later works, such as the women in *Darpa Churna*,[32] *Grihadaha*, *Pather Dabi* and *Charitraheen*. These women registered strong statements of individual protest as admirably unconventional and forth-right women who had the courage to think and act differently in an age and society that was conservative and delimiting.

Is Sarat Chandra the 'Outsider' of His Own Novel, Parineeta?

There has been much debate on a long and analytical essay by Sarat Chandra called *Narir Mulya*.[33] Academics argue that some of his creative works such as novels and short stories often contradict the arguments he has placed criticizing the position of women in society. There are also counter-arguments that solidly support Sarat Chandra for his forthright views of women and the inner strength they have shown through several of his cre-ative works. The female characters in *Parineeta*, exemplified by Lalita, her maternal aunt Gurucharan's wife, Lalita's cousins Annakali and others and Sekhar's almost faceless sister-in-law, contradict Sarat Chandra's progres-sive arguments pleading the cause of women in this essay. The only two relatively strong women with views of their own is Girin's sister Manorama who lives a very happy-go-lucky life unfettered by obstacles that might not permit her to play cards which she loves to play or go to the theatre in a group and Sekhar's mother Bhuvaneshwari who has very progressive views about her son marrying a girl of his choice, even if it is Lalita, an orphan brought up in her uncle's home.

---

[31] *Narir Mulya*—Woman's worth.
[32] *Darpa Churna*—Cracking the ego.
[33] Sharat Chandra Chattopadhyay, *Narir Mulyal*, *Sharat Sahitya Samagra*, vols. I and II (Kolkata: Ananda Publishers, 1986).

Sarat Chandra Chattopadhyay's vision of a woman's liberty and her struggles for attaining selfhood was filtered through the consciousness of his own cultural, social and literary heritage in relation to the new idioms that were relentlessly influencing and shaping a creative artist's imagination in that day and age. Despite his exceptional empathy with women, his perception of the 'ideal' woman was still shaped and influenced by the prevailing feudal, patriarchal conception of woman as naturally the giver and the nurturer. While denouncing the double standards exercised by society in devaluing women, he also felt the need to represent the failure of an acquired Western brand of feminism that threatened the dissolution of the family unit or the social structures, which were invested with so much of national emotions and which formed the very basis of Indian culture and tradition. In challenging existing social biases, Sarat Chandra's women protagonists, however, could not address the entrenched patriarchal values within the social edifice.[34]

Those who have read Sarat Chandra's works will agree that in most of his novels and short stories the incidents, events and narratives are centred on women. Madhumita Purakayastha[35] states that the narrative flow of most of his fiction is determined by his women characters or follows the destiny of his female protagonists. They are arguably more dynamic and unconventional than their male counterparts. But this argument stands in conflict with the female characters in *Parineeta*. Sarat Chandra does not give Lalita's aunt even a name one can identify or remember her by, thus relegating her to anonymity in history. Why? He fleshes her out as a skeletal woman burdened by child-birth on the one hand and poverty on the other. They have no servants and Lalita is the only one who is always beside her.

The child marriage factor is no issue because at the time when the novel was written (1914) child marriage was not illegal.[36] Lalita is not

---

[34] Madhumita Purakayastha, 'Cultural Relativism and Feminist Discourse in Sharat Chandra Chattopadhyay's Fiction vis-à-vis His Concepts on the Worth of Women', *IOSR Journal of Humanities and Social Science* 16, no. 2 (September–October 2013): 58–63.

[35] Ibid.

[36] In 1891, the Age of Consent Act (according to which sexual intercourse with unmarried or married girls below 12 years of age, with or without their consent, was to be treated as rape) had been passed, despite overwhelming protest by Indian nationalists. However, fearing social unrest, the viceroy had issued a subsequent executive order 'that made it virtually impossible to bring cases of premature consummation of child marriage for trial under the Consent Act' (Mrinalini Sinha, *Colonial Masculinity: The 'Manly Englishman' and the 'Effeminate Bengali' in the Late Nineteenth Century* [Manchester: Manchester University Press, 1995], 138). In spite of this corrective measure, the psychological impact of the Consent Act on the Bengali *babu* was far reaching indeed! For between the legal binding of the Consent Act and the impossibility of its implementation, there opened up a chasm of vulnerability (Arora, Poonam. "Devdas: India's Emasculated Hero, Sado-Masochism and Colonialism". *Journal of South Asian Literature* 30, nos 1 and 2 (1995): 253–76.).

oppressed, marginalized or sidetracked in her uncle's home. But the focus of her life is linked to Sekhar who she considers her husband whether they are married in custom and convention or not. Can one interpret this as Lalita's determination to stick to her choice reaffirmed accidentally or through destiny through the exchange of garlands at the precise moment of *shuva vivaha*?[37] Marrying Girin would have given her a better life, perhaps, than marrying Sekhar. Again, it is her belief that she is already a married woman, and during her time a woman could get married only once to one man. So, once a parineeta, she cannot accept anyone else as her husband. She does and achieves all this without confiding her inner feelings to Sekhar or anyone else even once during the entire story or film. What is surprising is that in the original novel Lalita is only 13 years old, while in the film she appears to be around 18. A strong pointer to the position of girls and women in Hindu society during his time is how little girls internalized marriage as the be-all and end-all of their existence. Bimal Roy makes Lalita's determination to stick to what she considers her destiny more logical and credible than in the novel by adding years to her age. Does that make her a strong woman? Not necessarily, but she certainly comes across as a determined woman who will not shake from the decision she has taken, never mind that she considers it her destiny or an accident of faith.

The fact remains, however, that Sarat Chandra is certainly an 'outsider' compared to the woman characters in his other stories and novels, as the following analyses of the two other films by Bimal Roy, namely, *Devdas* and *Biraj Bahu* will try and establish.

Biraj Bahu (1954)

Biraj was married off to Nilambar Chakrabarty when she was a little girl. The couple is childless. Nilambar is pious, generous and loving, but unemployed. His devious younger brother takes advantage of his naiveté to force a partition of the home and buy off their joint land under an assumed name from the lender it was mortgaged to when it is time to get Punnu, their little sister, married. Nilambar and Biraj are reduced to a wretched existence.

To make matters worse, Deodhar, a wealthy young man, who is the son of a neighbouring zamindar who has bought huge tracts of land across the river in Rajpur, arrives in the village. He strikes a tent on the river bank, struts around with his dog and his gun and attracts attention by shooting into the air. He sees Biraj when she comes to collect water in the river. He is

---

[37] *Shuva vivaha*—The auspicious moment of wedding.

captivated by her beauty and tries to bribe Biraj's erstwhile maid Sundari to lure her to his boat. After several dramatic twists and turns, Biraj is tricked into his boat. But she jumps off before he can do any harm. She runs away from the hospital in the middle of the night to see her husband one last time. He had promised that he would bless her at the time of her death and that she would die at his feet.

The audience is introduced to the main characters in the next seven minutes. Biraj, married when she was a little girl to the much older Nilambar, lives with her husband, his younger brother Pitambar, Pitambar's wife and their little sister Punnu. The finer nuances of characterization are built subtly through movement, expression and dialogue. Biraj, child-less, loves Punnu like a mother would, pinches her cheeks when she unties the calf from the cowshed and sets it free and is devoted to her husband. Nilambar goes to *keertans*[38] the whole day or performs rituals and sings at cremations for people who have no one to help them. At home, he reads out from the Ramayana, chants *stotras*,[39] offers prayers to the Krishna icon or engages himself in childlike banter with his beautiful wife whom he loves dearly. His younger brother Pitambar is diabolic, shrewd, cunning and a liar to boot, though his wife is an innocent young woman. The financial status of the family is given in suggestion: There are cows in the cowshed and Biraj lays a generous plate for the family, with milk and dessert to finish off a square meal. The family also has a maid, Sundari, and an occasional helping woman, Tulsi.

These opening scenes spell out in sharp contrast the disaster that befalls Biraj and Nilambar over the rest of the film. The maid is sacked, Biraj takes the help of a poor woman to sell small toys of river clay she makes herself and she feeds Nilambar with food she buys with the money but deprives herself. Nilambar remains oblivious to all this. The relationship faces problems because Nilambar is still jobless, still goes to keertans and the couple become poorer by the day. Biraj repels Deodhar's advances and rebukes him for parking a tent on land that belongs to them. His determi-nation becomes stronger and he tells Sundari to act soon. During these days of grinding poverty, while the younger sister-in-law is away to attend to her

---

[38] *Keertans*—Refers to a genre of religious performance arts, connoting a musical form of nar-ration or shared recitation, particularly of spiritual or religious ideas.

[39] A *stotra* is a Sanskrit word that means 'ode, eulogy or a hymn of praise'. It is a literary genre of Indian texts designed to be melodically sung, in contrast to shastras which are composed to be recited. A stotra can be a prayer, a description or a conversation, but always with a poetic structure. They are chanted or sung in a given tune to a given rhythm, individually or collec-tively by a congregation of worshippers in prayer in public places like temples or in the privacy of one's own home. (Source: Hindupedia—The Hindu Encyclopedia).

ailing father, Biraj and Nilambar have a big fight and in his state of having taken an overdose of *bhang*[40] Nilambar tells her to get out and go away. Biraj is stunned, not so much because she is thrown out but because she finds Nilambar suspecting her going out after sunset to meet Deodhar when she had actually gone to ask Tulsi, the old maid, for a fistful of rice because her husband was coming home after two days and there was not a single grain of rice in the house. Deodhar's abduction of Biraj through dubious means with the help of Sundari, who is bent on revenge because Biraj threw her out, opens the floodgates of tragedy. The film closes with Biraj returning to her husband's place only to die, metaphorically and literally, 'at his feet'. On this night of lightning, rain and thunder, as Biraj and Nilambar are arguing and Nilambar throws a brass bowl at her and she begins bleeding from the forehead, the lightning filters in through the window of the room, suggesting the lightning change in the equations between husband and wife.

The rains, the darkened clouds, the changed ambience of the village Biraj totters through in her sick and starved state sustains almost till the end of the film, metaphorically building up and leading to the tragic climax of Biraj's brief and tragic life.

Bimal Roy's minute detailing of interiors, scenes and characters is incredible. The scene where the younger sister-in-law comes to the partition fencing to very apologetically request Biraj to accept a little help from her when Biraj is facing severe financial crisis is one example. Or take that small scene showing Biraj trying to cook some gruel for herself on a makeshift oven under a tree and a passer-by handing her alms taking her to be a beggar. It is emotionally hurting to see her accept the alms but this is what could happen in real life. On the other hand, one cannot miss the melodramatic touches of Sundari wanting to confess when she is dying of snakebite, or a physically injured Biraj suddenly jumping into the river when she finds herself in Deodhar's *bajra*.[41] Roy consciously uses the allegory of the mythological Ram–Sita story when Biraj is trudging back home with Mohammed Rafi's 'Suno Seeta ki kahani' (meaning: listen to the story of Sita) on the soundtrack. The sweet banter exchanged between Biraj and Nilambar when he reminds her how she had let the bird out of the cage because she felt a caged bird will fly back, and how he used to tweak her ears when she was a

---

[40] *Bhang*—(Hindi: भांग) It is an edible preparation of cannabis known as hemp in English. Bhang in India and Nepal is distributed during some Hindu festivals like Holi, Janmashtami and Shivratri, and consuming bhang at such occasions is common. (Source: Wikipedia, the free encyclopedia).

[41] *Bajra* is the Bengali word for a decorative boat formerly used by landlords and moneyed people in Bengal that was fully equipped with kitchen, music room, living room, toilet, staff and staff quarters. One finds frequent mention of the bajra in classical Bengali literature.

child, are feather-light touches exploring the romanticism of love between a couple even when there is a vast difference in their ages.

The editing is seamless, coming from Hrishikesh Mukherjee. The soft fades and the gentle mixes lend a lyricism to the entire film, absent in contemporary Hindi cinema, replete with razor-sharp editing and frequent jump cuts. Dilip Gupta's camera, especially in the climactic scenes of rain, thunder and storm, when Biraj is trying to find her way home, look like delicately executed charcoal sketches in movement. The same applies to art director Sudhendu Roy's recreation of a village home in Bengal. The simple courtyard, the *tulsi*[42] plant, walls choc-a-bloc with glossy but old pictures of gods and goddesses, a small temple in a corner with a beautiful, black idol of Lord Krishna are restrained in design and expression, devoid of the gloss and glamour one saw in many Hindi mainstream films of the time. The scenes inside Deodhar's bajra are orchestrated, cinematographed and edited beautifully. The camera cuts from the rolling bottles of liquor on the table in Deodhar's room to the unconscious Biraj lying on the bed to the lantern swinging from the ceiling to the easy chair rocking along with the swinging of the bajra are captured in a collage of fast-moving shots against a dynamic but low-key soundtrack.

Kamini Kaushal as Biraj won the Filmfare Award for Best Actress the following year. Her performance, with its low-key smiles, anger, hurt, humiliation and shock, comes across beautifully. The only drawback is her plucked eyebrows that stand out like a sore thumb towards the end of the film. The scene where she looks into the mirror, is shocked to find all her beauty gone and says, "Accha hi hua" (meaning: what has happened is good) is touching. The comment is addressed to her beauty which attracted Deodhar to her in the first place, initiated and then lead to abduction which reverses the story of her life forever. Her values, her wish to go back to her husband are still intense, but circumstances continue to work against her.

The other moving moment, albeit a bit overdone, is when the younger brother destroys the bamboo fencing between the two homes in remorse when Biraj fails to return. Abhi Bhattacharya as Nilambar passes muster but sounds artificial when he has to laugh loudly. Pran as Deodhar is his usual villainous self but has a small role. The time-leap from the beginning when Punnu is a little girl and in the end when she is married and the mother of a baby does not show in Biraj's looks, though it is quite clear in Nilambar's graying sideburns.

---

[42] Tulsi plant—Holy basil, or tulasi (also spelled *thulasi*), is an aromatic plant considered to be holy but is not permitted inside the house and is always positioned in the courtyard.

The high point of *Biraj Bahu* lies in Salil Chowdhury's extremely atypical musical score. It reminds one of S.D. Burman who made Bengali folk music in Hindi cinema his trademark. Chowdhury's music always carries his distinct signature. In *Biraj Bahu*, he is different. He departs from his regular oeuvre of fusion, much before the word came into being, to enrich the film with beautiful Bengali folk songs from Bhatiyali[43] to keertan. Hemant Kumar's 'Mere man bhula bhula kaahe dole' haunts you much after the film is over.

Seen in retrospect, more than six decades after it was made, Bimal Roy's *Biraj Bahu* would appear to be thematically passé, sentimental to an extreme and overly melodramatic. But in terms of cinematic expression, it still stands tall among all celluloid interpretations/transpositions of Sarat Chandra classics made in any language. The most outstanding quality of a Sarat Chandra classic placed on celluloid by Bimal Roy is that it is completely faithful in terms of the period, place, social relationships and characters to the literary work it is based on. Watching *Biraj Bahu* more than five decades after it was made is like reading the classic more than 90 years since it was written. Roy retains the flavour of the original so beautifully that one can stretch one's hand to touch the characters, as if transported to a village in Bengal 90 years ago in a time machine called cinema.

"How many times have you read *Biraj Bahu*?" Roy had asked Kamini Kaushal before shooting for *Biraj Bahu* began.

Kamini Kaushal reminisces in the documentary *Remembering Bimal Roy* directed by his son Joy Roy:

> "I read it twice," I told him. He wanted me to read it twenty times. I did. When shooting began, I was so completely in harmony with the period, the characters and the ambience that I didn't even feel I was acting. I understood why he had asked me to read the original novel in translation 20 times.

After *Biraj Bahu*, Bimal Roy brought the beautiful marble statuettes of Radha and Krishna he had used in the film during the song 'Mere man bhula bhula kahe bole' (meaning: why do you take away my mind with your words?), synced by Nilambar and sung by Hemant Kumar, and installed them in the annex of his bungalow in Bandra's Hill Road where the twin gods reigned many years after he had passed away.

---

[43] Bhatiyali is a form of folk music in West Bengal and Bangladesh. Bhatiyali is a boat song, sung by boatmen while going down streams of the river. This has been explained in greater detail in the chapter on music dance and song in this book.

Biraj, the Displaced Outsider by Compulsion

Biraj Bahu is a complete stereotypical village-centred novel of all times, spilling over with syrupy and tear-jerking twists and turns. There are the typically cliché characters of a village scenario—the moneylender, the maids, the two brothers with characters polarized by completely black and completely white mentalities, their wives in close bonding, a small sister-in-law who grows up and is married off for a handsome dowry that Nilambar cannot afford and Pitambar refuses to help with, the avenging maid Sundari, the archetype villain Deodhar and, of course, Biraj and Nilambar presenting a picture of a perfectly happy couple who do not have children but never express any sadness in their barren marriage because they find happiness in being with each other. Biraj is the epitome of the most ideal *bahu–bhabhi* there ever was who never once leaves for her maternal uncle's home leaving her husband. Even the cows in the shed seem peaceful and in harmony within these surroundings. In this sense, Biraj simply cannot be considered an 'outsider' at any point of the text.

But she 'becomes' an outsider by virtue of a twist of circumstances only towards the end of the 120-minute film. The circumstances that lead to her ostracization begins with her husband who suspects her of having gone to the *ghat* (river bank) when she refuses to tell him where she was after sunset when he was away attending to the cremation rights of someone who had passed away. It is a night of rain and thunder and as she walks out of the house and the compound of their home, she walks towards the river bank. The camera cuts back and forth from the ripples of waves in the river to Biraj's distraught face, suggesting that Biraj was probably contemplating jumping into the river waters. From this point on, Sarat Chandra, the author turns his back on her, despite the image he had so carefully built, expression by expression, gesture by gesture, over the story only to make it collapse by turning Biraj into an emotionally superhuman martyr.

However, the very next minute, we find that Biraj after all is as vulnerable as any woman of her time, place and position would be because she gives up the idea of jumping into the water when Sundari sees her and asks her to step into her boat, lying that she would take her to her home. Biraj is almost in a kind of dazed stupor and is drawn into things and places she does not quite understand at that point. She faints out of weakness of having starved for days together and of the shock of having been practically thrown out by her once-loving husband who strikes her for the first time in their life together.

Her faint body is carried by the boatmen and by Deodhar's men into his bajra. When she regains consciousness and realizes where she is from the shaking of the boat and the bed she is lying on and seeing the smirk on

Deodhar's face, even in her physical condition, she tries to escape and finally does. Deodhar warns her that the boat has sailed far away from Rajpur, her village, because he had earlier asked his boatmen to cut the sails off and let the boat sail free. So, when Biraj jumps into the waters of the river, she lands up in a village some distance away from Rajpur.

She suddenly realizes with shock that she is really 'a nowhere woman with no home and no one' as she keeps saying in the end. We see her once with a young housewife in the new village. She looks at a mirror the wife hands her and is shocked to look at her image, bereft of her *sindoor*[44] and her bindi. The kind woman brings her some and she puts it on her forehead but it is faint and blurred. "Where is your home, sister?" asks the young woman. "I do not know, dear," says Biraj, realizing that, perhaps, she never had one. She runs away again. Is it to go back to Rajpur and to her husband? Or, is it to find out whether she has a home at all or not? She repeats several times that she has "no home, no one," perhaps to go back to and we empathize with her and also understand her predicament.

The physical journey of Biraj as an insider belonging to a definite, close-knit family in a village with a definite identity to a village whose name she does not know to find herself in a hospital bed with an anonymous doctor and nurse by her bedside, her evolution to a complete outsider is complete. She runs away from the hospital, longing to go what she once considered 'home', but has no idea where it is and how to go there. The camera captures her shorn looks, the sari on her body slowly reducing to tatters and she looks like a widow.

In retrospect, Bimal Roy, in his own directorial way, offers his perspective to Biraj by turning her into a metaphor and a symbol for all self-sacrificing, committed, loyal wives, sisters-in-law and daughters-in-law who, within the patriarchal village society and economy, do not really have a home to go back to once they are out of it, never mind if this is by circumstance or by self-will or even if they are thrown out, mostly, for no fault of theirs.

Maybe there is no reason or logic but this state of 'homelessness' resides in the very germ of womanhood from the minute she is born. But Biraj finally limps back home, nearly dead, and as she tries to scramble up the wall of her home, she falls again in a faint. Nilambar, half-crazy with grief, hears the loud thud outside the window and comes out to see. It is Biraj, his wife. She dies at his feet as she had made him promise. She made it her sole mission in life. Her death symbolizes, however, that she was

---

[44] *Sindoor* is vermillion powder that a married woman puts on the parting on her hair and *bindi* is a dot on the centre of her forehead to depict that she is a married woman and that her husband is alive.

an outsider who lived as an outsider without being aware of it and died an outsider. The home was never hers; her husband was an apology of a husband who lost faith in his loyal wife who had not eaten a morsel of food for days yet begged for rice from a maid to feed him. He had no clue about her enforced starvation and did not notice her frail body and ailing face. Why? The only sense of 'belonging' that was genuine was in Biraj's bonding with Pitambar's wife who is her sister-in-law and whose faith in her 'didi'[45] remains unshaken till the end. But then, by the same logic, the younger woman who is often bashed up needlessly by her insensitive and cruel husband Pitambar is, like Biraj, an outsider too, isn't she? Perhaps that is why Sarat Chandra kept them childless so that they do not leave anything behind when they go because they had nothing they could call their own to begin with, not even their bodies.

Devdas (1955)

Background

Devdas (1935), produced by New Theatres, is an all-time hit. It made P.C. Barua (1903–1951) a star overnight and revolutionized the concept of cinema as entertainment into (a) cinema of social concern and (b) literature expressed through celluloid. Sarat Chandra, a then-frequent visitor at the New Theatres studio in south Calcutta, told P.C. Barua after seeing *Devdas*, "It appears that I was born to write Devdas because you were born to recreate it in cinema." It was a rare tribute from a writer to the actor–director of a film based on his story. Over time, the character of Devdas became synonymous with the name of P.C. Barua. Till today, the image of P.C. Barua the man is inseparable from the image of Devdas, the character he played.

Sarat Chandra Chattopadhyay (1876–1938) wrote *Devdas* in 1901. But he could not find a publisher till 1917. Sarat Chandra was sympathetic to the woman, repressed at home and tortured outside. He was partial to those who, for no fault of theirs, incurred the disapproval or displeasure of the family or community. *Devdas* continues to be Sarat Chandra Chattopadhyay's most successful and controversial novel.

P.C. Barua used Sarat Chandra Chattopadhyay's novel as his raw material, creating his own structure and transforming what was purely verbal into an essentially visual form. Avoiding stereotype and melodrama, P.C. Barua raised the film to a level of noble tragedy. The film's characters are not heroes and villains but ordinary people trapped within a rigid and crumbling social

---

[45] *Didi*—Form of address for one's older sister by Bengalis.

system. Even the lead character, Devdas, has no heroic dimensions to his character. What one sees are his weaknesses, his narcissism and his humanity as he is torn by driving passion and inner conflict. *Devdas* established P.C. Barua as a front-rank filmmaker and New Theatres as a major studio.

Both P.C. Barua and K.L. Saigal were cult figures after *Devdas* became a hit. The character of Devdas and the film of the same name have 'become a reference-point in the romantic genre'. Never before had an Indian film won such commercial and critical acclaim. *The Bombay Chronicle* hailed it as "a brilliant contribution to the Indian film industry. One wonders as one sees it, when shall we have such another." It ran to packed houses in all the major cities, people returning to see it over and over again. A Bengali magazine wrote: "Pramathesh Barua who became famous overnight with his superb direction of Devdas, shows in this picture the same skill in handling psychological themes."

The climax of the film was P.C. Barua's original contribution to the story because Sarat Chandra had written it differently. Had Devdas the film ended the way the novel did, the audience might not have understood it. P.C. Barua decided that when Parvati would hear that her Devdas was dying under a tree outside her house, she would run out to see him. But as she would rush out, the doors would begin to close on her. This door is a metaphor for the social taboo against a married woman rushing out to see her former lover, crossing the threshold of her marital home. It was unthinkable in those days. "Barua conceptualised this entire scene. It was not there in the novel. When Sarat Babu saw the film, he was so moved that he told Barua that even he had never thought of ending the novel the way Barua had done," informed Jamuna Barua. Sarat Babu went on to tell P.C. Barua that this actor's entry into films was solely to give life to Devdas, the character he had created through the written word.

Devdas turned into a folk hero for all time. P.C. Barua metamorphosed into a cultural icon of his time since he directed and brought to life the Devdas character. Yet, the story goes that P.C. Barua was under severe mental stress during the making of this film because he was still coping with his grief over the death of Kshiti (Amala Devi) who had passed away before he began to make the film. The script of *Devdas* was being written while P.C. Barua was already shooting *Rooprekha*.[46] After finishing the casting, P.C. Barua discovered that he had not found the Parvati he was looking for. Kanan Devi was approached but she had to decline because she was already under contract with Radha Films. He then chanced upon Jamuna, sister of Sitara and Jaya Gupta of Varanasi, who was chosen to portray Parvati.

---

[46] *Rooprekha*—Name of a film directed by P.C. Barua.

Sometime during the making of the film, the reel-love story turned into a love story in real life. P.C. Barua married Jamuna. As soon as work on *Devdas* was complete, Jamuna gave birth to their son who, to rhyme with the film that brought the lovers together, was christened Debkumar.

Devdas was released in Chitra Talkies on 26 April 1935. There are several scenes in *Devdas* that marked the entry of the jump cut to heighten the drama through a new editing strategy. When Devdas vomits blood during his travels, the camera cuts in to show a plate of floral offerings falling off Parvati's hands, far away in her matrimonial home. In a night scene on the train, as soon as Devdas calls out to Paro, the scene cuts once again to show the doors and windows burst open in Parvati's room as Parvati screams out in sleep in the middle of a nightmare. These scenes set out P.C. Barua's creative imagination in explaining through the language of cinema the psychological stress his characters were reeling under, as also the telepathic bonding the lovers shared, without reducing these to melodrama or using sentimental dialogue.

According to filmmaker late Phani Majumdar, who began his career as secretary to P.C. Barua, his best performance is in *Devdas*. He describes, in particular, the scene where Devdas, after his beloved Parvati has been married to another, wanders aimlessly, drinking and shooting down birds at random. Manorama, a friend of Parvati who spots him from a distance while carrying a pot of water back home, is scared to cross his path. But Devdas merely comes close to the girl and asks her how she is, thus building a scene to an unpredictable anti-climax in a film spilling over with dramatic twists and turns and human tragedy. This is an example of how P.C. Barua had gained both command and control over the medium of cinema. As an actor, P.C. Barua abhorred melodrama. He kept his face almost deadpan, used minimum body language and left it to his audience to read from his emotions and from the total mise-en-scène.

P.C. Barua did not create Devdas—he 'was' Devdas. So powerful was the impact of his portrayal on screen, so close it grew to his private life, that to the Bengali audience, Devdas was synonymous with the actor who played the character. By the time the film was released, P.C. Barua became aware that he had contacted tuberculosis (TB) and, drawn inescapably to the bottle like his screen parallel, wasted himself away, slowly and surely, to die an untimely death barely 15 years after he had lived the character of Devdas on screen. P.C. Barua is reported to have said:

> Devdas was in me even before I was born, I created it every moment of my life much before I put it on the screen. Once on the screen, it was more than a mirage, a play of light and shade. Sadder still, it ceased to exist after two hours.

Devdas is one of the most often made and remade films in the history of Indian cinema. There have been one Tamil (P.V. Rao, 1936), one Malayalam (O. Mani, 1989), two Telugu (Vedantam Raghaviah, 1953; Vijaya Nirmala, 1974), four Hindi and three Bengali versions over the years, and perhaps a few more. Lyricist and filmmaker Gulzar had once decided to make *Devdas* with Dharmendra in the title role. Asked why he wanted to make it, Gulzar said: "The greatness of *Devdas* lies in its never-changing adolescence. I had chosen Dharmendra for the role because I felt that he had and continues to have the youthful quality to play Devdas." But the film never got made.

In addition to these many 'official' versions of *Devdas*, the story and its tragic characters have also served as crucial referents for such major Hindi films as Guru Dutt's *Pyaasa* (1957) and especially his *Kaagaz Ke Phool* (1959) which involves a dissolute director remaking *Devdas* as a film-within-a-film. Guru Dutt is yet another key figure in Indian cinema whose tortured personal life unfortunately resonates with the tormented and self-destructive *Devdas*.[47] There are parallels drawn between other contemporary and more recent films that feature the figure of the self-destructive urban hero, such as Raj Kapoor's portrayal in a Devdas-like character in *Phir Subha Hogi* (1958) directed by Ramesh Saigal, which was an Indianized and relocated, loose adaptation of Dostoevsky's *Crime and Punishment*. *Muqaddar Ka Sikandar* (1978) directed by Prakash Mehra could be read as offering a completely different and contemporised version of the post-middle twentieth Century Devdas. This comes across in the personification of the larger-than-life screen image of Amitabh Bachchan reflecting what Devdas would look like in 1978. He is a micro representation of the working class, an angry young North Indian of the post-Emergency era. This strips the character of Devdas of the typical, upper-class, Bengali Brahmin, cultured bhadralok.[48]

Bimal Roy's Devdas

P.C. Barua's *Devdas* was photographed by a new young cameraman at New Theatres. His name was Bimal Roy. In the course of time, this cameraman became a producer and director in Bombay and directed the same film, this time in Hindi, under his production banner, Bimal Roy Productions, 20 years later. Bimal Roy's *Devdas* stands independent of its inspiration and

---

[47] Creekmur, C.K. (2007). Remembering, repeating, and working through Devdas. In H.R.M. Pauwels (Ed.), Indian Literature and Popular Cinema: Recasting Classics (pp. 173–190). Abingdon: Routledge.

[48] Ibid.

Balraj Sahni and Jaywant in *Do Bigha Zamin*
Photo credit: Subhash Cheda

Do Bigha Zamin
Photo credit: Subhash Cheda

Nirupa Roy and Balraj Sahni in *Do Bigha Zamin*
Photo credit: Subhash Cheda

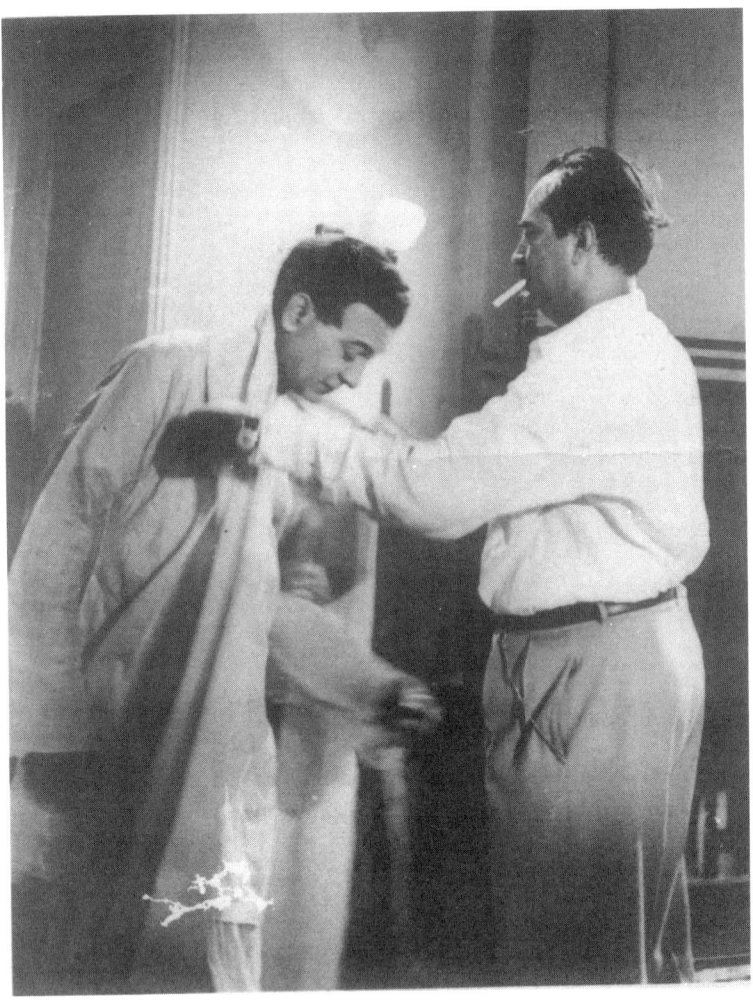

Bimal Roy with Motilal on the Sets of *Devdas*
Photo credit: Subhash Cheda

Devdas as a Boy with Parvati
Photo credit: Subhash Cheda

Devdas **Lobby Card**
Photo credit: Subhash Cheda

Vyjayanthimala in *Devdas*
Photo credit: Subhash Cheda

Dilip Kumar and Vyjayanthimala in *Devdas*
Photo credit: Subhash Cheda

Dilip Kumar and Suchitra Sen in *Devdas*
Photo credit: Subhash Cheda

Ashok Kumar and Nutan in *Bandini*
Photo credit: Subhash Cheda

Ashok Kumar and Nutan in *Bandini*
Photo credit: Subhash Cheda

Nutan in *Bandini*
Photo credit: Subhash Cheda

Nutan in *Bandini*
Photo credit: Subhash Cheda

***Bandini*, Prison Scene**
Photo credit: Subhash Cheda

Closing Shot from *Devdas*
Photo credit: Subhash Cheda

Sujata, **Opening Scene**
Photo credit: Subhash Cheda

Sujata
Photo credit: Subhash Cheda

Sunil Dutt and Nutan in *Sujata*
Photo credit: Subhash Cheda

carries the typical signature of its new maker, producer and director Bimal Roy. This individuality lies in the approach, style and interpretation. The difference lies in the camerawork because Bimal Roy paid very close attention to the visual details of his film, having evolved from a cameraman to a director. Without the use of dialogues, he could build up a situation by manipulating the visual power of cinema. Bimal Roy's signature lies also in the scripting of the music, the songs and the lyrics, created to gell with the period, the characters and the place setting of the narrative.

In an interview, Nabendu Ghosh said that they had originally planned to cast Meena Kumari as Paro and Nargis as Chandramukhi.[49]

> We wanted Meena Kumari as Paro, and Nargis as Chandramukhi. Meena Kumari would have been the ideal Paro—she had Paro's quietness. Unfortunately, she could not do the role because [*husband*] Kamal Amrohi laid down certain conditions, which Bimalda did not agree with. I remember Meena Kumari broke down—she was that keen to do the role. Nargis refused—she wanted the lead role of Paro. Then we approached Bina Rai. She refused, too. Suraiya, too, wanted Paro's role. We then had to go for Suchitra Sen. She was very happy. It being her first Hindi film, we had to dub certain portions. She is a legend, yes. But her face was more cultured and sophisticated than required for Parvati. That is why I say Meena Kumari would have been ideal—she had the simplicity of a middle class young girl who is not very educated.

Ghosh went on to explain that he personally did not approve of Vyjayanthimala (as Chandramukhi),

> [B]ut we had no option—no one wanted to play Chandramukhi, and we were committed to our distributors. We were in dire straits, and Bimalda's unit was big. He never compromised in the making [*of his film*]. That meant expenses. And we needed money. Vyjayanthimala came to our rescue. She came to Bimalda and said, "I am ready if you think I can do it." She was, of course, a very good actress, but she was too young for Chandramukhi, as envisioned by Sarat *babu*.[50]

In 2005, *Indiatimes Movies* ranked the movie amongst the *Top 25 Must See Bollywood Films*.[51] *Devdas* was also ranked at Number 2 on the University

---

[49] Lata Khubchandani, 'I Did Not Approve of Vyjayanthimala as Chandramukhi', interview with Nabendu Ghosh. see http://www.rediff.com/movies/2002/jul/05ghosh.htm/ (Accessed on 12 January 2017).

[50] Ibid.

[51] See http://www.listal.com/list/india-times-top-25-mustsee (Accessed on 12 January 2017).

of Iowa's list of top 10 Bollywood films by Corey K. Creekmur. The film was also noted for its cinematography and lighting under Kamal Bose that enhanced the emotional torment of the tight-lipped protagonist played by Dilip Kumar.

Set against the backdrop of rural Bengal during feudal times, Devdas is the story of a doomed love affair between Devdas (Dilip Kumar), son of the local zamindar, a high-caste Brahmin, and Parvati (Suchitra Sen), the daughter of a poor neighbour, also a Brahmin, but belonging to a slightly lower status in terms of caste, affluence and status. They grow up as childhood sweethearts. But when they decide to marry, Devdas' father puts his foot down, packing his younger son off to Calcutta for higher studies. Parvati's proud father arranges Parvati's marriage to a wealthy zamindar, a widower with children older than his young second wife. Learning about Parvati's marriage, Devdas rushes back to his village and tries to stop the marriage, in vain. Parvati is prepared to elope with him. She comes to his room at 2 AM at night but Devdas refuses. Paro leaves his room in the middle of the night, castigating him for his cowardice.

In Calcutta, Chunilal (Motilal) introduces him to an attractive and strong-willed courtesan, Chandramukhi (Vyjayanthimala), and initiates Devdas into the darker corridors of the city. Devdas finds an easy escape in drink and though he insists that he hates Chandramukhi, he keeps coming back to her for moral support. Chandramukhi falls in love with him and gives up her profession. "He is the only man I have met who insisted on paying and not making use of my services." When she dances, he hardly looks at her. This is something she has never experienced before. He rejects her and says he hates women like her. This also reminds the viewer that he had written to Paro too that he never felt love for her which, of course, was a lie. Why did Devdas shy away from relationships with both women?

Devdas meets Parvati once more, when he returns to the village to perform the last rites of his father. Parvati pleads with him to give up drinking. He evades a direct reply and instead promises to see her at least one last time before he dies. Chandramukhi gives up the life of a professional courtesan and concentrates on nursing the alcoholic Devdas back to health. He gives up drinking for some time and is advised to go on a holiday.

The film's characters are not heroes and villains but ordinary people conditioned by a rigid and crumbling social system. Even the lead character, Devdas, has no heroic dimensions to his character. What one sees are his weaknesses, his narcissism and his humanity as he is torn by driving passion and inner-conflict. Bimal Roy's *Devdas* reflects an almost identical approach. Seen in retrospect, the two women in his life, Parvati and Chandramukhi, are stronger than he is, as independent women with minds of their own, with Devdas being an unwitting catalyst in Chandramukhi's life.

Bimal Roy creates a build-up of the love between Devdas and Parvati by tracing their childhood through Devdas's pranks and Parvati backing him up all the time. Some of their 'signals' are echoed when they grow up and Devdas throws a stone on the roof of Parvati's house to call her, like he did when they were kids. Roy dots these with songs and two Baul numbers, namely Geeta Dutt–Manna Dey's 'Sajan ki ho gayi gori' (the fair girl has become her lover's) and the eternally beautiful 'Aan milo aan milo shyam saanwre' (please come and meet me oh my dark lover Shyam) drawing on the Radha–Krishna allegory to symbolize the tragedy of their love. The closure of the film is a marked departure from the original novel and follow's P.C. Barua's version. When Parvati hears that her Devdas is dying under a tree outside her house, she runs out to see him. But as she rushes out, the doors begin to close on her. This door is a metaphor for the social taboo against a married woman rushing out to see her former lover, crossing the threshold of her marital home. It was unthinkable in those days.

When *Devdas* was being made, Dilip Kumar was already established as one of the top triumvirate that defined Hindi cinema—Raj Kapoor, Dilip Kumar and Dev Anand. *Devdas* shows Dilip Kumar at the peak of his career where, in the title role of the tragic hero, he invests the literary character with his personal chemistry as an actor par excellence. Vyjayanthimala's Chandramukhi is embellished with her graceful dance style that evolves with the evolution in her character within the film from a popular dancing woman to a woman who, in love with Devdas, has unconsciously mutated to reflect the mainstream woman. For Vyjayanthimala, the character marked a turning point from glamour to pure histrionics, offering her scope to explore her potential as a dramatic actress without taking away from her the most outstanding gift she brought to cinema—her dance. Suchitra Sen as the grown-up Parvati is ethereal, the pride showing in that scene on the banks of the pond where Devdas uses his fishing line to mar her beauty. She carries the scar as a sad reminder of their doomed love story. She is courageous enough to come to Devdas asking him to take her away late into the night. He is scared and she goes away, embittered by what she considers a betrayal. Yet, when she gets married, like the ideal Indian housewife and mother, she moulds herself into the vessel she is poured into. It is a fine debut for Suchitra in Hindi cinema.

Motilal is the best Chunilal among the many versions of *Devdas* that have been made. He portrays to perfection the fine blend of the elite and the mundane, the lover of a joyful life who has enough depth to understand the tragedy of his friend. Baby Naaz as the child Parvati is a natural and delight to watch. Ram Kumar is no patch on her. Besides, Roy has fleshed out his character beyond its literary origins to make it a kind of witty, fun-loving and jovial counterpoint to the forever sad and depressed Devdas who he introduces to the *kotha*[52] pockets of Kolkata in general and to Chandramukhi in particular. He drinks and goes to the kotha every day and, in one scene, Chandramukhi tells Devdas that she had a tiff with him because he was pimping by bringing a rich customer to her after she had quit her 'business' which Devdas refers to as her 'shop' she has closed down. Chunilal appears like magic again towards the end of the film as he steps, as if from nowhere, into Devdas' first class coupe, urging him to drink. Devdas says that he has given up drinking, but when Chunilal disappears, as suddenly as he appeared, he leaves the bottle and the glass and Devdas picks it up. But the glass falls on the floor of the coupe and so does Devdas who is very ill.

Sudhendu Roy's art direction is so credible and earthy that it is almost impossible to believe that the entire village was constructed within Mohan Studios. In Chandramukhi's kotha, we see 'translucent' net curtains parting to offer a glimpse of the dancing Chandramukhi, the walls covered with floral wallpapers and the ornamental circular design on the dancing floor completing the picture. Kamal Bose's evocative and at times poetic cinematography keeps to the pace of the film. When Chandramukhi has quit soliciting, singing and dancing, the apartment is bereft of the ornate decorative objects and furniture and this is replaced with a small pooja corner with a lamp burning.

Hrishikesh Mukherjee's editing adds its own slow and sad rhythm to this immortal love that ends in tragedy. Once Paro is married and Devdas flitters between Calcutta and his village, there is frequent intercutting between Paro's life and Devdas's to demonstrate the catharsis happening in either of them. The film effectively uses the jump cut several times towards the end, mixed and merged with matching editing of sound during the last phase when Devdas is travelling at random, not getting down anywhere, on his last journey by train. Devdas does not know where he will stop and the old retinue is fed-up. The camera superimposes the names of the stations over the rushing train and we know which places it is running through. The sounds of the wheels on the train track are loud and disturbing till at one point the whistle of the engine begins to sound like a cry in moaning.

---

[52] *Kotha*—A house of ill repute which houses singing and dancing girls who also sometimes become mistresses of regular customers or indulge in prostitution. It is not a Bengali word but a Hindi–Urdu one.

Then, soon after Chunilal has left, the train stops at Pandua and Devdas can only hear the announcer who mentions Manikpur among others, urging passengers headed for these places to get off at Pandua. Devdas remembers that Paro is the wife of the zamindar of Manikpur and also his promise to see Paro one last time before he dies. He gets off the train to begin his last journey.

When Devdas vomits blood during his travels, the camera cuts to Parvati falling in a faint, far away in her village home. In a night scene on the train, as soon as Devdas calls out to Paro, the scene cuts to show Parvati screaming out in her sleep, in the middle of a nightmare. Her husband tells her she is mistaken. These scenes spell out the psychological stress his characters were reeling under, as also the telepathic bonding the lovers shared, without reducing these to melodrama or using sentimental dialogue. The similarity with P.C. Barua's *Devdas* is striking. This is the natural extension of the earlier *Devdas's* cinematographer taking on the responsibility of directing his own version of the same story and film.

At first glance, Bimal Roy's celluloid version of *Devdas* seems subtle and naturalistic with affinities to the then-emerging Bengali art cinema. The actors are restrained and convincing, and often placed within realistic situations created beautifully and, mostly, within carefully constructed studio sets. But a closer examination reveals that Roy's version is formally intricate and yet it does not needlessly draw attention to the technique. Roy introduces Devdas and Parvati as children, carrying them into young adulthood through a transitional dissolve focusing on the richly condensed image of a closed door. Then the camera focuses on white lotus bud in the midst of lotus leaves in the village pond where Paro has come to collect water. She dips the pot into the water and as we see the beautiful Paro now grown up, stepping out of the ripples, the lotus is in full bloom. This is a unique time-bridge created at that time by the director that includes nature in its fold. The composite image of the blooming lotus, the water-filled pitcher and the beautiful Paro walking out of the waters symbolizes the bloom of youth in Paro as well as the cyclical rhythms of the changing seasons as a subtle suggestion of the passage of time.

Poonam Arora, in her paper 'Devdas: India's Emasculated Hero, Sado-Masochism and Colonialism'[53], argues:

> Indian cinema has immortalized Devdas and Parvati not so much for their devotion to each other as for their mutual chastity, and to a lesser

---

[53] Poonam Arora, 'Devdas: India's Emasculated Hero, Sado-Masochism and Colonialism' (University of Michigan, Dearborn, 1997).

degree for their defiance of societal codes. In order to understand the psycho-social implications of the lovers' sexual chastity and Devdas's chastity vis-à-vis Chandramukhi, one must locate this chastity within the larger gender ideology of colonialism.

This writer begs to disagree with Arora. In support of her argument, Arora brings into it the Age of Consent Act brought in by the British Government in 1891 and later ratified by the same government. This does not enter into the Devdas–Parvati debate at all because during the time setting the story belongs to, the mindset of a young man and a teenaged girl would not have harboured sexual feelings at all.

If Parvati comes to Devdas in the middle of the night, it is most certainly not to offer sex but to propose that they elope so that (a) she need not marry a man old enough to be her father and (b) their love can culminate in marriage. She also refers at another point of her paper that the scar Devdas had made on Paro's forehead with his stick was a 'sexual scar'. He had done it in anger and he wanted to make a dent in her pride. Arora insists:

> The original scene, wherein the erotic and the violent get conflated, is obliquely repeated throughout the narrative. Even though Devdas does not literally possess Parvati, he nevertheless 'leaves a mark on her'. If, in Devdas's mind, Parvati's beautiful face is comparable to an unsustainable state of perfection, he claims his right to be the first to sully it, and she, in turn, is almost complicitous in permitting this violation.

This argument is not acceptable within the historical context the story and the characters belong to apart from the social framework in which the love story happens. It is true that Paro keeps caressing the scar later on and also looks at it in the mirror in her new home, but that has nothing to do with repressed sex. Arora reads a sexual undercurrent in the scene that does not exist. Arora goes on to add:

> [When] Parvati's mother notices that her daughter's face has been scarred on the day before her wedding, she exclaims in horror and panic. There is a suggestion, in the mother's response, that the scar is a signifier of her defilement or perhaps a violation of her chastity.

Even on hindsight and with several viewings of the film, this argument does not sustain the logic of the story and the mindset of the lovers because sex is neither a part of their social construct nor is it a part of their upbringing.

Other celebrated Bengali writers such as Rabindranath Tagore, Bankim Chandra Chatterjee and post-Sarat Chandra authors like Bibhuti

Bhushan Bandopadhyay have, for some reason or other, refrained from investing their writings with details on the sexual resonances of a man–woman relationship. Tarasankar Bandopadhyay perhaps was the pioneer in explaining, without detailing graphic sex, the physical shades in man–woman relationships, sometimes inclined towards the woman being sexually more aggressive than the man such as in *Bedeni*[54] (1943). Tagore suggested, mainly through innuendo, the finer nuances of sex in *Chokher Bali* and a strong, one-sided suggestive sexual attraction of Charulata for Amal in *Nastaneer*, among other writings, which is not permitted to reach culmination in terms of physical sex.

Santanu Mandal, research scholar at Viswa Bharati University, Santiniketan in his well-researched paper 'Love's Labour's Not Lost: 21st Century Reincarnation of Devdas', writes:

> The core of the story of *Devdas* is the absence of a mature sexuality and the failure to consummate love. Devdas clings on to his childhood myth of love while he rejects the adult love that he is offered both by Paro and Chandramukhi, even striking Paro in a typical act of impotence. His failure punishes the two women as Paro remains a virgin even after marriage (there is an ambiguity about her night time visit to Devdas's room although no direct reference is made to any sexual activity) while Chandramukhi, whom he abuses verbally with his words of revulsion rather than desire, retires to live alone, a reformed courtesan.

Mandal adds:

> Devdas converts both his desired women into maternal figures as they both come to tend to him in sickness, indulging him like a naughty child. The purity of their love for him is beyond question as Paro's devotion to him borders on the religious. This is seen clearly in Bimal Roy's film where her lighting of the lamp as he returns is meant to imply she is worshipping him, further emphasized by *Vaishnava*[55] songs of love and passion. Devdas's one act of heroism, after he has become alcoholic and contracted tuberculosis, then viewed as an illness with moral attributes, is to keep his promise to return to die at her house. The characters fail to stand up to society's pressure. Their own personal flaws of pride and ineffectuality ruin their lives as they are destroyed by themselves, their families and society.

---

[54] *Bedeni*—A Gypsy girl. It is the name of a novel by Tarasankar Bandopadhyay later made into a film by the late Anjan Das.

[55] *Vaishnava*—Relating to Lord Vishnu and specifically referring to his Krishna avatar.

This is an interesting argument to follow or to contradict when one arrives at trying to find out which of the characters in Devdas is the 'displaced outsider'.

Who is the 'Displaced Outsider' in Devdas? Is it Devdas, is it Paro or is it Chandramukhi?

The social relevance of Bimal Roy's *Devdas* lies in that it was the first film within mainstream Hindi cinema in Bombay to place on celluloid the social ramifications of a man of high birth who moves away from his feudal, upper-class roots in rural Bengal to the colonial city of Calcutta during pre-World War II years. It tried to explore the inner pain of this man, torn between the pull he feels towards his village roots and his wish to run away to the city to escape from the tragic reality of a lost love. His wilful manner of moving towards self-destruction could be read as his casual indifference to the village that he once belonged to, a village he now responds to with mixed feelings. Before his death, he tries, in vain, to run away from an anonymous death in the unfeeling city, by coming back to the village, in one last desperate attempt to renew lost ties. The harsh, heartless reality of the city has changed his perspective towards the village. He rejects the tempting illusions and fantasies the city once held for him. The city loses Devdas, but the village too refuses to accept him even in his ignominious, humiliating and tragic death. Only two women—Parvati and Chandramukhi—who operate like invisible, unwritten 'guardians of conscience' in the wreckage his life is reduced to, are left to grieve over his death.

In her voluminous research, *Realism and Reality: The Novel and Society in India: Myth and Reality*,[56] Meenakshi Mukherjee offers a sociological perspective and demonstrates that Sarat Chandra's popularity rests not on his creation of serious literature, but of emotionally extravagant domestic drama. Mukherjee concludes, "Hence, any literary evaluation of Sarat Chandra cannot quite be delinked from his cultural significance, and when the literary critics have finally given him up perhaps the sociologist will take up for further scrutiny the phenomenon that is Sarat Chandra." She notes that throughout his work, Sarat Chandra left the basic values undisturbed; he was permitted by his readers to critique certain other aspects of social behaviour.[57]

So far as Devdas the character goes, he is an 'outsider' within the mainstream. He is born into an affluent family but is not interested in

---

[56] Meenakshi Mukherjee, *Realism and Reality: The Novel and Society in India* (New Delhi: Oxford University Press, 1985).

[57] Ibid, 106.

property from his childhood. He is not interested in academics either, takes tobacco clandestinely even as a schoolboy and bullies Paro who is forced to act on his beckoning even when she does not like to do his bidding. He cries inconsolably when his strict father and diabolic older brother send him to Calcutta for studies. But he neither can fit into the city environment nor is he happy when he comes back. He does not really 'belong' anywhere, and if at all he has 'belonged' it is not to a place but to a person—Paro. When he comes back to the village on her father's death, he does not show any interest in appropriating his share of the property. He grows to love Chandramukhi who he was once repelled by, but in a different way.

It would be in context to discover how alcoholism in the male lead played a significant role in the shaping of the narrative in Hindi cinema around the time *Devdas* was made and how some of this spilled over into the real lives of some stars destroying their lives forever. In Ram Daryani's *Ghar Ki Izzat*[58] (1948), Dilip Kumar portrayed Chandra, a gambler and a drunkard who ultimately reforms himself. Mehboob Khan's *Andaz*[59] (1949) had Raj Kapoor who plays a playboy who often drinks. Kedar Sharma's *Jogan*[60] (1950) reflected the sufferings of the leading lady, portrayed by Nargis, who suffers because of her alcoholic brother who is not the hero of the film. Amiya Chakravarty's *Daag*[61] (1952), which brought Dilip Kumar his first Filmfare Award as Best Actor, was also about how alcohol can destroy the life of a good man. Dilip Kumar plays Shankar who becomes an alcoholic, reforms himself and becomes a drunkard all over again, so much so that he spends the money kept aside for his ailing mother's medicine on alcohol. The film was a box office hit because it had a happy ending.[62]

Some important films during the 1950s that tackled alcoholism in different manifestations were *Main Nashe Mein Hoon*[63] (1959) directed by Naresh Saigal, which had immortal songs created in and around addiction and featured Raj Kapoor as the alcoholic hero. In Mehboob Productions' *Awaaz*[64] (1956), Nalini Jaywant, who plays the daughter of an ill-fated old man, is forced to commit suicide because of the torture her alcoholic husband inflicts on her. In Guru Dutt's *Pyaasa* (1957), the frustrated and

---

[58] *Ghar Ki Izzat*—The honour of the home (the wife or bahu).

[59] *Andaz*—Style, this is the name of a Hindi–Urdu film which was a big hit at the time.

[60] *Jogan*—Jogan is a Hindi word which is actually a female counterpart of a *jogi*, or a yogi, that is a monk, someone who doesn't believe and use worldly things and tries to keep him away from worldly pleasures.

[61] *Daag*—The stain.

[62] Manidipa Mukherjee, 'Such a Long Journey', *High Spirits* XXVII (September, 1995).

[63] *Main Nashe Mein Hoon*—I am drunk.

[64] *Awaaz*—Voice.

alienated poet Vijay roams aimlessly across the streets through the red light areas of the city ironically belting out the song 'Jinhe naaz hain hind par woh kahan hain'[65] (where is the person who is proud of his homeland Hind?—meaning India). This signifies that the failed alcoholic hero was not entirely new within mainstream Hindi cinema by the time *Devdas* made its entry. The role was not completely unique for Dilip Kumar either.

Alcoholism became a common addiction among many leading actors in Indian cinema. P.C. Barua could be considered a pioneer in leading this 'movement' towards conscious self-destruction, followed by his alter-ego K.L. Saigal who became a star overnight with the Hindi *Devdas*. Motilal, one of the most underutilized actors in Hindi cinema, once owned a helicopter. But his addiction to the bottle did not leave money even for his decent burial as he spent everything on gambling and drinking. Guru Dutt, his wife Geeta Dutt and Meena Kumari were also alcoholics. Geeta Dutt and Meena Kumari died of excessive drinking and Guru Dutt committed suicide. But the difference between Devdas and these real life alcoholics lies in that while Devdas began drinking and died of this addiction because he was almost thrown out of the family—first by his father, with good intentions, and then by his much older brother when his father died (but by then, he was beyond caring)—the same does not apply to real life people like Motilal, K.L. Saigal, Guru Dutt and Keshto Mukhjerjee who had no credible reason to become drunkards beyond cure. The best exception to this is Dilip Kumar himself who, unlike his predecessors who portrayed Devdas, loved his drink but mostly in company and did not ever get addicted to it.

The movement between the village and the city that abets Devdas' descent is fundamental to the historical experiences of Indian modernity and the consequent alienation from tradition; he is spineless, cruel, narcissistic and a virtual Hindu Hamlet in his frustrating inability to act, especially when action seems most necessary.[66] Devdas, therefore, is a very complex character whose failure, frustration, alcoholism and tragic death is rooted in his inner desire to remain an 'insider' through marriage to Paro, but he veers between the two polarized realms of displacement and rootedness only because he could not marry the only girl he ever loved. In the final analysis, his tragic end at Paro's door, his dying body lying prostrate under the big tree with a crowd slowly gathering in numbers to see this dying stranger, writes the finish to his displacement and his final affirmation of becoming

---

[65] Mukherjee, 'Such a Long Journey'. The line means where are those people who take pride in Hind? (Hindustan, a synonym for India).

[66] Creekmur 'Remembering, Repeating and Working Through Devdas', 173–190.

an outsider, part of it circumstantial, part of it self-willed and part of it dictated by societal norms. Devdas is, therefore, a displaced outsider, partly by circumstance and partly of his own volition. His 'outsiderness' culminates in his untimely and painful death, bringing the tragedy full circle.

Towards the end of the film, Devdas is shown to be in constant physical pain; he presses his abdomen even as he talks; he cannot walk straight and collapses on the floor of the coupe. The question that arises here is: Is the physical pain more unbearable for him than the psychological pain of having loved and lost one woman and of not being able to replace Paro with Chandramukhi who also loved him? Another feature that highlights his 'outsider' quality is that throughout the story and the film, except as a boy, Devdas hardly smiles, much less laughs. His smiles and his laughing are more in sarcasm and irony and often directed at himself than they are natural expressions of human emotion of happiness and good feeling.

Sarat Chandra's novels and short stories are mostly women-centric. Most of his chief protagonists are female and the flow of the narrative in most of his fictional work is determined by his woman characters or follows the destiny of his female protagonists. They are arguably more dynamic and unconventional than their male counterparts.[67] The beauty and complexity of his works can be attributed to his women characters.[68]

Devdas is a classic exception to this theory. The chief protagonist is a male and the story is titled after his first name, not his family name, probably in order to strip him off his roots at the outset and set him apart from the mainstream where, during the time he belonged to, family antecedents were paramount to a man's identity formation and personality. The narrative follows the destiny of Devdas who almost writes his destiny leading to a kind of suicide soon after he gains adulthood and comes back to his village. It is, therefore, quite extraordinary to discover the way Sarat Chandra is able to sustain the strength and the dynamism in Paro and Chandramukhi, the two women in Devdas' life, that is lacking in his own character.

Devdas' character becomes the archetype of a disillusioned man who seeks his identity through self-inflicted sufferings. He could see no option except the inevitable self-destruction in the face of an oppressive social milieu in which true happiness could not materialize in the true unity of the lovers. The character had, and still has, a universal appeal for the Indian mindset because the theme also represents escapism and indecisiveness whereby the failures of the individual are attributed to the external

---

[67] Purakayastha, 'Cultural Relativism and Feminist Discourse', 58–63.
[68] Jayanta Bandopadhyay, *Sharat Shahitye Byakti O Samaj* (Kolkata: Karuna Publications, 1406 [Bengali year], 2000 [Gregorian calendar]), 15.

social factors.[69] This writer disagrees with the logic of 'external social factors' because Devdas had the choice of running away with Paro when she approached him and suggested that they elope. If she was willing to elope, risking the social ostracism that might bring upon her and upon her family, what made him hesitate? His expressed inability to choose between his parents who he loved dearly and Paro who is also loved seems to be a very convenient excuse in retrospect to escape both risk and responsibility. He hardly kept any connection with his parents when he went to Calcutta, and his giving away his share of the property to his widowed mother, who anyway went away to Kashi, was his way of rejecting the family he belonged to, which was an extension of his rejection of Paro, strongly suggesting that he was unable to sustain close emotional relationships with anyone including his brother and sister-in-law and Chandramukhi.

Paro: The 'Outsider-Insider'

Paro is mainly a mainstream woman who surrenders to her father's choice of marrying her to a widower who has children older than she is. But her surrender is dictated by Devdas's rejection of her when she comes in the middle of the night to his room and suggests that they elope. Her love for Devdas remains as intense as it was before, and even as a little girl she gets easily bullied by him who orders her about. Even though her married life which, as the story suggests, is never consummated, she is not displaced physically except by reason of marriage to the landlord of Manikpur. She summarily gives away her entire jewellery to her married daughter. According to her husband, she never wears jewellery and when she tells him that she gave them away to Yashoda, their daughter, he says, "I got them made again for you," she just smiles. She has no fascination for jewellery, which is very uncommon for the time and the space she belongs to. She becomes an indispensable female head of Manikpur family and the stepchildren dote on her, as do the servants and her generous and kind-hearted husband.

Paro has no reservations at all about eloping with Devdas before marriage. Nor does her love for Devdas dilute due to her marital responsibilities. But these are the only two features of her quality of perhaps becoming an 'outsider' subject to Devdas's acceptance of her suggestion. For all practical purposes, she remains an insider. She tries to break through the doors of her home to reach out to 'someone lying under the tree outside' in response to her having imagined her name cried out by Devdas. She would have broken out nevertheless if her husband had not called out to his son and the servants to pull the shutters of the main entrance. Her sari trails behind

---

[69] Ashok Raj, *Hero*, vol. I, *The Silent Era to Dilip Kumar* (New Delhi: Hay House, 2010), 163–164.

her and her hair is all astray as she rushes like a woman possessed, oblivious to the shock waves she generates among the members of her family. This marks her out as an 'outsider' and also lays the foundation for the contemporary woman of today who copes very well with the two roles of being an outsider and an insider at the same time, never mind how difficult this contradiction might appear to most of the world.

Chandramukhi: The Twice-displaced Outsider

Bimal Roy makes several references to the devotional love that Parbati and Chandramukhi have for Devdas. Parbati, having known Devdas all her life, cannot think of anyone else as her husband. But as fate would have it, Devdas's inability to stand up for himself results in her marriage to someone else. However, that does not stop Paro's love for Devdas. On the other hand, Chandramukhi, who has constantly caught the attention of so many men, cannot see past her love for Devdas. Knowing that he can never be hers, she changes her life altogether for spiritual attainment.[70] This argument by the Mishras does not stand the test of the story, at least for Paro though not for Chandramukhi. Paro's love for Devdas is purely emotional that would later graduate to its fruition in sex which is kept away from the narrative and from the romantic text. But this does not happen because Devdas practically shoves her away from his room as the clock strikes three in the night. He says he is afraid of the social scandal that would surround Paro. But if Paro is not afraid, why would he, a man, be afraid?

Prostitution on celluloid, mainly in Indian popular cinema, occupies one point of continuum of representations of women, a continuum along which are also situated some commonly available and highly socially visible representations, such as in advertisements. All films with prostitutes as principal or important characters are mainly motivated by prospects of raising the film's commercial viability. In rare cases such as in Bimal Roy's *Devdas* or Kamaal Amrohi's *Pakeezah* have the directors addressed themselves analytically to the social and economic situation of the business of prostitution.

It is never quite clear, in the text or in the film, whether Chandramukhi was a courtesan who only sang and danced to entertain rich customers, whether she was a prostitute or whether she was both. It was perhaps not considered necessary by the author because the inferences make it clear that she was both. We are not given any idea even by suggestion about the social history she belonged to before she entered the trade or whether she was born into it. But since the right to a normal life as a normal woman in

---

[70] Mishra Maitreyee and Manisha Mishra, 'Marriage, Devotion and Imprisonment: Women in Bimal Roy's Devdas and Bandini', *Commentaries—Global Media Journal* 3, no. 1 (June, 2012).

the mainstream has denied her, we can assume that she is displaced when Devdas meets her for the first time.

In this sense, we meet Chandramukhi as one who is already displaced from the mainstream. This gets translated in the different celluloid versions of *Devdas* including Bimal Roy's. Bimal Roy inflects the image of Chandramukhi with lyrical, romantic and humanist emphasis. Let us examine these areas a bit in detail. The lyrical quality is present in the song–dance numbers in Chandramukhi's kotha where she performs to a paid clientele and then only to Devdas who has paid earlier but not accepted her 'services'. The fact that her services included sexual services is lucidly brought across when Chandramukhi tells Chuni that Devdas is 'the only man who gave money without taking [her] service'.

The romantic emphasis in the film text arrives after Chandramukhi has given up her profession for good and has taken up a life of spirituality and faith in God. It is her deep admiration, respect and love for Devdas that forms the basis of this new 'displacement' from an old life as a professional entertainer shunned by mainstream society to a spiritual person.

When Devdas comes looking for her after his father's death and is away from alcohol for one year during the mourning phase, someone opens the door. Her back is turned to Devdas but when she turns around to face him, he sees that it is Chandramukhi transformed. The spacious rooms of her apartment are shorn of the ornate furniture, the floor matting and the musical accompanists are missing and she is shorn of jewellery and her *zardozi*[71] costumes and is wearing a simple, red-bordered white sari, much like a religious minded, Bengali married woman. When Devdas comments on the change, Chandramukhi says, "the change is not outside, it is inside too," guiding him to a pooja corner with a lamp burning in front of the statuette of a god figure. "So, you've given up shop?" he asks, missing out on the tragic double entendre in his use of the word 'shop'. When he asks her why she did not leave this place earlier, she simply says, "Just to see you. I knew you would come back one day." "My perceptions about everything have changed after you came into my life. I have been in this business of love many times but I have loved only once," she adds in the same vein.

The humanist angle to Chandramukhi's character comes across when she practically rescues Devdas from a street drain where he is almost prostrate, nursing his bottle, sozzled out of his wits, very sick and semi-conscious. The build-up that leads to this scene is touchingly established. From Paro's

---

[71] *Zardozi*—It is a Persian word that means sewing with gold string. *Zar* meaning gold and *Dozi* meaning embroidery. Zardosi attained its summit in the seventeenth century, under the patronage of Mughal Emperor Akbar. Available at http://www.craftrevival.org/CraftArtDetails. asp?CountryCode=India&CraftCode=002944 (Accessed on 1 March 2017).

interaction on her not using jewellery at all, the camera cuts to Chandramukhi dressing up in front of the mirror. She says, "I am going to search for my husband." The soundtrack fills with the music of percussion instruments and dancing bells which changes to a *thumri*[72] as Chandramukhi goes looking for Devdas in the red-light neighbourhood. She does not find him. While riding back on her horse-drawn carriage, she hears his drunken voice belting out lines of a song. She gets off the carriage and approaches him asking him to come home. He fails to recognize her and asks her, "You know me, beautiful?"

She takes him to her abode and like a spoilt child he demands liquor, questioning her right to deliver speeches to him when he can hardly walk straight. Chandramukhi begins to dance for him without any instruments but some very melodious music on the soundtrack. He pays attention to her and begins to walk out when she stops him by begging him not to leave. She then sings 'Jise tu kabool karle who adaa kahan se laoon' (meaning: from where will I bring the style that you will accept?) in *mujra shaili*.[73] She nurses him back to some semblance of good health and, according to the doctor's advice he begins his long train journey that is also his last. Chandramukhi begs of him to take her along, but he refuses. He hands her a thick bundle of currency notes and insists when she refuses it. She stands on the balcony and watches his carriage going away till it turns round the corner and disappears. They never meet again.

Without drawing artificial parallels with the mythical Radha, Chandramukhi's second 'displacement' comes full circle as she personifies the transcendence of human love into the divine. The irony of her life is that when she is a courtesan, she is an outsider in the mainstream, repelled by the only man she fell in love with. When she leaves that ostracized life for good for love for the same man though she knows her love will never be reciprocated nor recognized, she is still not accepted by the mainstream and remains as much as 'outsider' as she was when her story began. But by then her mindset has changed for good and she no longer cares whether she is ostracized or whether her transcendence to this ascetic lifestyle has 'redeemed' her socially or not. So, drawing upon the same mythical love triangle of Radha, Krishna and Meera, would it be appropriate to find parallels between Meera, a creation of mythology, and Chandramukhi, a creation first of Sarat Chandra and then of Bimal Roy?

---

[72] *Thumri*—Thumri is a common genre of semi-classical Indian music.

[73] Mujra Shaili—Mujra is a form of song and dance that began with the courtesan singers and dancers during the Mughal era which incorporated the elements of native classical Kathak dance into the music. Shaili means 'school'. The Mughal era incorporated elements of the native classical Kathak dance onto music.

Bimal Roy invests his own version into the original story by introducing a scene that shows Paro and Chandramukhi meet somewhere in the middle of nowhere, in the fields near a water body. While Paro, the mainstream woman, very much an insider, is shown going back to her village in a palanquin drawn by palanquin bearers who keep humming the rhythmic beats they always do, Chandramukhi, the outsider, is walking down in the opposite direction with her servant Bhairon searching for Devdas when there is no correspondence from his end for three long months. They are walking along the aisle between two fields. Paro peeps out of the palanquin to see who the woman is. Chandramukhi sees this beautiful woman but they do not speak. Chandramukhi walks down to the pond to wash her face and the palanquin moves away. This perhaps is the director's directorial contribution to the author's original note where the insider and outsider meet once in their tragic lives psychologically and emotionally decimated by the man they both loved—Devdas.

CONCLUSION

Sarat Chandra still holds a strong position in classical Bengali literature as a rare male writer whose works offer a deep insight into women's minds, psyches and emotions and, most important, the courage of their convictions to stand by what they believe in, be it love, marriage, the 'sanctity' of virginity or the 'impurity' of being a non-virgin, even if they cannot stick to their convictions by reason of the social compulsions they feel responsible to abide by. Lalita resisted the social compulsion of agreeing to her match with Girin because she actually believed that she was married to Sekhar and even if Sekhar had not accepted her in the end, it is doubtful if she would have compromised with her life by marrying a different man. She would have preferred to die a 'married spinster' to marrying a man she considered an 'outsider' in her life.

Biraj of *Biraj Bahu* is fleshed out as an ideal, sacrificing wife who offers solid support to her husband when he becomes jobless. She makes earthen toys to be sold in the market to keep body and soul together, but he remains dedicated to his *keertan sabhas*[74] and his religious songs. She is perhaps one of the earliest working wives in the history of Bengali literature. She believes she will die at her husband's feet and she does, though she has been kidnapped through trickery into the villain's boat from which she tries to save herself by jumping into the waters of the river. She could have died

---

[74] *Keertan sabhas*—Gatherings of people who come to listen to keertans usually in and around temple complexes.

but her faith keeps her alive even when people take her to be a beggar, only because her faith in her belief in the destination of her death keeps her alive.

Paro and Chandramukhi of *Devdas*, in their own distinct ways, try to resist the rigid codes of conduct imposed on womanhood by patriarchy. The two of them, completely polarized by social class, caste and occupational distinctions, have their inner strengths as woman in common that could not save them from the common tragedy of losing the only the man they loved, but spelt out the power and ability of women to emerge 'from confining cultural systems through a reinforcing of their self-esteem'.[75]

---

[75] Purakayastha, 'Cultural Relativism and Feminist Discourse'.

IV. THE WOMAN QUESTION — SUJATA AND BANDINI

BACKGROUND

The Male Advantage[1]

The advantage of being a male director in a largely patriarchal set-up is that, unlike his female counterpart, he does not have a political agenda of any kind. His principal function is to express himself in the language of cinema. Second, he has the responsibility of vicariously carrying the economic burden of the producers and financiers who have placed their faith in him by assuring that his film brings back the money invested in its creation. Beyond these two conditions, the director is free to play, express, use the language of film in any which way he chooses. It is the second condition, however, that, through its structured 'freedom', tends to bind him to certain fixed strategies in directing a film. As a consequence, he traps himself within what the box office demands, ending up in many cases playing to the gallery rather than being honest to himself and with the medium he is working in. Along the way, many male directors get sucked into the vortex of using women characters to titillate the audience through camera voyeurism, or portraying them as vulnerable victims, or projecting them as

[1] This section is an extract from the author's PhD thesis from the Netaji Open University obtained in 2007–2008.

truly negative vamps. Third, male directors are never 'ghettoised' like their female counterparts, solely on grounds of their gender. Male directors also have the unstinted support of a male-dominant industry where the finance, the distribution, the exhibition of films are also mainly a male domain. This is an advantage because men directors are looked at by the cinema industry with much less speculation than women directors. Men carry the advantage of numbers as well, because in India, which produces around 1,000 feature films a year, women directors are no more than a proverbial drop in an ocean.

In a majority of Indian films directed by men, the female protagonist occupies the position of a victim in the narrative. In other words, "victimhood is posited as an essential and eternal feminine quality, which then needs miracles of some sort to redeem the situation."[2] At the other extreme, one encounters the femme fatale or the dangerous woman violently eliminated or totally drained of antagonism. The femme fatale is eliminated because she threatens the patriarchal order in her ability to slide between both the registers of masculinity and femininity. In addition, however much cinematic convention may turn her into an object of desire, she would bounce back as a subject of desire.

Many of our cinematic conventions are embedded in the patriarchal unconscious and characterize the representation of women through a distortion of reality, through melodrama, through violence and through camera voyeurism, both in terms of their body and character. They are subjected to a series of gazes, whether voyeuristic, investigative or medical, in all of which the controlling look remains with the male. Otherwise, women who challenge the system are often seen as hysterical or abnormal, as if normality and abnormality are natural categories instead of being historically produced social categories. To make things worse, hysteria becomes a natural quality of women.

All this has resulted in the following:

1. It has created a monolithic image of woman, as if all women are the same and are dictated by the same needs and demands everywhere, across boundaries of time, space, language and culture. Whether she is portraying a moll or even the gangster, or whether she is portraying the simpering, sobbing martyr, most women lack the varying shades of grey between the polarities of black and white that real life offers.

---

[2] Lalita Sridhar, 'Films and Femininity: An Interview with Film Scholar Venkatesh Chakravarty', in *Infochange News and Features* (December 2003).

2. Men directors shy away from tackling and depicting female desire. Rarely do they venture into an exploration of female sexuality. Somehow, in their hurry to cater to a patriarchal audience, men directors have proved for many years that a woman cannot assert her desire beyond the patriarchally defined boundary of the one man who contains it. It took Aparna Sen to break the myth of the sexually faithful female in *Paroma*. In Dipa Mehta's *Fire*, the two women desire each other not because they choose to do so, but because their husbands cannot function for some reason or the other. Radha and Nita are victims of a social order rather than subjects of their own desire. Mahesh Manjrekar, in *Astitva*, reveals how natural it is for a married woman to enter into sex with another man when her husband is absent for long periods of time. But the director also tries to justify the woman's 'misdemeanour' by painting the husband as an unabashed male chauvinistic pig.

Shyam Benegal's *Ankur*[3] (1974) was not an exploration of the woman's sexuality, but a critique of feudal exploitation. Benegal's *Bhumika*[4] (1977), however, is a radical departure among creations by men directors. In the case of Usha, the protagonist (based on the autobiography of a famous star of the Marathi screen), her repeated acts of adultery are expressions of autonomy, which begins with sexual autonomy but ends with a search for coming to terms with herself, on her own terms, within her own space. Tired of the world of men and of their attempts to curb her independence, Usha decides to live alone, refusing a space even in her now grown up daughter's home. The end of the film finds her alone in her hotel room, where her grown up daughter comes to visit, understanding the mother's need to be left to herself. Usha's adultery cannot quite be termed adultery in the strict sense of the term because she leaves her husband when she begins to live with other men. Loneliness, she realizes and accepts, is the price she must pay if she is to retain her autonomy.

3. A situation of paradoxical reality emerges where on the one hand, men directors shy away from tackling the rather delicate issue of female desire and female sexuality and on the other, they pull out all the stops while portraying women as titillating objects of

---

[3] *Ankur*—The seedling.
[4] *Bhoomika*—The role.

male desire even as they treat them as victims of male oppression and violence.

4. Most Indian films are structured on the erroneous assumption that the audience is homogenous and patriarchal. Thus, even at a subconscious level, they design and tailor their scripts towards an acceptance from the patriarchal audience. But the audience is not a homogeneous category. It consists of heterogeneous people coming from different ethnic backgrounds, class, caste, gender, sexuality, educational background, financial status and ideological convictions. To complicate issues, audiences never remain the same. A study of audiences in the 1930s would produce a different result from a study of audiences in the 1990s. Instead of speaking of media effects, we should historicize media forms and conventions to locate the social causes that produce transformations in the media against the backdrop of political, economic, social, cultural and technological changes. This would tell us more about the media as well as the people who consume its products, and about society.

5. This leads to the creation of a culture of celluloid stereotypes, not only of the woman characters but also of the male ones. The problem with stereotypes is that they internalize and naturalize historically and socially constructed representations. In this, formal mechanisms or conventions of the media often close the gap between representation and perception. Beyond that, stereotypes legitimize the existing order of things instead of opening it up to a process of interrogation. Nonetheless, there is always a space for resistance.

INTRODUCTION

The treatment of women and their representation in the cinema of Bimal Roy deserves focus because none of the women in his cinema fall within a patriarchal reading. His soft, feather-light touches to the characterization of women was a permanent feature of all his films never mind if a given film dealt with a female protagonist or not, or whether it was a celluloid adaptation of a literary work, or whether it fell somewhere between these two main features of his work. Even for negative characters with more grey shades than white, there was a touch of empathy or rationalization he approached the character with. In a very minor cameo in his film *Do Bigha Zamin*, the character of a woman from a higher social class (Meena Kumari) is so touching that she makes an indelible mark on the viewer's mind. This woman is shown only through a beautiful lullaby she hums to her baby—"Nanhi kali sone chali hawa dheerey aana" (meaning—the little one is going to sleep, wind, please flow slowly)—and her role is confined to reading out letters to Paro, the unlettered wife of Shambu Maheto. Even the reading out of the letters delivered in the sonorous, sensual voice of Meena Kumari with a gentle smile cuts to focus on the shy smile on Shambu's wife's face. Very subtly, this reading of the letter by one woman to another creates an invisible bond of sisterhood between two women belonging to two different social classes within the same society at the same time.

His choice of subjects, most often drawn from literature and then converted into smooth and cinema-friendly screenplays, featured women who, by virtue of their presentation in the script, the way the actors projected and portrayed the characters, left a footprint on the sands of women portrayals in Indian cinema. The women in Bimal Roy's films had an identity of their own. Their stature was unimpeachable. They were emotionally 'independent'. They were not mere foils to the men or to the other characters in the film even if and when they were in love, and we're committed to their relationships. They created a niche for themselves.

It would perhaps be in the fitness of things in interpreting Bimal Roy's women by roughly classifying them into categories such as (a) mainstream women, (b) displaced women and (c) the woman as an outsider. The lines between and among these categories are rather blurred because they are consciously constructed divisions that the director might not have agreed with. But this writer wishes to classify them in this way so that analysis becomes simpler and the derivatives are not lost.

Within this artificial classification, the women have some things in common. The leading female characters of all Bimal Roy films are rooted in a simple, straightforward version of the 'family' as the basic unit of social existence and survival. They may be rural like Shambhu's wife in *Do Bigha Zamin* or uneducated like Sujata in *Sujata* or a devoted housewife like Biraj in *Biraj Bahu*, they belonged to a definite social backdrop. If and when some female characters in his films are characterized by ruthlessness, this is depicted as circumstantial and not a position the woman has chosen to live in. Chandramukhi in *Devdas* is a courtesan, but when she falls in love with Devdas, she voluntarily walks out of her profession not knowing what the future holds for her. Sujata is uprooted from her original roots of having been born of untouchable parents and transplanted on more 'respectable' soil. She remains unaware of this filial 'transplantation' from her roots to an adoptive family where the foster mother was not happy with her husband's having been forced to take on the responsibility of a baby of low birth, sometimes marred by inner questions about why her birthdays are not celebrated while her sister Rama's are. When she learns later that this 'family' has never been her own, she still clings on to it not because she has nowhere to go but because she has grown to love it as her own.

Kalyani in *Bandini* is a prisoner in the women's cell of a small town prison. In this sense, she has been uprooted from her original family that she has no way to return to. She tries to alienate herself from thoughts of a normal married life with the young jailor because, deep in her subconscious, she still loves the man she thinks betrayed her in love and life. Till she is a prison inmate, she tries her best to jell in with the prison crowd sharing with them her loneliness and offering to nurse the prisoner suffering from TB knowing it is an infectious disease.

The 'biological family', therefore, is not necessarily the norm, but it is still what the women in Roy's films adhere to and love to belong to. His women do not speak in symbols or in metaphors or rhetoric, unlike women in contemporary Bollywood films. In *Madhumati*, the protagonist of the film (Madhumati) is rooted in her biological family and is traumatized when the rich Pran tries to molest and rape her. Roy, therefore, did not ever attempt to use formal symbolism and yet did not reduce any of these women characters to stereotype or cliché. This also points out to the element of forced displacement in his women characters. In *Do Bigha Zamin*, the wife has to follow Shambu from the village to the city which also compels her to leave the family's primary occupation—farming. Lalita in *Parineeta* is already displaced at root because she is an orphan and it is her maternal uncle and his wife who bring her up.

The mainstream women in Bimal Roy's films are the ones who are firmly rooted to the soil they emerged from when the film began and, physically, they remain rooted to the same ground when the film ends. From point A to point B, however, their journey might have brought about changes within their psyche, their ideology and their mindsets, but they remain 'mainstream' women so far as the storyline goes. Examples are Rama and her mother in *Sujata*, Biraj's kind-hearted sister-in-law in *Biraj Bahu*, the wife and mother from an upper-class, educated family, such as the cameo character portrayed by Meena Kumari in *Do Bigha Zamin*, Parvati in *Devdas*, Shekhar's mother and Lalita's cousin Anna in *Parineeta* and so on.

This chapter is devoted to two displaced women in the cinema of Bimal Roy. One of them is Sujata and the other one is Kalyani in *Bandini*. Bimal Roy's two films with Nutan, *Sujata* and *Bandini*, saw him returning to realistic imperatives. These two films mark the best works of Bimal Roy in his most mature and mellow performance as director. Till this day, *Sujata*, based on a novelette by Subodh Ghosh (1909–1980), enjoys the status of an iconic classic both at national and international retrospectives of Bimal Roy's films. Its mechanisms of pleasure, blend of realism and idealism, and the humanitarian vision that it embodies denote a powerful, albeit fading, current in the symbolic universe of the 1950s. In and through *Sujata*, many of the oppositions that sustain between poverty and wealth, renunciation and worldliness, *dharma* and *adharma*,[5] desire and law are worked out in terms of the family-as-nation/nation-as-family ideal.

SUJATA (1960)

Background

Till this day, *Sujata* enjoys the status of a classic both at national and international retrospectives of Bimal Roy's films and of Indian films.

The only notable film based on the delicate theme of untouchability in Hindi before *Sujata* is *Achhut Kanya*[6] (1936) which turned out to be a big box office hit with music by Saraswati Devi that are hummable to this day. Produced under the Bombay Talkies banner, *Achhut Kanya* was directed by Franz Osten with the story by Niranjan Pal, dialogues by J.S. Casshyap, photography by Josef Wirsching, art direction by Karl Von Spreti and Sound by Savak Vacha. Devika Rani and Ashok Kumar portrayed the two leads in the film. The storyline goes as follows: Caste prejudice and class barriers prevent marriage between Kasturi, a Harijan girl, and Pratap, a Brahmin youth—both childhood friends and in love. Soon, Kasturi is forced into a loveless alliance with one of her own caste. When a chance encounter at the village fair brings the two lovers together, Kasturi's husband, inflamed by jealousy and suspicion, attacks Pratap at the railway level crossing, where he is employed as gatekeeper. While the two men are engaged in a fierce fight unmindful of a fast approaching train, Kasturi, in an attempt to save them, is run over and dies. Before this, only two other films had touched upon the caste problem is any significant way—Nitin Bose's *Chandidas* (1934) and V. Shantaram's *Dharmatma*[7] (1935).

Two significant films released in the same year, 1959, need mention here to place *Sujata* in perspective. One of them is Guru Dutt's *Kagaz Ke Phool* and the other is B.R. Chopra's *Dhool Ka Phool*.[8] *Kagaz Ke Phool* is placed within the setting of a film industry, a point-of-view narration by a noted director who has lost his gloss, his fame and his glory. He enters the

---

[5] *Dharma and adharma—Adharma* (Sanskrit) is derived from combining 'a' with 'dharma', which literally implies 'not-dharma'. It means immoral, sinful, wrong, wicked, unjust, unbalanced or unnatural. Thus, dharma means all that is moral, just, right, balanced and natural.

[6] *Achhut Kanya*—The untouchable girl.

[7] *Dharmatma*—The holy soul.

[8] *Dhool Ka Phool*—Flower in the dust.

studio floor that he shot his classic films on, to journey into the past. Said to be filled with autobiographical anecdotes and suggestions, the film journeys through his broken marriage and his affair with one of the leading ladies he gave a break to, now a famous star, to his present state of decay and death. There are two women characters in the film. One of them remains out of the visual frame, but nevertheless forms a strong presence for a part of the film. It is the director's wife. The other is the actress, enacted beautifully by Waheeda Rehman, who is said to have had an intense emotional relationship with Guru Dutt in real life. This real-life relationship is repeatedly referred to through suggestion right through the film. This inter-cutting of celluloid with real life in one of the best self-reflexive films in Indian cinema makes a strong yet subtle statement about women who find themselves trapped, marginalized, exploited and misused within the glitz and the chutzpah of the plastic world of cinema—whether she happens to be the wife of a filmmaker or the other woman in his life.

Dhool Ka Phool is the first post-Independent social comment on unwed motherhood in mainstream Indian cinema. The focus of the film, however, soon shifts from the tragedy of the woman to the tragedy of the illegitimate child, the 'flower born of dirt and dust' as the title of the film suggests. The father refuses to acknowledge the child as his own, the mother is married off too and the child is left alone to be brought up by a Muslim. The film was reduced to melodrama mainly due to the director getting lost within a host of arguments he initiated but failed to carry through. Within this scenario, it would be interesting to discover what position *Sujata* occupies within this time sequence. Other films released before and after *Sujata* are—*Lajwanti*[9] (1958), *Sone ki Chidiya*[10] (1958), *Deep Jele Jai*[11] (Bengali; 1959), *Anuradha* (1960), *Baishey Shravana*[12] (1960) and *Meghe Dhaka Tara*[13] (Bengali; 1960).

Subodh Ghosh (1909–1980)

Subodh Ghosh's stories are marked by a strong, vigorous narrative style and a lively universe of people and places drawn from the writer's formidable range of life experiences. It is no surprise that several of his stories were made into classic Bengali and Hindi films and that the awards he received came from both the literary and film worlds. Ghosh was born in Bikrampur, Dacca

---

[9] *Lajwanti*—The shy one (female).
[10] *Sone Ki Chidiya*—The bird in the golden cage.
[11] *Deep Jele Jai*—Lady with the lamp.
[12] *Baishey Shravana*—The 22nd day of Sraban, a month of monsoon in the Bengali calendar.
[13] *Meghe Dhaka Tara*—The cloud-capped star.

(now Dhaka), now in Bangladesh, and educated at St. Columbia's College, Hazaribagh. His literary works remain the favourite of filmmakers in Hindi and Bengali. Among the most popular films based on Subodh Ghosh's stories are: Bimal Roy's *Sujata*, Ritwik Ghatak's *Ajantrik*,[14] Mrinal Sen's *Ek Adhuri Kahani*,[15] Basu Chatterjee's *Chit Chor*,[16] Nabyendu Chatterjee's *Parshuramer Kuthar*,[17] Tapan Sinha's *Jotugriha*,[18] Gulzar's *Ijaazat*,[19] (an improvised and individualized version of *Jotugriha*) Prabhat Roy's *Shedin Choitromash*[20] and Suraj Kumar Barjatya's *Main Prem Ki Diwani Hoon*,[21] which incidentally is an updated and much more sophisticated and glamorized version of *Chit Chor*. Winner of the Sahitya Akademi Award, Subodh Ghosh also won the Filmfare award as the best story writer twice: in 1959 for *Sujata* and posthumously for *Ijaazat* (based on *Jotugriha*) in 1987.

These films are a mere drop in the ocean of novels, novelettes and short stories penned by one of the most popular among contemporary writers of fiction in Bengali literature. Ghosh began his career with a novel named *Ekti Nomoshkare*, which has been widely translated in major Indian languages including English. His range of works stands testimony to his versatility and in his ability to move back and forth through genres ranging from the historic research-based work *Bharat Premkatha*[22] to a collection of folk tales aimed at children captured in *Kingbodontir Desh*,[23] to the tackling of private issues like adultery (*Kinu Goyalar Goli*[24] made into a moving Bengali film), or divorce resulting from a barren marriage such as in *Jotugriha*, or the man in the margin, such as in *Shuno Baranari*[25] (made into a film with Uttam Kumar and Supriya Debi in the lead) and in *Thogini* (made into a film with Sandhya Roy in the title role) which narrates the story of a young girl who is initiated by a parasitic father to con young men into marriage and then run away with the booty to settle down in another place in search of another prey. Ghosh's rich imagination finds ultimate expression in his ability to humanize a dilapidated car in the last dregs

---

[14] *Ajantrik*—The pathetic fallacy.

[15] *Ek Adhuri Kahani*—The unfinished story.

[16] *Chit Chor*—Heart stealer.

[17] *Parasuramer Kuthar*—The axe of Parasuram.

[18] *Jotugriha*—House of lac.

[19] *Ijaazat*—Permission.

[20] *Shedin Chairtramaash*—That day in the month of Chaitra.

[21] *Main Prem Ki Diwani Hoon*—I am crazy with love.

[22] *Bharat Premkatha*—The classic love stories of Bharat (India).

[23] *Kingbodontir Desh*—The country of legends.

[24] *Kinu Goyalar Goli*—The bylane called Kinu Goala.

[25] *Shuno Baranari*—Listen dear woman.

of its existence a la Jogoddal, which Ritwik Ghatak chose to immortalize in *Ajantrik*. He is still renowned as one of the best short story writers in Bengali literature and is taught as such within the syllabus for Bengali literature in most of the universities where Bengali is offered as a major for postgraduate studies and doctoral and postdoctoral research.

Synopsis

An untouchable girl is sheltered in infancy in an emergency, when her kinfolk die in a plague epidemic, by an engineer, Upendranath Choudhury (Tarun Bose), and his wife, Charu (Sulochana), of Brahmin caste. The family assumes the arrangement to be temporary, hoping a suitable home would be found for the child. In the course of various postponements of finding the girl a home, the family becomes attached to the child and she is brought up with their own daughter of similar age. The untouchable girl is named Sujata meaning well born. In later years, as the girls grow, Sujata (Nutan) is sometimes referred to by acquaintances of the family as their daughter. Charu always parries this, but says that Sujata is 'like' her own daughter. Sujata within this ambience of affection, warmth and love is aware of this phrase that she is in some way different from the girl she regards as her sister.

Sujata's low-caste roots do not particularly trouble the parents till it is time to arrange the marriage of their own daughter, Rama (Shashikala). Rama's marriage has been fixed long ago with another Brahmin family whose scion is the handsome and promising Adhir (Sunil Dutt). Adhir's family, consisting solely of a highly conservative aunt who is fiercely protective and proud of her Brahmin roots, is deeply disturbed to discover that an untouchable girl has so long lived in Upen Babu's house as one of their own. However, she insists that the girl should be married off to a man of her caste before Adhir and Rama can be married to avoid the embarrassment her presence would cause during Rama's wedding. Destiny, through one of those unexplainable sleights of hand, plays another trick. Adhir falls head over heels in love with Sujata during his visits to the house. He does not shy away from professing his love to her. Sujata is initially confused with the surge of strange feelings within her in response to Adhir's approach, but ultimately surrenders to her own feelings and makes no secret of it to Adhir.

All hell breaks loose when Adhir tells his widowed aunt that he has fallen in love with Sujata and wishes to marry her and not Rama. Charu is outraged. Her feelings of outrage change to feelings of anger and condemnation for Sujata because she holds the innocent girl responsible for having spoilt the alliance between Rama, her daughter, and Adhir. That the marriage of her own daughter has been frustrated by the untouchable girl they have sheltered is something she cannot bear. During one of her tirades against Sujata, she falls off the stairs and loses a lot of blood. A blood transfusion is needed. No match is found within the family or even from Adhir. Ironically, it is Sujata's blood group that is found to match Charu's, a girl she insisted on saying was 'like her daughter'. Sujata donates her own blood to save Charu's life and Charu finally learns that blood has no 'caste' and accepts that Sujata is as much her daughter as Rama is. The film closes with the suggestion of an acceptance of Sujata's marriage to Adhir with the parental sanction of both families.

Adhir, a college teacher with a romantic bent of mind, is burdened with the responsibility of carrying forth the heritage of tradition. He finds himself torn between his love for an untouchable girl, considered to be a social outcaste in spite of having had an open and respectable upbringing, and that of fulfilling the wishes of his domineering and fundamentalist aunt. For him, at times, it appears to be a losing battle between the progressive forces brought about by a democratic India and a post-Tagorean Bengal and the pressures of oppressive tradition that forms part of his genetic and social legacy. Despite the fact that his character is not fully fleshed out, Sunil Dutt shines as the low-key-yet-clear-in-his-convictions Adhir who is a perfect foil to Nutan. He realizes it is her film and at no point tries to corner the limelight for himself. The rest of the cast supports the lead pair perfectly.

Sujata, dealing with caste prejudice is more humane than most films made on untouchability. Bimal Roy is one of the first Indian directors noted for simplicity and understatement in the treatment of his films. *Sujata* is one of the best examples. One never finds him loud or ludicrous, except, perhaps, slightly, in the scene of the telephonic song where Adhir sings a Hindi song to the tune adapted from a Tagore original by S.D. Burman. In the other technical departments too, the film excels. The chiaroscuro cinematography using a diffusion lens and backlighting for many close-ups of *Sujata* in her myriad moods adds to the lyrical rhythm of the film. *Sujata* is a sensitively directed film with the romantic scenes between Adhir and Sujata taking on a lyrical, poetic rhythm. The story is told in a series of deft, restrained episodes never ever lapsing into self-pity that could have easily marred the film. The director in Bimal Roy insisted that such a marriage is not only possible but is more importantly necessary.

Analysis

Bimal Roy is one of the first Indian directors noted for simplicity and understatement in the treatment of his films. *Sujata* is one of the best examples of this. In the other technical departments too, the film excels.

The chiaroscuro cinematography using a diffusion lens and backlighting for many close-ups of Sujata in her myriad moods adds to the lyrical rhythm of the film. *Sujata* is a sensitively directed film with the romantic scenes between Adhir and Sujata taking on a lyrical, poetic rhythm. The story is told in a series of deft, restrained episodes never ever lapsing into self-pity that could have easily marred the film. And unlike P.C. Barua, whose *Devdas* Roy had photographed before remaking the film himself, where a death or two would have seen the story out of its tangled web.

When the film opens, one hears the sound of stones being broken on a hill. A bridge is being built. There is news of a cholera epidemic in basti number 2 that houses the coolies who work at the stone-chipping site, and they are on the run for fear of being infected. The following day happens to be the birthday celebration of the site engineer Upen Babu's little girl, Rama. Against this prologue, the title graphics begin to come up. A couple of coolies approach Upen Babu with a tiny infant in the arms of one. They inform Upen Babu that the infant girl is the sole survivor of trolley-coolie Bundan's family. Both Bundan and his wife have succumbed to cholera. Bundan was of low caste and no one in the village is willing to take care of the baby because not a single person belongs to that caste. Wolves were waiting to pick up the baby when these coolies brought her to Upen Babu. This marks the entry of Sujata into Upen Babu's family as an infant. She remains completely unaware of her genetic roots till she is grown up. Unlike her more liberal, progressive-thinking husband, Charu tries her best to resist forming a bond with Sujata. She could neither deny the maternal spirit within her nor send Sujata off to an orphanage. Sujata's adoptive father Upendranath Choudhury is a pro-gressive man who learns to accept the untouchable girl who circumstantially found place in his household as his own daughter. But from time to time, he buckles under his wife's staunch refusal to give Sujata an equal position to Rama, their biological daughter. Sujata's lover Adhir, however, makes a con-scious decision to break away from patriarchal and feudal norms by refusing to marry anyone other than Sujata, her low-birth notwithstanding.

The film is shot with rich lyrical, tonal quality and evocative fram-ing that bring out the human emotions of the story. And helping to lift the film several notches is its evergreen musical score by S.D. Burman. It is laced with such masterpieces like 'Jalte hain jiske liye' (For whom [the lamp] burns), 'Kali ghata chhaye' (Dark clouds are gathering), 'Hawa dheere aana' (Wind please flow slowly), 'Bachpan ke din' (Those days of childhood) and 'Sun mere bandhu' (Listen, my dear friend) rendered by Burman da himself. 'Jalte hain jiske liye' is perhaps the piece de resistance of the film. It must rank as one of the best romantic solos in Indian cinema and one of singer Talat Mehmood's finest songs. 'Hawa dheere aana' remains to date one of the most enduring lullabies ever in Hindi cinema. Geeta Dutt is in full form in this delicate little lullaby making prime use of her voice with the minimum orchestral support of just a *jal tarang*, and Asha Bhonsale impresses with 'Kali ghata chhaye'. Other songs include the cute Asha–Geeta duet 'Bachpan ke din bhi kya din the' and the Mohammad Rafi solo number 'Wah bhai wah'. And to push its humanistic message, the film includes an elaborate stage performance of Tagore's dance drama *Chandalika*.

Posing the toughest problem of all in class and genealogical terms, namely the 'pollution' of blood and the 'mingling' of blood structure the narrative.[26] The opposing views on untouchability are counterposed in dramatic conflict along various points in the narrative. The viewer's identification with and empathy for the central character of Sujata is ensured through every means available to mainstream cinema—star quality (Nutan, Sunil Dutt and Shashikala in the three main roles), beautiful musical score (S.D. Burman) and the apt placement and choreography of songs that chart every dramatic event that takes the story ahead—from the scene where Rama sings a paean to their bonding as sisters as kids, through the birthday scene to Sujata's humming to herself in the garden to the boatman's song where Adhir and Sujata come close for the first time in the film; cinematic techniques like the close-up, the silhouette shot on the banks of the river, the point of view shots and framing, the narrative pleasures of romance and a happy ending after the suspense and the catharsis come across eloquently, underlining the director's command over the craft of cinema and his control and supervision of his technical crew.

The Women in *Sujata*

Through *Sujata*, Bimal Roy gives the women a voice they can call their own, not only through the soft characterization of Sujata herself, who is almost like a painting done in watercolours, subdued, feminine and diffident, yet grateful to her adoptive parents without knowing the truth of her status, but also through the other female characters in the film. Rama for instance, is diametrically opposite of Sujata. Their upbringing is clearly filled with markers that show the difference. Rama has a good education, but the script is completely silent about why Sujata was not allowed to continue her education. If Charu had objections, what was Upen Babu doing? The apparent 'equality' is thus shown up to be a façade. Is Sujata really a 'daughter' of the house? Or is she a convenient handmaid to help Charu run the household with clockwork and silent efficiency?

---

[26] Chakravarty, *National Identity in Indian Popular Cinema*, 112.

Rama is loud, but the loudness is a cover for her tender feelings for the sister she loves dearly. She is the first and the only person within Upen Babu's family to wisen up to the mutual attraction between Adhir and Sujata. In fact, she consciously makes herself scarce and leaves when Adhir comes to their house to allow the lovers to be with each other. She plays tennis, participates in her college functions, throws lavish birthday parties and is generally a fun-loving young woman who remains unspoilt by the care and attention her mother showers on her. The difference between Sujata and Rama is tellingly captured in the song 'Bachpan ke din'. Rama is a carefree lady of leisure, plonking the piano, while Sujata is soft-spoken and hard-working, enjoying the song even as she expertly folds the laundry. Rama's character is truly endearing. She is probably the person who has accepted Sujata unconditionally. She calls her Didi, stands up for her sister when Adhir's aunt scoffs at Sujata's illiteracy and giggles teasingly with her sister while pointing out knowingly that she knows Adhir's taste. She does all this with a casual air without either her or the director making a major production of this, heart-warmingly underlying the fact that this is nothing special—this is how 'any' sibling would behave.

The two women with negative shades, Charu, as Sujata's adoptive mother, and Bua-ji, Adhir's widowed aunt, present a microcosm of women who belong to the time and place-setting Sujata represents. Charu is gullible enough to succumb to the machinations of Bua-ji who questions her looking after a girl who is an untouchable by birth. This begins to change her attitude towards Sujata, which was already different from the treatment she gave to her biological daughter Rama. The central mother–daughter relationship is calibrated really well. The mother's innate goodness is captured as well as the paradigm shifts in her attitude towards Sujata. Sujata yearns for her mother's affection, but is made aware of being an *achhut*[27] by her foster mother in a fit of pique.

Bua-ji, played by Lalita Pawar, noted for her negative roles in mainstream Hindi cinema, is much in control under the directorial baton of Roy. She brings to Upen Babu's home, a pundit in order to 'enlighten' the family about the demerits of having an untouchable girl under the same roof as theirs. Pundit-ji says that a kind of poisonous gas emanates from the bodies of untouchable people. This gas pollutes the bodies, minds and spirits of people born into high or upper castes. When Upen Babu asks him, "have you actually seen this gas?" He retorts by telling him, "have you seen vitamins?" Upen Babu's is not convinced by the pundit's argument. This infuriates Bua-ji who threatens to go away to Kashi for good.

---

[27] *Achhut* means 'untouchable', attached to a person of very low caste whom higher caste people do not touch even by mistake.

Neither, Charu nor Bua-ji is really bad. It is their upbringing within a framework of old-age and an outdated belief that makes them behaves the way they do. One point common between the two is their apparent lack of education. If Charu appears to be slightly more open than Bua-ji, it is because she is married to a progressive man like Upen Babu and is also much younger than Bua-ji and is distanced from her through age. The difference between the two is more of degree than of kind. If Charu finally accepts Sujata only when she learns that it is her blood that partly runs in her veins, then Bua-ji too bends under the pressure of the deep affection and love she feels for her nephew who refuses to marry any woman other than Sujata.

Gandhi, Buddha and *Sujata*

Mahatma Gandhi is a palpable and physical presence in *Sujata*, the film. Many shots have been used with Barrackpore's Gandhi Ghat as the backdrop. Interestingly, all these shots are focused exclusively with either Adhir or Sujata in the frame and no other character in the film is ever present here. In some shots, the camera pans up to close into Gandhi's empanelled mural on the wall, including him as an omniscient but a silent presence in the film. Using Gandhi-ji's sayings and example in his narrative in the touching scene where Sujata runs out of the house in a night of rain and storm to the Gandhi Ghat, probably to commit suicide, Roy makes palpable his desire for an egalitarian world. When Sujata is stopped from attending Rama's stage programme, Adhir leaves the show midway and meets Sujata. He conveys the programme's message and boosts Sujata's self-confidence with the film's best line: *Aatma ninda aatma hatya se bhi bada paap hai* (Criticizing the Self is a sin worse than suicide).

There are several references to Gandhi in the film. In one poignant scene, as they stand together along Barrackpore's Gandhi Ghat, Adhir tells Sujata that once, when out of the blue, some people donated a sum of ₹13,000 to Gandhi when everyone was ready to reject him for having taken in an untouchable girl within the Ahmedabad Ashram. Gandhi stood his ground and refused to let the girl go away even when he knew that the very existence of the Ashram would stand threatened by this move.

Sujata is ideological in the sense that it presents the possibility of the ideal society in the here and now under the spirit of Gandhi, who is a sort of patron saint to Sujata, saving her once from suicide and unfailingly offering comfort, strength and hope in her darkest moments. In fact, the very idea of the narrative situation, that of an 'untouchable' being 'adopted' by an upper-caste family, is taken from the teachings of Gandhi.[28]

---

[28] Ibid., 113.

Roy departs from the original source by incorporating an abstract from Rabindranath Tagore's dance drama *Chandalika* within the main narrative as part of a programme in Rama's college. The original Subodh Ghosh story used an annual sporting event as a strategy for taking Adhir away from the scene back to where Sujata was, at home. This change from the sporting event in the literary source to the staging of the dance drama *Chandalika* where Rama is shown portraying the title role is a pointer to Roy's perceptions of the appropriate.

Chandalika (The untouchable girl, 1933) is a full-fledged dance drama based on a Buddhist legend under the umbrella title of *Sardulakarnavadana*. It is the story of a low-caste girl called Prakriti, who refuses to acknowledge the handicaps that are attached to people born low such as not being allowed to touch or be touched by people of higher birth. While she is grappling with the tragedy of her birth, a disciple of the Buddha named Ananda steps in to ask her for drink of water to quench his thirst. When she tells him that she cannot give him water to drink as she is an untouchable, he insists, saying that there is no such thing as high or low birth and being born human is the only caste there is in this world. Having quenched his thirst, he leaves but Chandalika has already fallen in love with him. She approaches her mother, who has occult powers, and implores her to use them and bring Ananda back to her. Her mother appeals to her not to distract a spiritual person from his penance, but Prakriti insists.

However, as she watches the transformation of Ananda being brought back to her, through her mother's magic mirror, she realizes that this man is not the Ananda she has met; it is only the body, which is the shell that protects his soul and his spirit. Her claim over his body will not get her his soul. She asks her mother to stop her magic chant and, in the original Buddha legend, she renounces the material world of her own will. In *Sujata*, the audience is shown the segment where Ananda is asking Prakriti for a drink of water and when Prakriti is afraid of satisfying his thirst, he explains to her the philosophy of humanity and her life changes forever. In Upen Babu's home, the scene shifts to the garden with an exchange between Sujata and Adhir and these shots are intercut with the shots of the dance drama at the college.

The 'Progressive' Upper Caste and its Attitude to Dowry

In response to the urgings of Bua-ji and his wife Charu to find a match for Sujata before Adhir's marriage to Rama can be finalized, Upen Babu places an advertisement in the matrimonial column of a newspaper. One Haricharan arrives at Upen Babu's home to make enquiries. It turns out that they used to attend the same class in college. Haricharan thinks that Rama is the proposed bride. During the conversation, when Upen Babu asks him about his expectations for the proposal of his son in marriage, Haricharan puts up a strong protest. He carries on a brief tirade against the system of dowry in a Hindu marriage. He goes on at length about the insignificance of money when compared with man's integrity, culture and capacity. "The family background is not important," he says. "What is important is the man himself. If the man is not good, what will I do with his ancestry, tell me? Will I lick it up? He Ram, when will our society open its eyes?" When Upen Babu asks him what his son is doing, Haricharan informs him that though the son is a graduate, he is not interested in a nine-to-five job because he is a man of 'independent spirit'. He goes on to add that business which interests his son calls for funds, especially in an age of competition. Upen Babu is intelligent enough to grasp the underpinnings of this comment. He assures Haricharan that he would offer every kind of support in setting up the son in his own business.

However, as soon as Haricharan learns that the girl in question is not Upen Babu's daughter, or even a close relation, but an untouchable, he leaves in a huff, warning Upen Babu to stop fooling people with false matrimonial ads in newspapers. This is when the interval sign flashes on screen. This scene is cinematographed in a straightforward manner, in the lounge of Upen Babu's bungalow. Mani Chatterjee puts up a realistic portrayal as Haricharan, his mood-swings captured effectively both through dialogue as well as through expression. This scene is a telling comment on the hypocrisy that defines the genteel intellectual class of upwardly mobile Brahmins.

Blood Transfusion in *Sujata*

The climactic scene where Sujata's blood is transferred to Charu following her fall from the stairs is Bimal Roy's personal contribution that does not exist in the original novel. Reel 95 has the blood transfer sequence. Charu lies unconscious on the bed. When the doctor informs Upen Babu that his wife needs blood immediately, each family member and even Adhir lend them to find if there is a match. There is no match. Finally, they call upon Sujata. Surprisingly, her blood matches perfectly with Charu's. In reel 96, the camera captures a top-angle shot of Sujata and Adhir following the blood transfusion. "My blood is poisonous, go away from this breath for your own good," she tells him. She has penned a letter addressed to him which lies on a table. As Adhir slowly walks out of the room, the letter flies away in the soft breeze to land somewhere, unknown to Adhir. It is later discovered by Upen Babu and he reads it out to Charu when she comes back to her senses—in more ways than one.

The question is why did Bimal Roy incorporate this scene into the film when it was nowhere in the original? Does it make more sense? Yes, it does. It stands out as a living irony to all that has gone before in the film, beginning with the coolie coming to Upen Babu's house carrying a newborn infant in his arms, right till the time when Charu falls off the stairs, calling for a blood transfusion. The blood transfusion is a culmination of the argument Bimal Roy began the film with—that the innate goodness of a human being is what counts above everything else.

But then, he could have achieved this with a male character as well, wouldn't he? Not really. Had the infant been a boy instead of a girl, Upen Babu might not have taken the responsibility of taking the infant into his home in the first place. The girl being brought up within the four walls of a home with the biological child of her foster parents—also a girl, made it possible for Bimal Roy to explore and to express all the myriad emotions he had in mind, ranging from sisterhood to motherhood, to love, to rejection, the father–daughter relationship, the rigours of housework, the direct links to nature in the garden scenes and everything that goes along with the business of day-to-day life. The colour and thickness of blood do not really differ from one man or woman to another is the message of the film. He underscores this when Rama's blood does not match her own mother's blood group, yet Sujata's does. Some critics found this bit of concrete symbolism a bit too loud when placed within the subtle and lyrical mood of the rest of the film. But considering that the audience is a medley of caste, class, education, urban–rural background and sex, perhaps it is this cosmopolitan nature of the Indian audience that might have triggered this incorporation. In retrospect, it does not seem forced or melodramatic in the least.

Chakravarty[29] insists that the film is the culmination of an ultimate vision, since it integrates within the construct of the nation, the self-sufficiency implicit in the modern bourgeois family and the ties of blood and genealogy that characterize Indian notions of family. She critiques the blood donation by saying that Sujata's giving blood to save her adoptive mother's life is the ultimate test to prove herself so that it is now alright for the Choudhury family to accept her within its own caste identity and social milieu. Sujata must transcend the conditions of her birth before she can truly 'belong', and the agent of her 'upliftment' is not something that she 'does' but something that is—her 'blood'; its 'type' matches that of the dying Charu. According to Chakravarty, therefore, while making the point that caste is not a matter of polluted blood, *Sujata*, the film, actually reinforces the existence of caste by making the breaking of caste barriers dependent on accident.

---

[29] Ibid., 114.

Nutan in and as *Sujata*

Sujata has seen yet another sparkling performance from Nutan in the central role. 'Yet another' because, with sterling performances in heroine-centric films such as *Paying Guest, Tere Ghar Ke Samne,*[30] *Baarish,*[31] *Sone Ki Chidiya, Seema, Dilli Ka Thug*[32] and others, Nutan had established herself as one of the finest actresses of the Hindi screen. Irrespective of director, role or banner, Nutan always gave her best without the need to glamorize herself unless the role demanded it. It is perhaps surpassed only by her performance in the other Bimal Roy film she did, *Bandini*. Nutan enacts the role of the untouchable girl with stunning grace and is able to convey her hurt, her trauma with just a glance or a gesture. She proves once again what a thinking actress she was and as one who tried to fathom the inchoate motivations of the characters she played. She could convey much more with just a look or a fleeting glance than most actresses could with expansive dialogue. In fact, Lata Mangeshkar singled her out as the heroine whose expressions came closest to suggest that she was actually singing the song herself.

One story that did the rounds of the studios after *Sujata* became a box office hit wherever it was released was that Nutan did not initially agree to don the dark make-up Bimal Roy had planned for the character of Sujata that she had to portray. According to Bimal Roy, Sujata had to be dark-skinned in order to distinguish her from the rest of the family, as she was an untouchable and Upen Babu belonged to the highest caste of Brahmins. Nutan was insecure about wearing dark-toned make-up and stood her ground for some time while Bimal Roy patiently waited for his leading lady to agree to his idea. She relented at length on the condition that the make-up would not be black. The real life irony in this story lies in that Nutan looked perhaps the most beautiful among all her screen roles as Sujata in the dark make-up with that tiny bindi in the middle of her eyebrows, wearing a simple Bengali cotton sari with the *pallu*[33] tied around her waist as she goes about silently doing her household chores.

She does her work to the dot and one could clock her precisely. When Adhir asks Rama where Sujata is, Rama looks at the wall clock and says, "If it is four, she must be up on the terrace picking out the washing." Sujata's world collapses around her when she overhears her mother saying that she wants Adhir to marry Rama. Roy, a master of semiotics, shows Sujata

---

[30] *Tere Ghar Ke Samne*—In front of your house.

[31] *Baarish*—Rains.

[32] *Dilli Ka Thug*—The thief from Delhi.

[33] *Pallu* is the Hindi equivalent of the end of the sari the woman wears. It has many socially and metaphorically significant associations in literature and cinema.

retreating to another room and switching off the lights—her hopes. Even when Adhir insists that he does not believe in caste distinctions, Sujata turns down his marriage proposal. Sujata does not sacrifice her love because of her caste, but because of her devotion to the only mother she has ever known. It takes a convoluted catastrophe to open the floodgates of Charu's heart.

An interesting departure from the original, among some other important ones, is in Bimal Roy's naming of his central character Sujata that is also the title of the film. In the Subodh Ghosh original story, the girl's name was Ambalika whereas the novel has the same name as the film, *Sujata*. Perhaps, the decision sprung from the fact that the film was being made in Hindi for an all-India audience and thus, Sujata—meaning a girl of high birth—would carry many meanings, metaphorical, literal, social, for the national audience. It also evolves into a strong and a satiric comment on casteism because Sujata is born to untouchable parents, but her adoptive parents of high birth choose to name her Sujata. Does biological birth determine the 'birth' of a child, metaphorically speaking? Or is it the environment she is brought up in that shapes her to what she becomes as an adult? Or, rather, is it her inner being that determines her 'birth?' All these questions get raised through the film in so low-key a manner that one tends to miss them completely unless one was actually looking at them closely.

Ambalika is a name that has no direct link to the subject of the story, underlined in the title—*Sujata*. But Sujata as the name of the central character narrows the focus to the essence of the story that gently and almost caressingly comments on the ironies of casteism, sheds light on little-known areas of the differences that lie between natural and adoptive motherhood and, last but not least, on the universality of love that knows no barriers of caste, class, race or birth.

The character of Sujata is a poignant issue of impersonation.[34] While exploring and trying to negotiate the right 'match' for Sujata, it is discovered that she fits neither into the caste she is born into nor into the caste she has been imbibed in and adopted by. She is a 'Brahmin' among untouchables and an 'untouchable' among Brahmins. She, along with the audience is always conscious of her split identity. The fact that Sujata is an untouchable by birth is almost incidental, though it has a crucial importance in the unfolding of the narrative. Sujata's associations are with nature and we see her at regular intervals in close proximity and in happy harmony with nature, watering the plants and flowers in the garden, cinematographed with the upper half of her face seen rising from a cluster of flowers, a Chandramallika flower being the only ornament she adorns her hair with

---

[34] Chakravarty, *National Identity in Indian Popular Cinema*, 85.

and so on. The song she sings to herself in the garden—'Kali ghata chhaye mora jiya tarsaaye, aise mein kahin koi mil jaaye'—is also a paean to nature, heralding the coming of rains.

On a night of rain and storm, she runs out on the banks of the Gandhi Ghat, wishing to end her life. The end of her sari gets caught in a sculpted mural of Gandhi with an inscription that stops her from taking the ultimate step. These scenes are used as subtle markers to stress the ironic fact of her birth juxtaposed against her natural and biological sense of inner alienation from the world of people close to her, as they are of high birth and do not really come from the world she does. Nature, perhaps, has a better understanding of this untouchable girl than people like Adhir's *Bua*[35] and her adoptive mother Charu do.

During the birthday song sequence where Rama (Shashikala) plonks on the piano as her friends belt out 'Tum jeeyo hazaaron saal saal',[36] the scene cuts to a flashback showing Rama and Sujata as little girls. Rama is sitting on Charu's lap and eating milk pudding out of her mother's hands. Rama is dressed in a brand new party frock. A surprised Sujata asks Charu why she is feeding Rama, why Rama is sitting on Charu's lap, why she is wearing and new frock and so on. Rama says that it is her birthday. The child Sujata begins to pester Charu to celebrate her birthday as well, because she, too, would like to wear a new frock, to sit on her Ammi's lap, to eat milk pudding out of her hands. Charu fails to cope with Sujata's demands and gets extremely irritated. She asks the ayah to take Sujata away. But Sujata puts up a fight with the ayah, refusing to leave, till she is forcibly taken away as she thrashes about in the ayah's arms and screams and shouts in protest. As the flashback ends with a dissolve, the scene shifts to the beautiful garden of Upen Babu's house.

Close shot: Sujata (Adhir in voice-over.)

CUT

Long mid-shot: Sujata and Adhir. Adhir comes close to Sujata. The camera tracks towards the two.
Sujata: You came away.
Adhir: And why did you come away?
Sujata: You will not understand.
Adhir: I have already understood.
Sujata: No one on earth has the power to understand all this.

---

[35] *Bua* means father's sister or paternal aunt.
[36] *Tum jeeyo hazaaron saal*—Live for a hundred years my child.

Adhir: I have the power. But that's just a one-time thing Sujata. Then, why are you so unhappy?

Sujata moves away.

Sujata: Which one-time thing are you referring to?

Adhir: This thing about your Ammi always refers to you as 'like my daughter, instead of 'my daughter.'

CUT

Voice-over: *Why are you crying Sujata, you are indeed Upen Babu's daughter.*

CUT

Close-shot: Adhir

Adhir: Who in this world can deny this truth?

CUT

Close-shot: The camera moves behind Sujata. Adhir enters frame.

Sujata: Do you accept this?

Adhir in voice-over: Absolutely.

Sujata: Tell that to me again, just once?

Adhir: Why once? I'll say it over and over again, a thousand times. The truth is that you are Upendra Babu's daughter.

CUT

Sujata and Adhir move to the left. Adhir in frame.

Adhir: Sujata, when is your birthday?

Sujata: Must be there somewhere, in the dark.

Adhir: I don't understand.

Sujata: When you've understood this much, why can't you understand that no one knows when my birthday falls.

Adhir: I say.......

Sujata: To whom?

Adhir: To the twinkling stars in the sky. The stars were twinkling exactly the same way that day too, Sujata. If I tell you that I'd like to give you a birthday gift in remembrance of that day, will you accept it Sujata?

Sujata: I've got it already.

Adhir: You've got it? How?

CUT

Close-shot: Sujata and Adhir.

Sujata: You have bestowed the dignity of being human to one whose birthday is unknown to the world. I do not wish a gift greater than the fact that you have recognized sorrow as sorrow per se.

CUT

Long mid-shot: Sujata and Adhir

Adhir: Sujata!

CUT

Mid-shot: Coconut leaves

CUT

Mid-shot: Sujata and Adhir. Sujata is leaving.
Sujata: But I am scared. All this happiness is something I might not be able to bear!

End of birthday scene (Reel Three)[37]

From this scene, Adhir appears to love repeating Sujata's name. His tone of voice is soft and caressing in tone and pitch when he talks to her, especially when he pronounces her name. This comes up in the film again and again, juxtaposed against Sujata not addressing him by his first name ever. Her references are always to *Adhir Babu*, perhaps to acknowledge her realization that in some way, she is inferior to him. Sunil Dutt exudes sincerity. His character is the embodiment of good and Dutt makes him believable. Nutan carries the film's dramatic weight outstandingly well on her responsible shoulders. She is often quiet, yet her expressive eyes illuminate her character's innermost thoughts and feelings.

In his deftly crafted screenplay, Nabendu Ghosh etches a fully fleshed-out character and as the film moves along, one feels as if Ghosh wrote out the character with Nutan in mind. Roy interestingly uses nature to convey Sujata's moods. Another garden sequence expresses this link between Sujata and her love for nature. There's a subdued yet entrancing romanticism in this love scene, where Adhir conspires with himself to meet Sujata in the garden lauding the fact that *tumhara sabse bada gun yehi hai ke tumme gun nahin hai* (your greatest quality is that you have none.)

Garden Scene in Upen Babu's House
Mid-shot: Sujata is in the garden, watering the plants. Adhir comes and stands close to her. A startled Sujata moves a bit away from him to the left.
Sujata: Rama must be studying in her room now.
Adhir: No, she isn't. I just met her. She's gone out to play.
Sujata: Oh!

CUT

Long mid-shot: Sujata enters the frame from the left followed by Adhir.
Adhir: Sujata, in this garden, you are really in full bloom.

CUT

[37] Original screenplay, Courtesy: National Film Archive of India, Pune.

Close mid-shot: Sujata
Voice-over of Adhir: *Do you know which is your best quality?*
Sujata: Quality?

CUT

Mid-shot: Sujata and Adhir
Adhir: Yes. Your best quality is that you have none.
Sujata: How is Bua-ji keeping now?
Adhir: Is this an answer to my question?
Sujata: Then tell me what to say.
Adhir : Can you pick out my best quality?
Sujata: You have tons of talent. I have no capacity to elaborate on them at length.

CUT

Mid-close-up: Sujata and Adhir
Adhir: Okay then. Let's hear my negative points.
Sujata: Negative points?
Adhir: Yes, my biggest fault.
Sujata: I don't know and I cannot even begin to understand all this.
Adhir: You don't understand? My biggest fault is that I come here just to look at you.

CUT

Mid-shot: A shriveled leaf

CUT

Close-shot: A shy Sujata

CUT

Sujata: Ammi is inside. Won't you look her up?

CUT

Adhir and Sujata begin to move from the left.
Adhir: Come along, I'll look her up.

CUT[38]

There are other sequences where Sujata's oneness with nature comes across movingly. A fluttering fern mirrors Sujata's state. And when a devastated Sujata goes out near Gandhi-ji's statue in the middle of a thunderstorm, the whole cosmos seems to be weeping with her or the silken serenade over the phone—'Jalte hai jiske liye'.

"Sujata is a floating signifier," writes Chakravarty.[39] Her natural parents are dead when the film opens and her entry into the dominant social

---

[38] Ibid. National Film Archive of India.
[39] Chakravarty, *National Identity in Indian Popular Cinema*, 85.

order must be initiated through a reconstruction of genealogy and blood links. In spatial terms, she must move from 'outside' society to inside it, from a 'natural' state of marriage and domestication, from poverty and dependence to wealth and social position. Membership into the family is sanctioned through marriage into the same higher caste she has been adopted by.

The transgenerational insight into the characters and personalities of the four women is brought across with conviction and without resort to any melodrama or sensationalization of the several issues involved—caste ostracism; adoption and its implications in a family where a natural child already exists; the love between a high-caste, highly educated young man and a low-caste, uneducated young woman; suicide as the easiest and shortest but dispensable escape route for girls like Sujata; the strong bond of sisterhood that sustains between two girls brought up by the same set of parents within the same family, though they are not real sisters at all; the possibility of marriage between the two social unequals based solely on love; blood transfusion as proof of caste being purely a social condition without any basis whatsoever in science, history or even God; and so on. Its mechanism of pleasure, blend of realism and idealism, and the humanitarian vision that it embodies, denote a powerful, if fading, current in the symbolic universe of the 1950s. Sujata's 'voice' is structured into the complexity of the environment that shapes and defines her quiet submission to everything that she goes through, everyone she interacts with, in her low-profile, quiet way.

Sujata won the Best Film, Best Director, Best Actress and Best Story-writer awards at the Filmfare awards in 1960 at a time when awards for Indian cinema at home were highly valued and were not a part of an anonymous medley of the indifferent and manipulated spate of private awards. Roy took some liberties with the original. But these celluloid improvisations enhanced the richness of the film's texture. It is one of the most beautiful celluloid representations of romanticism that evolved into a strong social statement against untouchability, spreading the message of the universality of love that extends not only beyond caste, class and status but also beyond blood. *Sujata* gives the woman a voice, mainly through her silence, her subdued personality and her acceptance of her marginalized existence within the framework of a family she is eternally grateful for. She does not respond, except through silent tears when Adhir sings to her through the telephone. She never answers back when reprimanded. She expresses her confusion when she discovers that Bua-ji avoids anything she touches but does not express anger at this condemnation. Her 'voice' is defined more by her silence than by its articulation. And from within this silence, Bimal Roy makes her 'voice' her statement.

BANDINI (1963)

Jarasandha (1902–1981)

Bandini, based on *Tamasi*, a Bengali novel by Jarasandha, is seen as the culmination of Bimal Roy's command over the language of cinema and his artistic mastery. Jarasandha's career began as a jailor in the northern parts of Bengal and culminated when he retired as jail superintendent. He began writing about his experiences as jailor, creating a completely new genre in Bengali literature where the characters, most of them criminals, were behind bars. Tapan Sinha made a beautiful film based on a few stories in his first volume of a four-volume series called *Louhakapat* (1958; *The Iron Door*). *Bandini* is the story of Kalyani, a woman prisoner charged with murder.

Jarasandha is the pen name of Charu Chandra Chakraborty. He catapulted to fame in 1952 when the first volume of *Louhakapat* got published. He had a brilliant academic career, winning the 7th position in the Entrance examination from Hare School, Calcutta, and an equally good result in MA in economics from Calcutta University. He was born on 23 March in 1902, in a remote village of Faridpur district, now in Bangladesh. He passed his BCS Examination to be appointed as a Jailor at Alipore Central Jail. He wrote a number of books that won him a unique position in the Bengali literary scene such as *Tamashi*, *Ashray*,[40] *Louhakapat*, *Ekush Bochhor*,[41] *Mashirekha*,[42] *Aboron*,[43] *Ebari Obari*[44] and *Paadi*[45] just to name a few. He wrote short stories for children too, which won wide acclaim. He passed away on 25 May 1981 in Calcutta.

Many of his novels and novelettes were adapted for Bengali films, but *Bandini* is the only Hindi film made on his work. Other films based on his works are—*Paadi* starring Pranati Ghosh in the lead, *Aparna* starring Tanuja as a con woman forced to extort young men for money by a gang she gets involved with and *Nyaydanda* (Scales of Justive) starring the veteran actor Radhamohan Bhattacharjee in the lead as a famous judge who turns nostalgic about his judgements and questions some of them in retrospect. This has shades of a Tarasankar Bandopadhyay novel *Bicharak*, also made into a film starring Uttam Kumar, Arundhati Devi and Deepti Roy in the lead.

---

[40] *Ashray*—Shelter.
[41] *Ekush Bochhor*—21 years.
[42] *Mashirekha*—A mark made in black ink.
[43] *Aboron*—Veil or cover.
[44] *Ebari Obari*—This house and that house.
[45] *Paadi*—The journey.

Background

Bandini is the first Hindi film to depict the story of a woman prisoner imprisoned for life for a murder she committed and confessed to without making any plea for forgiveness or harbouring any sense of guilt. The story told mostly in flashback from Kalyani's point of view. For most of the time, she is present within the cinematographic space of the film either visually or within the sound ambience of the film, also used at times as a strategy to move back into her past. Bimal Roy used imagery and sound beautifully to convey the changing and sometimes volatile moods of Kalyani, enacted by Nutan in the most powerful performance of her career. One noticeable change Bimal Roy made in this film is changing the name of the original character of the prisoner from Hena to Kalyani. Kalyani is derived from the word 'kalyan' meaning 'welfare' and is turned into an adjective in Kalyani that defines a woman who is born to work towards the welfare of fellow-beings. This is borne out at several points very clearly, and subtly at different points, over the film as we shall soon see.

There are very few films featuring the protagonist as a prisoner in Hindi cinema. Even if she is placed behind bars, she is shown as trapped by negative characters that have conspired against him, or her imprisonment is temporary and her space within the prison occupies little time in the narrative and cinematographic space of the film.

The film that comes to mind immediately is *Anjaam*[46] (1994) starring Madhuri Dixit and Shah Rukh Khan where the heroine is imprisoned for some time. The threat of rape and violence runs through the film. But no rape is actually committed, off or on-screen, on Shivani throughout the film. This 'threat' is posed more by the representatives of law than by the psychopathic male protagonist. This is a very good cinematic illustration of custodial rape—rape committed by custodial people, or people in 'power' positions who use and abuse this official power by raping women who are in their 'custody'.[47] The author has chosen this example because it offers

---

[46] *Anjaam*—The consequence.

[47] *Custodial* or power rape is said to be one of the reasons that led to the passing of the Criminal Law 'Amendment' Act of 1980 after three years of parliamentary enquiry and mounting public pressure. This is said to be an 'improvement' on the earlier functioning Criminal Procedure Code 1973 and the Indian Evidence Act 1872. Apart from increasing the minimum punishment for any kind of rape from two years of rigorous imprisonment to seven years which could stretch to life term, one of the principal introductions was that of a new section called 'custodial rape'. 'Custodial rape' is defined as rape committed by a male in a position of authority or custodial control over a woman. Such a male, by the very power and status he enjoys, should have had abused his official position to rape the woman who would otherwise have refused. That is, had he *not been in the position of official power* over the woman at that point of time.

a complete contrast and counterpoint to the relatively compliant women prisoners presented in *Bandini* including the jail warden. It also portrays an extremely negative and violent image of the police of either sex who are in charge of the prison inmates.

The trafficking of women in the jail and Arjun Singh's physical intimidation of Shivani constantly reinforce the possibility of rape. Consequently, both situations offer opportunities to Shivani to disrupt the rape script by recuperating violence. She subverts the first attempt to be 'picked up' by throwing up over the prospective 'client'. She subverts the second attempt by brutalizing and finally killing the jail superintendent who is about to hand her over to 'special guests'.

Her encounter with Arjun Singh results in the most direct rupturing of the rape script. Having cornered her in an abandoned barn, Arjun Singh towers over Shivani who is on the floor. With self-assured arrogance, he unbuckles his belt, unzips his trousers and pulls them off. Just as he about to bend over her, she plunges a knife through his thigh. From this point onwards, the roles get reversed. It is she who begins to chase her would-be-rapist and finally traps and kills him. Her use of the knife and the sword in the process displaces the gendered polarization of the grammar of violence wherein only the male body is empowered and assumed to be able to wield weapons.[48]

This, however, does not in any way immunize Shivani from cinematographic violence perpetrated on her by the camera, the lighting, the sound effects. She is still the 'object' of the spectator's 'gaze'. Though the narrative and cinematographic space 'pretend' to position her as the central 'subject' of the drama, in actual fact, Shivani is an example of extreme objectification of the woman's person and body, which must invest her with the qualities of a 'killer' in order to free her from this 'objectivity' and from the male 'gaze'. It is as if the entire concept of freeing herself from such narrative and cinematic objectification is totally determined by and dependent on her empowering herself with the 'qualities' of revenge through a spate of killings. The suggestion that this very venture to kill is an 'autonomous' decision of Shivani is undercut by her wilful death after killing the man responsible for the tragedy her life has been reduced to. Had the script permitted her to stay alive, her autonomy would have been firmly established

---

(Emphasis, mine.) Despite the passing of the amended law several years ago, rape continues and most of the situations are of custodial rape. The four most notorious cases of custodial rape that have drawn nation-wide media attention are of Mathura, Rameeza Bee, Maya Thyagi and Guntaben. All these cases involved gang-rape committed by policemen.

[48] Chakravarty, *National Identity in Indian Popular Cinema*.

and acknowledged. Her 'autonomy' is diluted also because each time she commits a murder, she invokes the memory of her dead husband and dead children almost as an explanation of the killings.

An example of the 'misleading quality of sound' deliberately structured to heighten the drama in the narrative is found in *Anjaam*. It demonstrated imaginative sound effects within the cinematic and narrative space. The best of these is structured in a particular series of shots when the female protagonist Shivani (Madhuri Dixit), with the active help of her fellow inmates in jail, sets out to kill the jailor, also a woman. The women are shown preparing to perform a devi pooja within the premises of the female section of the prison. As they get ready to begin, Shivani is summoned to the jailor's room. Shivani and Nisha (Himani Shivpuri), her close friend in the prison, exchange a long and silent look eloquent with meaning. Nisha begins the ritual chants while still looking at Shivani. Though the chants are apparently used to invoke the goddess, they are intended to cushion any noises of struggle between Shivani and the jailor. The chants, disguised as chants of religious invocation, are essentially a sound-and-music 'aid' to help Shivani in her mission. The elaborately performed slaughter of the jailor is intercut with the women performing the pooja. The terrible retaliation unleashed on the jailor is juxtaposed against celebratory shots of Nisha playing the flute with a flourish. Here is an example of 'using a sound-and-myth sign in reverse'. In Hindu mythology, it is Krishna who is identified with the flute. In *Anjaam*, we find a woman, imprisoned (wrongly) for having murdered her mother-in-law, playing the flute. The trapping, the chasing and the brutalization preceding the slaughter are shot with the attentive deliberateness of a ritual.[49]

Synopsis

Kalyani, an inmate of a women's ward of a prison in pre-independent India, is determined to serve out her full term. She resists the subtle but strong overtures of the prison doctor, Deven, though he wants to marry her. She is afraid to marry him because of her scarred past and his pure one. She is determined to sustain the social difference between herself and Deven and believes that her presence in his life will destroy his future because of the social stigma she will carry as a social and emotional baggage with her into his life forever.

---

[49] Shohini Ghosh, 'Deviant Pleasures and Disorderly Women—The Representation of the Female Outlaw in Bandit Queen and Anjaam', in *Feminist Terrains in Legal Domains—Interdisciplinary Essays on Women and Law in India*, ed. Ratna Kapur (New Delhi: Kali for Women, 1996), 167–168.

Kalyani writes her story in a notebook for Deven to read, and the film cuts back to a flashback, going back to Bengal in the 1930s. As the mother-less daughter of the village postmaster, Kalyani gets emotionally involved with Bikash Ghosh, a political activist, an anarchist always on the run from the British police. Once, Bikash falls very sick, and while tending to him, Kalyani falls asleep and happens to spend the night in his room. To rescue her from scandal, Bikash tells everyone that Kalyani is his wife. Before leaving the village, he promises Kalyani's father that he will come back and marry his daughter. But he never does.

The father and daughter turn into targets of ridicule and become social outcasts, forcing Kalyani to run away in the darkness of night to save her father from further humiliation. As she runs away, the soundtrack fills up with a beautiful situational song rendered by Mukesh 'O jaanewale ho sake to laut ke aana' (Oh please come back if you can you outbound traveller). She takes up an ayah's job in the woman's ward of a hospital. A particular patient, a neurotic woman, makes life difficult for Kalyani. One evening, when the patient's husband is visiting, Kalyani is made the butt of her insults. Kalyani discovers by chance that this is the woman who Bikash married, leaving her in the lurch. The same night, a telephone call informs her of her father's sudden death in an accident. These three incidents, piled one upon the other, disturb her deeply. Later that night, Kalyani poisons the woman not in a fit of rage exactly, but as if in a trance-like state conse-quent upon seeing her father's innate dead body on the hospital bed.

But having read her diary, Deven is still willing to marry her and his mother is prepared to accept her too. As she waits for the train to take her to Deven's home, she runs into the terminally ill Bikash, waiting for the steamer on the other side of the matted wall of the waiting room. The young boy with Bikash tells her that Bikash's marriage was a part of his commitment to the freedom struggle and in adherence to the rules drawn out by his party where he had to marry this woman with a mental problem. Just when the steamer sounds its hooting, ready to set sail, Kalyani rushes up the shaky wooden plank to join him. S.D. Burman's voice belt out 'Mera saajan hai us paar, main is paar, o mere maajhi ab ke baar, le chal paar' (My lover is on the other side of the river, I am on this bank, Oh My dear fisherman, take me across for once). The lines 'Main bandini hoon piya ki, main sangini hoon saajan ki' (I am the prisoner of my lover, I am the com-panion of my beloved) fill the soundtrack, spelling out the basic ideology of Kalyani. She is a prisoner of love from the beginning to end and the physical reality of her actual imprisonment is just a symbolic representation of this love. The fact that she has landed behind bars for committing a murder is traced back to her feeling of being betrayed in love.

Analysis

The imaginative and aesthetic use of sound and imagery through black-and-white frames to express the loneliness, the sense of alienation and the total lack of guilt that Kalyani experiences within the prison is unforgettable. Standing all alone in a corner of the jail compound facing the prison's high wall, Kalyani can hear the hoofs of the horse on the soundtrack pulling the horse carriage carrying Deven away. Just before she is to kill Bikash's wife, Kalyani sits with her back to a grilled window, her face in relief against backlighting, the sounds of a welding machine somewhere in the neighbourhood hammering nails of sound into the sinister ambience of the evening. Her hands tremble a bit when she pours the poison from the bottle, but her eyes burn with the determination of something terrible she has decided to do regardless of its consequence. Later, it appears as if she committed the act in a kind of trance and came out of it when the murder is discovered the next morning. Incidents build up towards this murder and carefully set up to establish her psyche. The friend, whose husband had helped her get the job in the hospital, calls her up to inform her that her father has met with an accident in the city. He had come searching for Kalyani. Kalyani rushes out. When she reaches the hospital, her father is dead. She walks back, silent. The recalcitrant patient screams out to her.

The scenes in the hospital shown in flashback offer some of the best examples of ambience or ambient sound[50] in Hindi cinema. The murder, unfolded in flashback, is committed in the nursing home where the victim is admitted as a mental patient and where Kalyani works as an ayah. The night before the murder, Kalyani is shown seething with cold anger at her repeated insults by this patient. She sits against a window throwing sparks and flashes of light, apparently from a welding unit. Her dark face is framed by the backlight from these sparks and flashes. Her face is dimly visible. The loud and irritating sound of welding juxtaposed against Kalyani's silence both heightens and intensifies her intent to kill the one who humiliated her (who is also the woman she identifies as having snatched her lover and destroyed her life) in cold blood. Kalyani pumping the pressure stove to make tea, the sound of the lit stove, Kalyani happening to overhear a conversation between the woman and her husband, the woman throwing away the cup and saucer while screaming at Kalyani, Kalyani's silence juxtaposed against the irritating and eccentric outpourings of the

---

[50] Ambience is widely used as a synonym for ambient sound. Ambient sound consists of noises present in the environment. See http://www.filmsound.org/terminology/adr.htm (Accessed on 3 March 2017).

mentally sick woman, Kalyani letting out a crazy scream when the murder is discovered, are some examples of ambient sound.

Every frame is carefully designed, well-orchestrated and spilling over with layers of meaning. Kalyani and Deven are constantly shown together in their early meetings without any barrier between them. But when Deven proposes, we see a door between them. Kalyani turns down his proposal without having to look at him. The door could be read as a signifier of the barrier Kalyani feels exists between the honest, respectable, kind and committed prison doctor and herself, a prisoner committed for life for murder.

After this scene, the two are always shown from two sides of a given space with a barrier between them. If he is outside the room, she is inside, and he sees her through the bars of the window. From Kalyani's point of view, she sees him standing outside through the bars of her cell window. The final point of separation comes when she does not see him at all but hears the sounds of the horse's hoofs and the rolling wheels of his carriage. The call of the prison guard announcing *sab theek hai* (everything is fine) spells out the opposite—nothing is fine. This spells out the irony behind the walls of a prison where prisoners, stripped of their human identity, are mere numbers, where life is reduced to an eternity of waiting either to go out to an unkind world that will not accept them, or to die inside. The prison guard's call is used three times in the film. The first time it happens, we see a freedom fighter being taken into the prison. The second time, Deven has resigned and is going back home. The last time the guard calls out 'sab theek hai', the freedom fighter is being put to the gallows. These function as subtle and underplayed counterpoints in the film. The song 'Mat ro maata, laal tere bahu tere' while the freedom fighter is being marched to the gallows and his family cries outside the prison gates appears a bit melodramatic in retrospect because it does not belong.

Bimal Roy uses the spaces within the jail compound and the bars of the prison as powerful symbols depicting openness and imprisonment. They represent everything, the seclusion of the prisoners, separating them from others and imprisoning them within their hold. The open spaces within the prison are seemingly open, but they offer respite for Kalyani to think, to retrospect and, in some ways, to create a distance between her and the other prisoners. The other women prisoners are placed in these spaces to do their prison jobs such as grinding flour on a big grindstone, singing songs that carry resonances of the home that they have left behind, get into fights and even make sarcastic comments about one of the jail officer's generosity towards Kalyani. Kalyani remains immune to these and keeps to her own.

The bars on the other hand symbolize Kalyani's quiet acceptance of her destiny spent in the prison. When one of the woman prisoners is diagnosed as suffering from TB and the female warden collects the others to ask who would like to volunteer to nurse her, Kalyani steps forward. When there is an appeal made to her for an early release, she says she does not want an early release. When the jail doctor adds an egg to her menu because she is looking after a TB patient and needs better nourishment than the others, she puts her foot down and says no. The fellow prisoners throw barbs at her for this 'special treatment' but she does not respond. It is as if she does not mind remaining a prisoner forever, perhaps because she suffers from a sense of remorse for a crime she realizes the gravity of much after she has committed it. It is not a cold or calculated murder, but murder committed on the spur of the moment out of a sense of deep rage, frustration, grief and revenge. In a manner of speaking, she feels guiltier at that point of time for her father's death than for the murder she has committed. The script remains quiet about her feelings of guilt and the director leaves this for the audience to read into and conclude. One can even see the flowering of spring from behind the bars that signifies the passage of time on the one hand and the lack of change in the lives of the inmates behind the bars on the other.

Bimal Roy remained staunchly faithful to Jarasandha's original story. The Bengali film version, *Tamasi* (1958) of the same novel retained the name but changed the texture of the story, turning Bikash into a negative character and suggesting Kalyani's union with Devatosh (In the Bengali version, this was his name) in the end. Roy changed the original name of the girl from Hena in the story to Kalyani in the film, picking the name of another female prisoner from the original novel.

In *Bandini*, Nutan communicates mainly with her eyes because she talks very little in the film. Nutan stripped the character of Kalyani of any highly charged emotion or theatrics. She underplayed the character, fleshing Kalyani out as a quiet but determined woman with a dignity that belied her prison backdrop and her murderer status. Her mental state is expressed through a flood of fleeting emotions on her face, especially in the scenes leading up to the murder and afterwards. When the body is discovered the next morning, she pulls at her hair, her sari falls off her chest and she screams out that she is the one who has killed the woman. Nutan had almost given up films after marriage. She was pregnant when *Bandini* was being made. Bimal Roy persuaded her to accept the role. Nutan once said, "Two of my best roles were penned by Nabendu Ghosh for *Sujata* and *Bandini*. These films by my favourite director Bimal Roy brought out two unknown aspects of womanhood and fired an intensity not seen in any other film of mine. Nabendu-da and Bimal-da formed one of the greatest script-writer–director combination duos of Indian cinema." It marked a new beginning in her career. The critical success of *Bandini* saw her career move from strength to strength.

CONCLUSION

Is Sujata an 'outsider', a 'displaced' woman or a victim of forced migration? The three categories are extremely blurred and ambivalent where the Indian woman placed in this film is concerned. She is displaced soon after her birth, but she is not aware of it till after a long time. A phrase her foster mother uses each time she is introduced to someone '*beti jaisi*'[51] is what triggers her curiosity about why her mother, who, she believes is her natural mother, uses the word *jaisi* after *beti* while Rama as their natural offspring does not even need an introduction. Another intriguing aspect that strikes her is that while Rama's birthday is celebrated with great pomp and show, her birthday is unknown even to her. As a little girl, she cries and rants and demands a birthday party which her mother ignores completely. As she grows up, she knows her birthdays will never be celebrated but she has no clue as to why. She accepts this difference quietly and internalizes this as a part of her life but the pain remains. She makes complacence and silence her principles in life and has no complaints about it. It is only at the end where the script inserts the blood transfusion that makes her finally happy with the fact that her 'mother' has accepted her. It is an 'acceptance' somewhat compromised by the blood transfusion where no one's blood group matches the adoptive mother's, except this low-caste, untouchable young woman's. This marks her entry within the mainstream family, which now makes her an 'insider' enriched and enhanced by her suggested marriage to Adhir belonging to a high caste that raises her caste as well.

Bandini could be said to be Bimal Roy's ode to purity, the most striking aspect of the film being its simplicity. It also stands apart in being a woman-centric film in an industry which has traditionally been the playground of heroes (and anti-heroes). *Bandini* makes no attempt to iconize the character of Kalyani nor does it place her on a higher pedestal or make her a martyr to any cause. Unlike many films with the woman as the protagonist, Kalyani does not have any agenda—individual, social or collective, and nor does Sujata. They are very ordinary woman belonging to common roots placed in positions of crisis over which they have no control. Kalyani is not just condemned guilty but she is an actual convict, and the film makes no effort to clear her of her crime.[52]

Roy's love for realism is reflected in the gentle fleshing out of the all characters in the film never mind the footage or the significance they occupy. Be it the gentle but firm Kalyani, serving her term in the jail, or the two men in her life, or the middle-aged female warden who looks after the

---

[51] *Beti jaisi*—Like a daughter.
[52] Ziya Us Salam, 'Bandini', *The Hindu*, 1 October 2009.

woman's ward, played eloquently by Chandrima Bhaduri in one of her rare, significant film roles, or Kalyani's gentle father who is a postmaster, but is very spiritual, or the sympathetic jailor, or the slightly villainous officer in the prison, or Deven's mother who surrenders to her son's wish to marry a woman jailed for murder, all emerge as real people and not idealistic or Utopian. Kalyani's friend and her husband who help her get the hospital job and then inform her of her father's hospitalization are also gentle, sympathetic, ordinary individuals kind towards a girl placed in dire circumstances without being judgemental about her.

There is a small sub-plot in the film showing a police officer's wife helping a freedom fighter to escape from imprisonment by letting him go through the back door of her quarters without the husband knowing of it. This, author Jarasandha said, was picked from real life. Bimal Roy does not create any circumstances to concoct a rationale for her crime—murder. In *Bandini*, the use of bars, grills, walls, barbed wire and other barriers are representative of physical distance. Bimal Roy uses these physical barriers to show the physical as well as mental confinement of characters. Such barriers are also used as a foreshadowing technique, symbolic of what is to come.[53]

Kalyani has two different facets in her character. One is Kalyani as prisoner within the prison walls, sometimes shown in long shots, sitting in front of the formidable prison wall, like a tiny, vulnerable cog in a large wheel—firm, silent, serious, unapologetic and unsmiling. The other dimension of Kalyani comes across in the flashbacks in her village home— coy, very feminine, wearing coloured saris, her forehead dotted with a small bindi surrounded by a circle of tiny dots, smiles a lot, talks some and sings songs dedicated to the love of Krishna and Radha while fetching water from the nearby river. She shares a strong bond with her father who is educated in the Vaishnava scriptures, its influence reflected in the songs she sings 'Mora gora ang lai le' (Take away my fair skin) and 'Jogi jab se tu aaya mere dwaare' (The day you, my saint, came to my door). The change in the girl's character, approach, attitude and language after she leaves her village home reflects a woman trapped in an unforgiving world created by circumstances beyond her control.

Viewed in retrospect, Kalyani is one of Hindi cinema's first celluloid women who lived life on her own terms and did not ever compromise to social and filial pressures. She is feminine, soft and gentle, even apparently submissive. But beneath this soft exterior, lies a mind made of steel that

---

[53] Mishra Maitreyee and Manisha Mishra, 'The Outsiders: Women as Social Outcasts in Bimal Roy's Films'. Paper presented at the International Conference on Communication, Media, Technology and Change, Istanbul, Turkey, 9–11 May 2012.

can make decisions even at critical moments of her life and throw away the certainty of a secure future in favour of surrendering to her emotions and offering succour to the only man she ever fell in love with. *Bandini* is Bimal Roy's most complete film. It has depicted the 'complete' woman with an appeal that transcends the personal to enter the political, a significance that is more universal than individual.

Kalyani in *Bandini* is both an outsider and a displaced human being. She becomes an outsider when she is trapped in the scandal of having spent the night in Bikash's hut when he had a raging fever. When Bikash fails to come back and live up to his promise of marrying her, she leaves her home and her father for the unknown not knowing what the future holds in store for her. She leaves in the belief that perhaps her going away will rescue her father from being constantly subjected to the ridicule of the villagers who once had deep respect for his knowledge of the scriptures. She, thus, becomes a social outcast. She is displaced from her roots—her village home, her father, her childhood and her growing years and forced to find shelter somewhere out there in a world fraught with unknown dangers. In the end, she rejects a life of security and shelter with Deven who is willing to marry her to choose to nurse the only man she ever loved, Bikash, in his dying months. Where will she go after he passes away? She does not know and nor do we. Finally, she has learnt to make her choice—of remaining an outsider, an out-of-the-box woman who carries the inner strength to move on, not knowing where to but knowing why.

V. THE ROLE OF MUSIC, SONG AND DANCE

INTRODUCTION

We do not quite realize the value of music because it is so deeply embedded in our minds and our lives that it does not really have an existence separate from what we are and what we stand for. Music, per se, is a powerful means of communication. It provides a means by which people can share emotions, intentions and meanings, even though their spoken languages may be mutually incomprehensible. It can also provide a vital lifeline to human interaction for those whose special needs make other means of communication difficult. Music can exert powerful physical effects, produce deep and profound emotions within us and be used to generate infinite subtle variations of expressiveness by skilled composers and performers. Music can and has been used to communicate. These are underlined by certain biological, cognitive, social and cultural processes that help in communication.

Music is a tremendously powerful channel through which people develop their personal and social identities. Music is used to communicate emotions, thoughts, political statements, social relationships and physical expressions. But, just as language can mediate the construction and negotiation of developing identities, music can also be a means of communication through which aspects of people's identities are constructed. Music can have a profound influence in developing and sustaining our sense of identity, values and beliefs, be it classical Indian ragas or Western schools of music or folk forms of different places—Jazz, the Blues, Heavy Metal, the Beatles and fusion—which have developed an identity of their own in recent years. Different research studies in social and developmental psychology are beginning to chart the various ways in which these processes occur.

Music in Indian cinema is both an extension and a reflection of the life of Indians soaked in music and songs of every imaginable kind used in every imaginable way, be it a wedding ceremony, a birth in the family, a death, a festival, to celebrate the different seasons of the year such as spring, summer, autumn and winter, or just to celebrate happiness, sadness, mirth, mourning and grief. Music and songs are an integral part of Indian life and it has been so since the beginning of our cultural history. Schools have a prayer song and a school song sung as daily ritual before the day's business is to begin. Temples have their entire range of *bhajans*[1] and keertans; wandering minstrels in different parts of India practise their own schools of devotional music such as the Bauls[2] of Bengal and the Varkaris[3] in Maharashtra. Sachin Dev Burman, who scored the music for Bimal Roy's *Devdas*, *Sujata* and *Bandini*, who hailed from Tripura, said:

> Nobody who is born in Tripura who does not have music in him. The farmers sing while working on the fields; the boatmen cannot row without a song on their lips; the weavers, the daily laborers, they also sing at their work. I am also from Tripura. Perhaps that is why my life has been spent singing.[4]

Therefore, a film without songs and music is unimaginable and might not be considered really 'Indian' at its core. Sometimes, risks have been taken by courageous filmmakers to break the tradition and make films without music, such as B.R. Chopra's two films *Kanoon*[5] and *Ittefaq*.[6] But, broadly

---

[1] *Bhajans* are songs with a religious theme or spiritual ideas in a regional language. They do not have any prescribed form or set roles and are lyrical, based as they are on melodic ragas.

[2] Bauls—The Bauls of Bengal have been explained in detail later in this chapter. They are groups of mystic wandering minstrels who forever keep moving from place to place within Bengal and Bangladesh.

[3] Varkaris—These are also wandering mystic minstrels and are part of a collective movement within the Bhakti spiritual tradition geographically more associated with different parts of Maharashtra than elsewhere in the country. They are worshippers and sing the praises of Lord Vithhala.

[4] Shyamal Chakrabati, 'Sachinkarta', in *Smarika*, ed. Mohan Swaroop Maheshwari, (Sachin Dev Burman Smriti Samaroh, Film Society of Jaipur and Sangeet Natak Akademi, 4–9 April 2009), 26.

[5] *Kanoon*—Law.

[6] *Ittefaq*—Coincidence.

speaking, these were exceptions and became popular because they belonged to the genre of mystery and murder, the former being a courtroom drama and the latter a murder mystery with a twist in the end. Kidar Sharma's *Munna*[7] also did not have any songs, but. for the most part, music and songs have been one of the major attractions of Indian cinema, crossing borders of genre, filmmaker, time, language and space.

In Indian cinema, music and songs are understood to function as an additional source of entertainment to raise the commercial value of the film at the box office. But this is not their only function. Music and songs in Indian films serve to reinforce, alter and/or augment the emotional content of a cinematic narrative. Songs are used to communicate or enhance the meaning of a given mood or scene, or add to the larger scope of the narrative itself. It reflects the overall strategy of the director, his music director, sound designer and lyricist in constructing a multi-faceted music and song track. Music effectively composed, used, positioned and choreographed within the film can elicit emotional response in different ways among the audience and can also convey the dramatic intentions of the film and its maker.

Songs in Indian films are used as a time-leap or time bridge—to denote the passing of time that can condense years in a character's life within a few minutes of screen time. Songs and music are also used as editorial strategies to make parallel cuts from one scene to another, or from one place to another or from one person to another while the song is either lip-synced by a single character or played in the background. Songs and music can enhance the level of ambiguity of a given scene without wasting footage on superfluous dialogue where a single strain of a musical note or a song can communicate much more in a better way than dialogue can. The more ambiguous the meaning of the visual image, the greater is the influence the musical score in the process of interpreting the scene.[8]

The relationship between the visual and auditory components in cinema is both active and dynamic, affording a multiplicity of possible relations that can evolve—sometimes dramatically, as the narrative unfolds; sometimes naturally, as a natural extension of the actions taking place; and sometimes to heighten the given mood of the situation or lighten the mood depending on the demands of the script and the approach, perspective and treatment of and by the director. Taken holistically, considering the aforementioned paradigms, film music is an inclusive concept especially

---

[7] *Munna*—Title of a Hindi film named after the lead character. It means 'small boy'.

[8] Scott D. Lipscomb and David E. Tolschinsky, 'Role of Music Communication in Cinema, Northwestern University', in *Musical Communication*, eds. D. Miell, R. MacDonald and D. Hargreaves (Oxford, UK: Oxford University Press, 2005).

with reference to Indian cinema, which defines, elaborates and explores the ability of a filmmaker to explore and use music and songs in the most creative way to add to the aesthetics of the film, to the unfolding of the narrative and to the quality of the larger film.

MUSIC AND SONGS IN THE CINEMA OF BIMAL ROY

The music and songs in the cinema of Bimal Roy are extremely versatile in their representation of different schools of Indian music such as different folk forms such as the Bhatiyali, the Baul, or the *ganasangeet* or marching songs, Tagore creations, beautiful, soothing lullabies used with precision to fit into the scene instead of disturbing the scene, mujra shailis and thumris, Hindi and Bengali transpositions of Tagore's music through in different films, sad songs, romantic songs, a patriotic song, a nonsense fun song, a pure Manipuri number performed on pure Manipuri music, but no song, a harvest song, a school prayer, songs drawing generously from the Vaishnavite cult of the Radha–Krishna legend and last, but never the least, songs that celebrate nature in its varied manifestations captured through the evocative cinematography of Bimal Roy's regular cinematographers Dilip Gupta and Kamal Bose.

Interestingly, once he came to Bombay, Bimal Roy did not do the cinematography for any of his films. Roy's lyricists map a rich world of the best lyricists in the history of Hindi cinema. It spans Kavi Pradeep to Pandit Bharat Vyas, Jyotirindra Moitra, Majrooh Sultanpuri, Sailen Roy (Bengali), Hasrat Jaipuri, Prem Dhawan and Shailendra to Sahir Ludhianvi, Rajender Kishen and Gulzar. The lyrics spanned a wide range, having used several dialects from the Hindi belt, including pure Hindi in lyrics other than Braj Bhasha, Bhojpuri and a mix of Hindi and Urdu.

In this chapter, I have tried to stick to the music, lyrics and dance in only those films chosen for content analyses within this book, with occasional comments on the music and songs in the films not included in this study, to present a holistic picture of the use, positioning and orchestration of the music, song and dance scenes in the cinema of Bimal Roy.

"Bimal-da's work is poetry in motion," says music director Tushar Bhatia, classifying the music in Bimal Roy's films into four categories: (a) as a cinematographer in New Theatres Studio, Calcutta, (b) as a director in New Theatres Studio, Calcutta, (c) as an independent producer–director in Mumbai with Bimal Roy Productions and (d) as a freelance director with production banners other than his own. "Bimal-da's aesthetic sensibilities were shaped and honed in New Theatres which spilled over to the films he made in Mumbai," says Bhatia, throwing light on background sound effects and the positioning and choreography of song situations in his early films. P.C. Barua's *Mukti* was cinematographed by Bimal Roy in 1937. The film was path breaking into becoming the first ever film in history to use Tagore songs in cinema. A song from the film, 'Diner sheshe, ghoomer deshe,'[9] sung by Pankaj Mullick was the first Tagore song with the music composed by Mullick after obtaining clearance from Tagore himself. "The effects could be seen all over again in Salil Chowdhury's music for Bimal Roy's *Madhumati*," informs Bhatia.[10]

If Bimal Roy could visualize songs that would become trendsetters for eons to come in the way they were shot,[11] his music directors—he alternated mostly between S.D. Burman and Salil Chowdhury—were equally involved, not only in the music they created for a given song, but also in the mood that sustained at that given point when the music and/or song would occur within the visual space of the film. For most music directors who worked during that time, the story was the hero. They took pains to know the story and the script, the scene where the song would be placed, its build-up and its follow-up. Both Bimal Roy and S.D. Burman shared the Bengal background and the common sight of Vaishnav/Baul singers of Baul songs, wandering with their *ektara*,[12] with bells tied around only one foot, singing their way from one place to another was a culture both were familiar with and attuned to. As Sathya Saran rightly states:

> Both Bimal Roy and S.D. Burman believed that a song was not only a song, and was more than just a pause in a story. A song was a means to carrying the story forward, of expressing emotions tat words and dialogue could not. The nuances of a song could reach the heart faster than a scene with mere dialogue in it.[13]

However, to be fair to the other music directors and lyricists who worked in Bimal Roy's films, the same would hold true. Salil Chowdhury, who wrote the story of *Do Bigha Zamin*, was deeply rooted to the Bengali identity and especially to Bengali music. He later widened the borders of his creations and his music by bringing in Western music and fusion into his compositions, but that did not take him away from his rootedness in Bengali folk, Tagore and other compositions.

---

[9] Translation—In the land of sleep at the end of the day.

[10] Lecture demonstration at Seminar on Bimal Roy at Nehru Auditorium, Calcutta, organized by Bimal Roy Memorial Trust, in a weeklong programme in January 2002.

[11] Sathya Saran, *Sun Mere Bandhu Re—The Musical World of S.D. Burman* (Noida, India: HarperCollins Publishers, 2014), 96.

[12] *Ektara*—As the name suggests, it is an indigenously made single string musical instrument usually used by Baul singers who make their own instruments.

[13] Saran, *Sun Mere Bandhu Re,* 96–97.

Long before he became famous for introducing the concept of fusion music—a beautiful blend of the Western and the Indian—Salil Chowdhury's music in Bimal Roy's films were rooted in the Indian identity, if not within the Bengali identity. Bimal Roy himself picked some original private Bengali compositions of Salil Chowdhury and asked him to use them in his films. One beautiful example is the famous song in *Parakh*—'O sajana, barkha bahaar aaye, ras ki phuar layee, ankhiyon mein pyar layee'[14] sung by Lata Mangeshkar—was picked by Roy himself from a Durga Pooja album in Bengali. The Bengali version was also sung by Lata Mangeshkar which went 'Naa jeyona, rajani ekhono baki, aaro kichhu ditey baaki, bole raat jaga pakhi naa jeyona'.[15] The lyrics in Hindi and in Bengali have different meanings because the Hindi lyrics were penned by Shailendra who wrote to fit the words to the music that was already there.

The picturization of the song sequence in *Parakh* (1960) is eloquent with the pitter patter of rains where the leading lady steps out of the house listening to the pitter-patter. Kamal Bose's eloquent camera pans across the cottage with the rains pouring off the awnings, drops of rain falling off the leaves of trees, the light of the moon shimmering on the small puddles on the ground as the very low key heroine (Sadhana) keeps singing a tribute to the monsoons. The rains are somewhere between a low drizzle and heavy showers. The lyrics are a fusion of romance enriched by nature and enhanced by the rains when the young girl is gushing with her feelings of love for the young school teacher.

Another song from the same film is performed as a stage dance in the village by Nishi and goes 'Yeh bansi kyon gaaye mujhe kyon rulayen',[16] translated in lyrics by Shailendra from the original Bengali composition by Salil Chowdhury. The Bengali lyrics went 'O baanshi keno gaaye, amaare kandaye, shey gechhey haraaye',[17] both versions were sung by Lata Mangeshkar. The song, like the former one, was a big hit among music lovers in Bengali and both songs are still sung by well-known singers of today. The camera shows a temporary stage built in a village space where the curtains go up to show a young girl looking at the figure of Krishna playing on his flute. A humorous touch is added when the entire audience bows when it sees the image of Krishna on stage. This image disappears and she begins to dance.

---

[14] Translation—Oh my beloved, the beauty of the monsoons have arrived; bringing with it a shower of juices and love in the eyes.

[15] Translation—Please do not leave yet (my beloved); the night is still young and there is a lot left to give; so says the night bird who never goes to sleep.

[16] Translation—Why does this flute sing to make me weep?

[17] Translation—O dear flute, why do you sing and make me weep because (my beloved) is lost?

The choreography of the dance number in the village performance was by Badri Prasad, a noted choreographer and dance director of Hindi cinema at that time. But, the dance itself was poorly performed by Nishi. However, in retrospect, the director must have kept the execution poor by design in keeping with the kind of audience—villagers interested only in 'entertainment' that made them happy, the poor execution seems justified in terms of the location, the audience and the performing artist. The opening line translated reads why does this flute sing so and make me cry dotted with a lovely orchestra between the *antaras*.[18]

There is another beautiful slow and mellow number in the film sung by Lata Mangeshkar and picturized on Sadhana in which cinematographer Kamal Bose shot almost the entire sequence in the light of the lamps in the scene. The lines go 'Mere man ke diye yuhin ghut ghut ke',[19] lip-synced by Sadhana in a very sad scene where the camera focuses on her moist eyes and pans across the places she moves in. However, other than the magic of the cinematography and the music by Salil Chowdhury, this particular number does not add much significance to the scene or the story as such.

A playful mood dominates 'Mila hai kisika jhoomka',[20] juxtaposed against the sombre and serious 'Mere man ke diye' sung by Lata Mangeshkar and lip-synced by Sadhana. 'Mila hai kisika jhoomka' is shot in open locations of fields where the young girl is motivated to sing, following the notes of a flute being played by a young cowherd as he rides on the back of a cow. She finds a little flower in full bloom and begins to sing, cheerfully, savouring the beauty of the flower and nature of which it is a part. The story of *Parakh* was also written by Salil Chowdhury, so it was comparatively easy for him to imagine what kind of music would go in which scene, shot on which character and why.

Parakh has a lovely, lilting Baul dance-and-song number sung by Manna Dey, however the name of the performer is not known to us. It is a completely different kind of a Baul song that is soaked in satire instead of invoking the Radha–Krishna mythology or the devotion that is the soul of Baul. It is a vigorous dance where the Baul performer, a comparatively young man, with *ghungroos*[21] on both his feet, playing with his ektara sings

[K]ya hawa chali re baba ruth badli
shor hai gali gali

---

[18] *Antaras*—Stanzas as in a song.
[19] *Mere man ke diye*—Oh the lamp of my heart.
[20] Translation—I have found someone's danglers.
[21] *Ghungroos*—Dancing bells worn around the ankle as anklets that keep rhythm to the dance movements.

sau sau choohe khaike billi
Haj ko chali
Pehle log mar rahe the bhookh se abhaab se
Ab kahin yeh mar na jaayen apni khau khau se
Are mithi baat kadvi lage gaaliyan bhali[22]

Though the dance performance and the costume and accompaniments are in the original Baul tradition, the lyrics present a different kind of mood which is a political satire, also very much a part of the Baul form of music, song and dance. Gour Khepa, one of the last vestiges of the original Baul tradition who passed away a couple of years ago, wrote, composed and sang at length about the environment and about how the young are hooked to the Internet and to social networking. He sang about sex openly without either embarrassment or shame. He dotted his lines with ribaldry and expletives galore and the audience would break into side-splitting laughter, but coming out of his mouth set in his smiling face, they did not sound bad at all.[23]

The origin of the word Baul is debated. Some modern scholars like Shashibhusan Das Gupta has suggested that it may be derived either from the Sanskrit word *vatula*, which means '(divinely inspired) insane', or from *vyakula*, which means 'desperate'; both of these derivations are consistent with the modern sense of the word, which denotes the inspired people with an ecstatic eagerness for a spiritual life, where a person can realize his union with the eternal beloved—the *Moner Manush* (the man of the heart).[24]

Considering that the music in *Parakh* is by Salil Chowdhury and the lyrics by Shailendra, the picturization of this particular Baul is a model lesson in conceiving and orchestrating a song situation with a gathering audience, mostly composed of small girls and young women, who laugh and smile and enjoy the performance as the sole form of entertainment for them.

The music of *Madhumati* is a different cup of tea. Each song, from 'Suhana safar aur yeh mausam haseen'[25] through 'Aajaa re main to kab

---

[22] Approximate translation—What kind of wind is blowing to change the ambience; there is noise in every by lane; the cat is proceeding towards Haj (a pilgrimage for Muslims) after having eaten hundreds of mice; earlier, people were dying of hunger and poverty; hope they do not die of greed now; (now) sweet words sound bitter while abuses and cuss words sound good.

[23] Gour Khepa would talk about fake Bauls and genuine Bauls and roundly critiqued the commercialization of the Baul culture in contemporary times when 'anyone dons a Baul costume of a saffron robe, pulls a patchwork shawl around him, keeps his hair untied and knotted and sings any song that comes to his mind'.

[24] Shoma A. Chatterji, *The Goddess Kali of Kolkata* (New Delhi: UBSPD, 2006).

[25] Translation—It is a beautiful journey in a happy season.

se khadi is paar'[26] to 'Zulmi sang aankh ladi'[27] to 'Ghadi ghadi more dil dharke'[28] to 'Papi bicchua'[29] to 'Toote hue khwaabon ne',[30] reaches far beyond being just a listener's delight and is placed firmly in posterity among the music archive of Hindi cinema. 'Dil tadap tadap ke kehe raha hai aa bhi jaa',[31] a duet, carries the essence of romance that forms the core of the story. Even 'Jungle me morenaacha', lip-synched by Johnny Walker in a scene too incongruous for a Bimal Roy film, was a big hit, probably because it was the only point of relief in a serious film. One can never forget Mubarak Begum's rendering of 'Hum haal e dil sunaayenge suniye ke naa suniye'.[32] This great mujra is a masterpiece of 'Daag Dehalvi', the heir of Mugalia Saltanat Bahadur Shah Zaffar. One listener Raghu Ram, commenting on this composition, writes on his YouTube feedback, "Shailendra as a lyricist is unfathomably deep in his poetic imagination. There is no option but to use the best in the business to compose music and sing the song, a rare but very precious jewel in the treasure chest of Indian film songs."

In 2004, a bunch of music lovers did a survey on the top 25 albums of individual choices. *Madhumati* topped the list, followed by *Guide*, *Pyaasa* and *Hum Dono*.[33] When *Madhumati* was released, Radio Ceylon played seven songs from *Madhumati* among its top 10. There is no hint of the Indian Peoples Theater Association (IPTA) and mass songs hangover. Each song defines the characters of the film and their evolution along with the story. This explains 'Suhana safar' sung by Dilip Kumar when the film opens and he is fascinated by the beauty of the hillscapes when he has not loved and lost and the 'Toote hue khwaabon ne' that he sings towards the end of the film. Mukesh sang 'Suhana safar', one of his career-bests and the latter was sung by Mohammed Rafi, though the character lip-synching the songs is the same and so is the actor.

Salil Chowdhury's love for Western classical music began as a young boy growing up in an Assam tea garden where his father worked as a doctor. His father had inherited a large number of Western classical records and a gramophone from a departing Irish doctor. Even as he listened to Mozart, Beethoven, Tchaikovsky, Chopin and so on every day, his backdrop was filled

---

[26] Translation—Please come, I have been waiting since when on this side.

[27] Translation—I have locked eyes with the cruel one.

[28] Translation—My heart keeps beating again and again.

[29] Translation—The sinful scorpion (metaphor for the beloved).

[30] Translation—My broken dreams.

[31] Translation—My heart beats are calling out to you to please come.

[32] Approximate translation—I will sing to you about the condition my heart is in whether you listen in or not.

[33] *Hum Dono*—We two.

with the mystique sounds of nature—the sounds of the forests, the chirping of the birds, the melody of the flute and the folk songs of the region. As a logical extension, he played the flute beautifully, and during his revolutionary phase in the freedom struggle, he always carried his flute with him and would begin to play it spontaneously. This musically nourished childhood within an ambience of nature and Western classical music left a deep and lasting impression of the young Salil Chowdhury. He became an excellent self-taught flute player and his favourite composer was Mozart. His compositions often used folk melodies and melodies based on Indian classical ragas, but the orchestration was very much Western in its construction. He developed a unique style one could identify with ease and get to love at the same time.

Shankar–Jaikishen composed the music for *Yahudi* (1958). The film was a period costume drama set in the era of the Roman Empire over 2000 years ago; it centred on the point of persecution at the time in the empires centre—Rome. The lyrics were jointly written by Shailendra and Hasrat Jaipuri. The ethnic Bengali music was redundant in the film.

Roshan composed the music for the four song numbers in *Baap Beti* which do not possess a Bengali identity or even reflect the scenario of any Indian village, but is located in a city which does not demand any specific kind of music. Therefore, the songs are either driven by emotions or by devotion.

Songs composed and written by Nobel laureate Rabindranath Tagore also played an important role in the cinema of Bimal Roy. The legendary music composer Rai Chand Boral, who was almost the staple music director for New Theatres' films, composed the music for the first few films directed by Bimal Roy. These are *Udayer Pathey* (1944), *Anjangarh* (1948), *Mantramughda* (1949) and *Pehla Aadmi* (1950). Though Tagore's compositions were first used in Bengali cinema in New Theatres' *Mukti*, it got consolidated in *Udayer Pathey* in which Roy and Boral used three Tagore songs in the film explained later in this chapter.

Rabindra Sangeet is a distinct genre of music. Tagore drew from all schools of music to create his own—Baul compositions sung by wandering minstrels, Western compositions based on symphony and harmonization of several scales, Hindustani classical ragas and even Carnatic ragas that have now become special areas of research and exploration by Tagore scholars and exponents of Rabindra Sangeet. His early creations bear the influence of keertan and *Ramprasadi*[34] tunes popular in Kolkata, where the poet resided during the early phase of his life. In the following years, from

---

[34] Sadhak Ramprasad Sen was a Shakta poet (devotee of Shakti) and saint of the eighteenth-century Bengal. His bhakti poems or devotional compositions known as Ramprasadi songs are still popular in Bengal addressed to the Hindu Goddess Kali and in devotion to the Goddess Kali.

his travels through Europe, he picked up the flavour of the music of the West and blended them into his compositions. He also composed songs on the love of Radha and Krishna in *Brijabhasha*.[35] His songs are compiled in the *Geetabitan*. The three volumes of 'Geetabitan' contain exactly 2,232 songs, classified into sections representative of every human emotion, from love (*prem*) to nature (*prakriti*) to devotion (*pooja*) and so on. 'Amaar sonar bangla, ami tomaye bhalobashi' (My golden Bengal, I love you) is the national anthem of Bangladesh. "The strains of his 'Jodi tore daak shune keu naa aashe tobeekla cholo re'[36] made popular at Gandhi's prayer meetings still receive a spontaneous response across the country," says Dr Reba Som, erstwhile Director, Tagore Centre, Kolkata, who has written the book, *The Singer and His Songs* on Tagore's songs.[37]

Mainstream Hindi filmmakers have generously drawn upon Tagore's music, songs, poetry in Hindi cinema. The credit for this goes to Pankaj Mullick. Among the earliest Hindi hits created by Pankaj Mullick are (a) 'Hare re re re re', (b) 'Phool kahe dhanya hoon main',[38] (c) 'Yaad aayen ke na aaye tumhari'[39] and (d) 'Pran chahe naina na chahe'[40] (a private disc). Mullick dedicated his life to the cause of Tagore's music and song on film, radio and gramophone. He is an icon for Tagore's music and songs in the world of Indian music.[41]

During the last 40 years of his creative life, Tagore fell back on a number of ragas such as *Todi, Bhairavi, Asavari, Sarang, Puravi, Iman, Malhar* and *Kedar*,[42] and blended them to create distinct and memorable variations. He did not introduce any new style, but blurred the lines between classical and regional modes. Today, we hear Tagore songs fused into other forms of modern music, both Indian and Western, of different schools. Young classical singer Sounak Chattopadhyay began to train in Rabindra Sangeet after becoming an accomplished performer of Hindustani classical

---

[35] *Brijbhasha* or *Braj Bhasha* language, also spelled Braj Bhasa, Braj Bhakha or Brij Bhasa descended from Shauraseni Prakrit and commonly viewed as a western dialect of Hindi. It is spoken by some 575,000 people, primarily in India. Its purest forms are spoken in the cities of Mathura, Agra, Etah and Aligarh. Available at https://www.britannica.com/topic/Braj-Bhasha-language (Accessed on 3 March 2017).

[36] Translation—If no one responds to your call, then move on alone. This was sung recently by Amitabh Bachchan for the music track of the film *Kahaani*.

[37] Shoma A. Chatterji, 'The Influence of Tagore on Indian Film Music', Paper presented at Tagore Conference, Calcutta University, Alipur Campus, 11 February, 2011.

[38] Translation—The flower says I am blessed.

[39] Translation—I may or may not harbour memories of you.

[40] Translation—The heart desires but the eyes do not.

[41] Chatterji, 'The Influence of Tagore on Indian Film Music'.

[42] These are all names of famous ragas from classical Hindustani music.

music. His album, titled *Nuton O Shonaton Rabindranath*,[43] integrates Tagore's songs in traditional style with Hindustani classical *bandishes*.[44, 45]

Sujata also used the original tune of a Tagore song, 'Ekoda tumi priye'[46] for a song with Hindi lyrics, but not a translation of the Bengali original, in the famous telephone song 'Jalte hain jiske liye'[47] with the music adapted by S.D. Burman from the original Tagore number. In *Prem Patra* (1962), one Tagore song was adapted by Salil Chowdhury. The original song 'Jetey jetey ekla pothey nibhechhe more baati'[48] was first sung by the very gifted and controversial Debabrata Biswas, who was ousted by Viswa Bharati University that accused him of playing around with Tagore's songs. Salil Chowdhury picked up only some of the tunes from the opening lines and an antara for which Rajinder Kishen composed the lines 'Saawan kee raaton mein aisa bhi hota hai'[49] as a duet lip-synced by Sadhana and Shashi Kapoor, where the camera pans across the two of them and then crosses over to focus on palms swaying in the breeze to enrich the happy mood in the lovers, one blind and the other playing proxy to the original girl he loves, forming a very lyrical comment on the irony of the love story.

Musical adaptations had been prolific in the 1950s and 1960s in Hindi films. Music composers Anil Biswas, S.D. Burman, R.D. Burman and Hemanta Mukhopadhyay were strongly inspired by Tagore songs and have often used his original music in many of their compositions.

UDAYER PATHEY (1944)

If music can be said to convey the scope of the film, then Bimal Roy has done it very effectively in terms of adding to the dramaturgy of the film in many of his films. *Udayer Pathey*, made before Independence, incorporated the complete music version in the chorus of Rabindranath Tagore's 'Jana Gana Mana' in Bengali which was repeated in the Hindi version of the film, *Hamrahi*, and became the National Anthem only after India became an independent nation in 1947. But the original screenplay of *Udayer Pathey* does not include this song.[50] It was probably added as an afterthought later by Bimal Roy.

---

[43] Translation—Rabindranath—New and till Eternity.
[44] Bandish is a fixed, melodic composition in Hindustani vocal and instrumental music.
[45] Chatterji, 'The Influence of Tagore on Indian Film Music'.
[46] Translation—Once oh beloved.
[47] Translation—The one for whom (my eyes) light up.
[48] Translation—While moving alone on the road, my lamp suddenly went out.
[49] Translation—Does this ever happen on a rainy night?
[50] *Udayer Pathey*, Original Screenplay in Bengali, Special Screenplay Edition, eds. Rahul Sen and Sanarendra Sengupta, *Bibhab*, Sarat Issue, Bengali calendar (1417), 85. Translation done by the author of this book.

The song 'Chalo beer chalo beer' used twice in *Udayer Pathey*, marks
the precursor of ganasangeet or marching songs always sung in chorus,
which were songs of awakening and consciousness later made popular
by the Indian People's Theatre Association and one of its leading members, Salil Chowdhury. The music for *Udayer Pathey* was composed by Rai
Chand Boral, one of the most outstanding music directors of his time, and
the lyrics of this song were written by Sailen Roy which narrates the ultimate
aim of the film and of its protagonist Anup to end the oppression of the poor
by the rich, of the proletariat by the bourgeoisie and bring about harmony
and peace in the nation and its people. The song, translated, goes like

Come all brave soldiers,
Towards the dawn where night will end.
Wipe the blackness off the night with light,
Bring along with your awakening,
Let the world awaken.
Break down the merciless chains
of the wealthy and the merchant class.
Let the cry of the masses come to an end;
Let the new flag of equality flutter in the sky,
Let selfishness be defeated to bring about the triumph of peace.

The beginning of the song was captured in a low angle tilted shot focusing on a mass of people walking along an ascending rough terrain, singing
together. As the song ends, the camera pans to a field with people gathering
from all corners to assemble together. Anup steps into the scene wearing a
Gandhi cap with his group. A banner shows 'Mill Workers' Association.'
The stage is set for a labour uprising. This song sets the trend for the
chorus peasant songs in *Do Bigha Zamin* which, though not overtly
Leftist, carries the air of a people's voice that cries out to draw attention
to the unfairness of the distribution of wealth and income among the
people. The songs were composed by Salil Chowdhury and the lyrics were
by Shailendra who became almost a Bimal Roy 'regular' later on.

Udayer Pathey also used three songs composed and written by
Rabindranath Tagore. The songs include 'Basante phool ganthlo, amar
joyer mala'[51] in a song–dance party scene in the home of the affluent industrialist's family. It is a song celebrating the spring season, but it can also be
read as a satiric song because it is a 'made-to-order' performance executed
by one Miss Sen to the song sung with the organ as accompaniment played

---

[51] Translation—The garland of my victory has been strung together with the flowers of spring.

by Lily Chatterjee, two guests from affluent and Westernized backgrounds who were guests at the party. This song–dance number is like a theatrical build-up of the next song sung at the same party by Gopa's friend Sumita a few minutes later. The song was penned by Sailen Roy and the lines that opened with 'Geye jai gaan geye jai', a melancholy song that stands in direct opposition of the spring song–dance number that went before. The following lines will establish this truth:

> Geye jai, gaan geye jai,
> Gaaner ei agnimala debo kaare
> Khunje na pai
> Nishidin paye jaader shikal Baaje,
> Tara je bondi shobai nijer kaache,
> Tara je jeebon tori nokol shonaye
> korlo bojhai.
> Amar e gaaner pakhi shonar khanchai daye na dhora,
> Kokiler gaan she to noy
> shonaye goda
> Gaane more milon-dolaye bhubon dole,
> E-gaane porer lagi apon bhole,
> Je shudhu milon-bhorey baandhbe bhubon
> Tarei je chai....[52]

No one among the invited guests or even Gopa's brother Shouren and his wife Roma cheer or clap. The only one who claps to the song in response is Gopa. This song rounds up the scene to build up to the next scene in which Sumita is accused of stealing from the table laden with birthday gifts which is proved wrong and she walks out of Gopa's house in tears.

The second Tagore song is woven around nature and opens with 'Oi malatilata doley, piyal torur kole poob hawatey' (There sways the creeper of the Malati flower beneath the Piyal tree in the eastern breeze) which functions with the design of determining the shape of the relationship between

---

[52] Translation in English by this author:
    I keep on singing, not knowing who I will gift this garland of fire to,
Those who hear the sound of chains in their feet forever,
Are prisoners within themselves,
They have filled their life-boat with fake gold.
This song-bird of mine refuses to be captured and kept in a golden cage,
The song of the nightingale is not bound in gold,
The world sways on the swing of harmony in my song,
This song makes one forget oneself in the service of others,
I aspire for my song to bind the whole world in unity.

Anup and Gopa later in the film. The third Tagore number, 'Chaander hashir baandh bhengechhey, uchhley pawre aalo, O rajanigandha tomaar gondhoshudha dhalo',[53] is a romantic song sung by Gopa on a full moon night while she is walking back with Anup from the workers' meeting in a slum. The lines translated, mean the dam of the moon's laughter has broken, spilling light everywhere, O dear night queen (rajanigandha, a long-stemmed white flower known for its beautiful fragrance it spreads only at night) please pour the nectar of your fragrance. This song is as much an ode to nature in the shape of the full moon as it is a prelude to the romance that subtly underscores the relationship between Anup and Gopa.

Another Sailen Roy creation, sung by Gopa in the film, is sung when Gopa is transformed from a rich industrialist's aristocratic daughter who has now taken sides with the struggling workers in his father's factory. She now wears simple saris like Sumita does and, though this is not articulated, she idolizes Anup and his beliefs and is in love with him. In a scene in her father's elaborately decorated drawing room, Gopa is introduced to an affluent gentleman. They are awkward with each other, when the awkwardness is broken with a request from the gentleman to Gopa to sing a song. Gopa readily agrees and begins to play on the organ to sing 'Tomaar bandhon khulte lage bedon kee je, notun jaale abaar ami jodai neejey'. This means 'I cannot express how painful it is to untie the bonds that tie me to you, yet I venture into a new bonding of my own volition.' This positioning of the song and its visual picturization underscores the effective manner in which the song augments the narrative to express the unspoken thoughts and unseen implications that underlie the drama of the scene and the major character within it—Gopa and the others she is addressing the song to. Her brother and the guest, a bar-at-law, are visibly uncomfortable. Very unpredictably, Gopa breaks into tears, bending over the organ, then, as suddenly, gets up and walks inside the house.

DO BIGHA ZAMIN (1953)

Do Bigha Zamin had four songs placed within the narrative and cinematographic text to depict the journey—physical, social, cultural and most importantly, cultural—of the protagonist Shambhu who is forced to leave his village and his traditional trade of being a peasant to move to the city to pull hand-drawn rickshaws. The songs in *Do Bigha Zamin* such as 'Mausam beetajaye' and 'Hariyala saawan dhol bajata aaya' reflect this mood of

---

[53] Translation—The moon has broken into laughter spreading its light all around, please oh *rajanigandha* (name of a fragrant night flower) please pour the honey of your fragrance into the night.

protest and rebellion. He called these 'songs of consciousness and awakening'. Music for him was a strong weapon of revolt, and the lyrics of songs he composed formed the 'blood' for this rebellious music.[54]

These two peasant songs of *Do Bigha Zamin* convey the quality and size of space also called 'depth in space' or 'physical volumes'.[55] This means how music combined with visuals and the song lyrics, often performed through dance, serves to make smaller spaces seem larger and spacious to enhance the sense of realism. This happens both in 'Mausam beeta jaye' and in 'Hariyala sawan dhole bajata aya'. The former is a song sung by the villages engaged in different occupations in a manner of bidding goodbye to a sad and forlorn Shambhu who is going to catch the train to Calcutta. This song has the repeated refrain of 'Bhai re' belted out by Manna Dey in a long drawl that suggests the collective unity among the villagers who go about their everyday work even when one of them is going to the city, and also the pain of Shambhu as the camera cuts to take a mid-close-shot of his face from time to time. When the song ends, the soundtrack suddenly switches to the loud sounds of a speeding train and we understand that Shambhu has finally left.

'Hariyala saawan dhol bajata aya, dhin tak tak manke more nachata aya'[56] is a song that welcomes the dark clouds covering the clear sky, a welcome sign for a village that has seen draught for two long years. It is complimented with a carefully choreographed group dance performed by the young men and women of the village intercutting with scenes of a young mother pulling at the cradle of a baby, young men playing the *dholak*[57] as they sing while the lyrics spell out how the green monsoon has arrived and dancing 'on the peacock of its mind, bringing life to the soil'. The dance performance is choreographed by Prem Dhawan to folk traditions which add to the visuals, culturally and socially.

There is one more chorus sung by a group of wearied daily labours in the Calcutta basti where Shambhu lives with his son. At the end of a work-weary day, it used to be a daily ritual by immigrant labour from outside Calcutta to gather together and sing a song together to relieve themselves of

---

[54] The World of Salil Chowdhury created by Gautam Choudhury is licensed under a Creative Commons Attribution. See http://www.salilda.com/nonfilmsongs/masssongtable.asp (Accessed on 3 March 2017).

[55] C. Gorbman, *Unheard Melodies: Narrative Film Music* (Bloomington, IN: Indiana University Press, 1987).

[56] Translation—The green monsoon has arrived playing on the drums, making the peacock in the heart break out in a dance.

[57] *Dholak*—Percussion instrument which is a two-headed drum usually used in South Asia in general and India in particular in Punjab, Haryana, UP, Bihar and so on during festive seasons.

their weariness, and also to entertain themselves through their own kind of music in a foreign place where they do not know the language or even the music. The song 'Gajab teri dunia O mere Rama' is picturized under the neon lights of the shops that have downed their shutters for the night. From the K.C. Das hoarding outside the shop, it is clear that the place is what is today called the Esplanade, a part of Chowringee. The camera pans up once to capture a middle-aged man, who, disturbed by the noise the song makes, comes out and tells them to stop their singing. But they go on, probably unaware of the reprimand.

The film also places a lullaby (*lori* in Hindi) in the village when Shambhu's wife comes to the home of a modern, educated housewife to get her husband's postcard read out to her as she is an unlettered woman herself. This lady (Meena Kumari), is putting her infant to sleep, pulling the strings of the cradle as she sings to the baby. Parvati, who is pregnant again, listens to the beautiful song till it ends and then steps into the home to call out to the lady. On the one hand, the song establishes the distinct class and status differences between the two women, and on the other, it draws attention to the subtle bonding between the two women, divided though they are by the neat fencing outside the affluent woman's home. She reads out the letter and when Paro coyly shies away from the endearments, the lady smiles, amused. The song 'Aja re neendiya tu aa' sung mellifluously by Lata Mangeshkar is framed and edited with aesthetic and dramatic precision without going overboard or distracting from the purpose of the scene—the reading of the letter. At some moments, as Paro listens to the lori, the camera superimposes her face with images flashing from her past, tending to Kanhaiya when he was an infant, and her face registers a soft smile.

It would be pertinent to give a brief glimpse into the background of Salil Chowdhury and his music here. Living through the World War II, the Bengal famine and the desperate political situation in the 1940s, he joined IPTA and became a member of the communist party. During this period, he wrote numerous songs and with IPTA took his songs to the masses. They travelled through the villages and cities in Bengal and his songs became the voice of the masses. They were powerful and stimulating songs of protest, which made people aware of the rampant social injustice that surrounded them. Salil-da's music and lyrics, during his post-Independence, commercial phase in Mumbai, was soaked in and reflected his concern for social injustice.

But Prem Dhawan was not only a choreographer. He was a lyricist and a music composer and has left behind a rich treasury of patriotic songs that will remain alive forever in the scheme of Indian film music.

Some of his most outstanding lyrics are 'Chhodo kal ki baatein'[58] from *Hum Hindustani*[59] (1960), 'Ai watan ai watan humko teri kasam'[60] from *Shaheed*[61] (1965) for which he also composed the music and 'Sambhalo ai watan walon'[62] in *Bharat Ke Shaheed*[63] (1973). There are more among his creations such as 'Mera rang de basanti chola'[64] in *Shaheed* and 'Ai mere pyaare watan'[65] from *Kabuliwala* (1961). He had memorable partnerships with the doyens like Khemchand Prakash, Hans Raj Behl, Salil Chowdhury, Anil Biswas, Ravi and Chitragupta.[66]

Dhawan joined the Communist Party of India and participated in many actions against the British. Later he went to Mumbai to join the IPTA. His views were of a communist and he was the founding member of IPTA in Punjab and found in this a platform to express the revolutionary ideas through songs, dances and writings. Here he came in contact with Pandit Ravi Shankar and with him and Sachin Shankar he formed a group and began to present their programmes in Punjabi all over the country; he also learned classical music from Ravi Shankar during this time. Later he learned classical dance from Shanti Bardhan, who had broken away from Ravi Shankar's elder brother, the great Uday Shankar's, dance troupe. Dhawan did the choreography in *Naya Daur* ('Udein jab jab zulfein teri'),[67] *Arzoo*[68] (1950), *Dhool ka Phool*, *Goonj Uthi Shehnai*[69] and *Waqt*.[70]

So, for *Do Bigha Zamin*, he was paired with none other than Salil Chowdhury as the composer and, since Shailendra was already roped in as a lyricist, Dhawan put in all his energy to choreograph the beautifully synchronized dance chorus hariyala saawan dhol bajata aya where the villagers are very happy expecting the rains after several seasons of drought, but the feelings fade away when the monsoon is hardly enough to soak their

---

[58] Translation—Leave the words of yesterday.
[59] *Hum Hindustani*—We are Hindustanis (from Hindustan, one name for India).
[60] Translation—Oh my motherland, I swear on you.
[61] *Shaheed*—Martyr.
[62] Translation—Take care O my countrymen.
[63] *Bharat Ke Shaheed*—The martyr of Bharat (India).
[64] Translation—Give me the orange colours of spring.
[65] Translation—Oh My beloved motherland.
[66] See http://creative.sulekha.com/prem-dhawan-unsung-hero_390590_blog (Accessed on 17 January 2017).
[67] Translation—Whenever your hair begins to fly.
[68] *Arzoo*—Desire.
[69] *Goonj Uthi Shehnai*—The shehnai began to play.
[70] Ibid.

soil that demands heavy rainfall. This song also conveys a 'sense of energy' through its visualization by the camera by Kamal Bose and the vibrant and dynamic performance by the chorus.

PARINEETA (1953)

According to the documented records available, originally, *Parineeta* contained seven songs, and since one song was repeated, namely 'Chale Radhe rani ankhiyon mein paani', that makes a total of eight. But when you watch the film today, you cannot see them all. Some seem to have been deleted though from these, the audio tracks are available for a few. *Parineeta* was produced by Ashok Kumar, though Bimal Roy held back the release of this film to allow *Do Bigha Zamin* to release first. But both films are memorable for their powerful storyline, their retelling on the celluloid format and the music and the songs. The music of *Parineeta* was scored by Arun Mukherjee, said to be a close relative of Ashok Kumar. He composed the music of *Parineeta* and of *Samaj*[71] (1954) as Aran Kumar and acted in the film *Jwar Bhata*[72] (1944) based on a Tagore novel. But after that no one seems to have heard of him or seen him. But his musical score for *Parineeta* will keep him alive in the minds of music lovers who will never be able to forget the songs 'Chale Radhe raani' and 'Gore gore haathon pe mehndi lagaake'. The lyrics were penned by Pandit Bharat Vyas.

The title music of *Parineeta*, as the credits flash on the screen in simple black and white, unfolds cheerful tunes of joy and mirth using lots of drums, flute, the *shehnai* and a dance orchestra in keeping with the times. As the credits end, the camera pans over the old Calcutta skyline kissing the tops of old houses till it peers through the trees at ground level to show glimpses of a horse-drawn carriage that rides towards a big mansion and stops. The music changes to a mellow mood, turning low-key as the dialogue begins and switching to a louder mode when there is no dialogue. The opening music is suggestive of a Bengali marriage that is the leitmotif of the story of the film.

The first song, a lovely song–dance number, is a stage performance when Lalita's cousins along with Girin and his sister and brother-in-law are in the theatre which Lalita dropped out of at the last minute because she guessed that Sekhar was angry about her going to the theatre with Girin in the group. It is performed as a duet by Gopi Krishna and Roshan Kumari who, in the course of time, were to become pillars of the Lucknowi *gharana* (one particular school of Kathak) of Kathak. The dance was choreographed

---

[71] *Samaj*—Society.
[72] *Jwar-Bhata*—Ebb and Tide.

by Gopi Krishna. The dance number, from the costumes the dancers wear—gypsy harem pants worn by the man with a zardozi jacket and a gypsy head-dress—appears to have been drawn from the story of Ali Baba and the Forty Thieves, as read in the lyrics of the song. The girl is dressed in traditional Kathak costume. The opening lines of the song go 'Ai bandi tum begum bano khwab dekha hai o maine khwab dekha hai main badshah banoonga',[73] which appears to be Abdalla singing to Morjina, the slave, because *bandi* in the song means 'slave' and 'begum' means queen, referring to Morjina who was once a slave and later became the queen by getting married to Alibaba's son, Abdalla. The lyrics and the tunes are filled with a joyful spirit and vibrancy suffused with the music of ghungroos, harmonium, *tabla* and poetry, plus the laughter from the members of Girin's group seated on special seats in the balcony of the theatre. The camera occasionally pans to focus on the smiling faces of Girin and company laughing away at the humorous lines of the song and the energetic performance. It was a duet sung by Kishore Kumar and Asha Bhonsle when they were yet to reach the peak they later did. But the song offers glimpses of their versatile talent not only in their singing, but also in their command over expressing the emotions through their singing.

The next is a Baul number sung by an ageing wandering minstrel who addresses Lalita as 'Lalita Maa' and waits till she gives him alms after his song is over. The song, thus, is placed in two versions in two different points in the film, once reflecting a happy mood to relieve a sad situation. The Baul comes singing when Lalita and Sekhar have a tiff over whether Lalita enjoyed the play she had gone to the evening before with Girin Babu. Lalita had withdrawn at the last moment, but Sekhar does not know this and Lalita is not willing to tell him. The song talks about Radha and Krishna teasing and taunting each other in a love filled with naughtiness where Radha is naïve and Krishna is naughty. The song goes as follows:

> Chale Radhe Rani ankhiyon mein paani
> apne mohan se mukhda mod ke
> chali radhe rani
> jamuna ke tat pe bansi ke bat pe
> natkhat ne usko gher liya
> dekho natkhat ne usko gher liya
> baato hi baato me jhagra bhya aisa....

[73] Translation—Oh dear slave girl, you will become a Begum (queen) and I will become a Badshah is what I saw in a dream.

baato hi baato me jhagra bhya aisa
baahon ke bandhan tod ke
apne mohan se mukhda mod ke....
apne mohan se mukhda mod ke

The rough English translation goes as follows:

Oh my queen Radha,
Where are you going with tears in your eyes
Turning your back on your Mohan?
See how mischief has surrounded him on the banks of the Jamuna
And on the body of his flute
Words led to such a quarrel
That you left the clasp of his arms and
Turned your back on your Mohan

The next number is a marriage song sung by the girls who are Annu's friends during the 'wedding' of Annu's female doll to a male doll organized strictly through the date and time given in the Bengali almanac picked with care by Annu's father Gurucharan who is Lalita's maternal uncle. It is a very happy song which, as the lyrics go, looking back, has strongly patriarchal lessons given to the 'girl' who is going to her in-law's home. 'Gore gore haathon mein mehndi lagaake naino me kajara daalke, chali dulhaniya piya se milne chhotasa ghunghat nikalke'. The song is sung by Asha Bhonsle as the lead singer with a chorus. The song is filled with the sound of little girls' giggles on the soundtrack, with drums and the shehnai as the supporting music for the song.

The song happens soon after Lalita has been garlanded by Sekhar in response to her unwittingly having thrown the garland around his neck at the precise almanac-decided minute of the wedding—eight in the evening. The clock in the clock tower seen in the distance chimes eight times and Sekhar tells Lalita that if any pair exchanges garlands at this minute, they become husband and wife. He professes his love for her and tells her to go downstairs and touch his mother's feet. As the song begins, from the little girls captured in a top angle shot, the camera cuts to Lalita coyly pulling the end of her sari to cover her head and looking into her reflection in the mirror with the dream-come-true look of happiness on her otherwise sad face, fantasizing her look as a bride which she now is but feels should keep it secret.

This particular song draws parallels, if one wishes to read it that way, with the institution of marriage as it existed at the time of the story, where a girl is almost like a doll who has no say in her marriage or in the choice of the groom. This is established when her uncle tries to make a match between Lalita and Girin. She is in love with Sekhar but cannot express it to anyone, including her sisters. The lines of the song extol the virtues a bride must follow in her in-laws and husband's home, such as please the husband, listen to whatever the in-laws say, not to answer back and always remember to control the veil over the head. For Lalita, it is a very welcome and happy quality to follow because she completely believes in this 'truth'. Viewed in retrospect, the parallels drawn between a doll's marriage and Lalita's position within her state could also be interpreted as a critique on the patriarchal society dictating terms to a helpless girl like Lalita.

Later in the film, the 'Chale Radhe Rani' song is sung by the same Baul. But the tone is very sad, the pace is slow and the lyrics are different because the situation is melancholy. The parallels are drawn once again with the Radha–Krishna story, but this time the Baul does not dance or swing to the beat of the song. He is sad and pensive and walks slowly towards the home where Lalita lives, then sits on a platform to sing the rest of the song. The situation is created when Lalita is going to Mungher with the entire family to Girin Babu's home for a climate change for her uncle Gurucharan who is not keeping well. She would have preferred to stay back, but has no choice. When the horse-drawn carriage filled with luggage on its roof comes to the door and everyone gets in, the strains of 'Radhe…Radhe' fill the air heralding the arrival of the Baul, coinciding with the departure of Lalita as Sekhar walks to the terrace to watch the carriage turn the bend. The song begins and the carriage moves around the bend. This time, the lyrics go like this:

> Chale Radhe Rani ankhiyon mein paani
> Apne Mohan se mukhda modeke…
> Chhodke bachpan ki wo rang raliyan
> Chhodke Gokul key yeh kunj galiyan…
> Chhodke Mohan ki meethi muraliyan
> Nainan ka naata todke
> Apne Mohan se mukhda modeke….
>
> Radha akeli mohan akela,
> Khel vidhata yeh kaisa khela
> Viraha ka yeh dil todke,
> Apne Mohan se mukhda modeke…[74]

---

[74] The author finds it difficult to translate this song. The essence of the lyrics spell out the pain of the separation of Mohan and Radha leaving behind the memories of sweet play as a child, the moments spent with Mohan in playful mischief, now having broken eye contact, Radha, what makes you go away turning your back on your Mohan?

The camera cuts between and among the singing Baul, Sekhar's face, Sekhar bending over the parapet of the terrace with the clock tower in the distance and Lalita sadly seated inside the carriage, shaking with its movement.

Parineeta's song list shows more songs, but three beautiful songs are not there in the DVD version of the film and there is no scope of finding out whether they were kept out of the film when it was first released or eliminated later. One song, probably sung by a female singer whose name does not appear anywhere in the credits, picturized on the varying moods of a pensive Ashok Kumar, runs only on the soundtrack. It goes 'Kab tak rahoge aakhir yun door door hamse',[75] but one cannot see the song in the whole film. The song has a fast swing to it and is very musically composed. Some songs can be heard on the music sites of the Internet, but cannot be seen visually in the entire film. One of them is a sad number sung by Asha Bhonsle that goes 'Tum yaad aa rahe',[76] a love song of separation and nostalgia. Another song is a solo Geeta Dutt number that is also a love song that talks about the tragedy of a change in the relationship (suggesting lovers) while the elements of nature have remained constant. The opening lines are 'Chaand hai wohi, sitare hai wohi, wohi hai chaman, phir bhi kyon udaas hai udaas mera man'.[77] One song was sung by actor Asit Baran Mukherjee, who portrayed the role of Girin in the film but was also a good singer and often sang in his films. The lines are 'Toota hai naata preet ka, par meet mila hame meet ka',[78] but we cannot see the visualization of this song in the complete film today.

BAAP BETI (1954)

The unique feature of the music and song tracks of *Baap Beti* lies in three things. First, all the four songs were sung by Lata Mangeshkar. Second, the music was by Roshan who scored the music for Bimal Roy only for this film, Third, Kavi Pradeep wrote the lyrics for this single Bimal Roy film and never again.

Since the background score of the film is no longer available anywhere, one has to focus on the four songs that reflect the versatility of music in Bimal Roy's cinema. The four songs spell out completely different moods though the voice is the same—Lata Mangeshkar's. The first is a devotional solo that goes 'Duniya bananewale Ramji, gajab ka hai tera intezaam', which

---

[75] Translation—How long will you keep away from me?

[76] Translation—You are forever in my memories.

[77] Translation—The moon is the same, so are the stars and so is the earth, then why, or why, is my heart filled with silent horror?

[78] Translation—My link with love has broken but I have gained the friendship of a friend.

sings about the surprises Ramji can spring with his strange arrangements. Then there is a school prayer with a chorus and the leading voice is Lata's. It begins with 'Andhere se ujale ke taraf le jaa hamey', which is a bit wistful but talks of hope of or reaching the light after walking through darkness. It is metaphorical for the little girl who feels she is in the dark because she does not know who her father is and, at the same time, is full of hope that one day she will find him and the darkness of her life will end.

The third song is a lullaby (lori in Hindi) which, in retrospect, seems to be a favourite with Bimal Roy who has positioned and placed three beautiful lullabies in three different films. The opening lines are 'Le chal re nidiyaan hamey chanda mama ke ghar udal khatole par'. Translated roughly, it means 'Oh Sleep, please take me to my dear Uncle Moon on your chariot' which personifies both sleep and the moon, referring to them as one who moves in the night on a chariot and the moon as 'mama' or uncle.

The last song, a cheerful number that begins with a lovely *sargam* voiced by Lata Mangeshkar goes 'Koel bole koo, papeeha bole pi, O jeenewale duniya mein has has jeeyo has has ke jee arey o rona na kabhi'. It has excellent orchestral backup and sounds topical to this day. It roughly means 'the cuckoo sings out cooh, the parrot sings pi, oh live in this world laughing away and never cry'.

BIRAJ BAHU (1954)

There are six songs in this film that repeats the pairing of Prem Dhawan for the lyrics and Salil Chowdhury for the musical score. The basic underpinning of the songs is pathos and devotion which cover an entire range of emotions and beliefs that spell out the larger philosophies of life. Without stressing on a single song that could be taken as the leitmotif of the film, the songs harp on the philosophy of giving, of selfless service to others and sometimes a single song portrays glimpses into the entire panorama of life.

Within the first two minutes, the credits come up against the backdrop of small village scenes and a beautiful Bhatiyali (boatman's song) 'Majhi re...Ram karega paar re naiyya',[79] on the soundtrack. These songs also are known as *maanjhi* songs. Bhatiyali is derived from the word *bhati*, which means the river-coast as these songs belong to the rivers and the river-coast areas. Bhatiyali songs reflect the sorrow, pain, joy and longing of the people of bhati regions. It narrates the customs of the fishermen, boatmen and farmers.

---

[79] Translation—Oh my dear boatman, who will take me across the river? This is a philosophical song where the boatman represents God and the river represents life with its ebbs and tides.

Bhatiyali songs are generally sung in high pitch. In the movie, as the boat plies along with the current, the vast endless rivers inspire a sense of wonder, longing to see his destination and the boatmen start singing in full-throated ease, giving expression to their feelings. The voice of the singer rises and falls in keeping with the movement of the waters that also rise and fall, and create ripples as the boatman draws his oars through the water. Bhatiyali is sung solo. Lyrics of all Bhatiyali numbers spell out feelings of longing for the soul of the Eternal (Super being). The dominant themes are love and pain. Bhatiyali may express simple joy too. This song is special because the music was composed by Salil Chowdhury, and because it is S.D. Burman, who is famous for his Bhatiyali songs which he has sung himself and also composed many of them himself.

The visuals we see against the song on the soundtrack show boatmen rowing their boats, fishermen drawing their nets from the river, village wives coming back with water pots hitched to their waists and farmers returning from their fields. The song fades and the sound of village wives blowing on their conch shells is complemented with visuals of the women stepping into the courtyard with lighted incense and earthen lamps to offer evening prayers to the Tulsi plant. These few shots, moving seamlessly from one to the next, establish the place setting, the period, the ethnography and the culture within which the narrative is placed. From silhouetted images, the visuals become sharper when the camera enters the courtyard. The place is Rajpur, a village in Bengal, the time is evening and when the camera finally comes to rest on Biraj, she is entering a dark room to light the tiny *kupi* (lantern) on the wall. The village, apparently, does not have electricity.

Nilambar has a song he sings in front of the tiny temple of Lord Krishna as Biraj listens enraptured and the others listen mesmerized in the midst of their work. The song, addressed to both Krishna and Rama and goes like this.

Mere mana bhoola bhoola kahe bole,
Prabhu sang preet lagale,
Prabhu bina kaun sambhale,
Jeevan ke yeh chhoti si naiyya,
Karde Raam havale

The rough translation of these lines goes as follows:

Why do you distract me with words?
Link yourself to God,
Who else can take care of you but God?
Surrender this tiny boat of life to
Rama.

It has a beautiful rhythmic beat and is a *bhakti geet*[80] that has philosophical implications elaborating on the devotional mindset of Nilambar who is oblivious to worldly responsibilities towards looking for a regular income that will help him tide over his family's needs.

The *bidayee*[81] song, 'Tera ghar abaad rahe', is played only on the soundtrack to express the pain of parting. But Bimal Roy built this scene up with a prelude of a sound design and some stotras that lead up to the wedding of Punnu, the younger sister. Nilambar followed by her departing for her in-law's abode. The soundtrack is filled with the loud noise of the wooden fence being built between the two sections of the home dividing the space of the two brothers following the quarrel they have. The sound of the fence being shaped and then fixed is punctured with the cawing of crows in the backdrop while a sad Nilambar sits in front of the small temple in his room and beings to recite devotional stotras voiced by Hemanta Mukhopadhyay in his mellow voice. The lines say 'Om namah vishwarupaya, vishweshwaraya, govindaya namo namo'. The camera cuts to show Punnu's marriage rituals which cut to Punnu and her husband coming to touch the feet of Nilambar to seek his blessings. Nilambar tells them to seek his brother's blessings too.

The bidayee song is voiced by Lata Mangeshkar and Shyamal Mitra with a chorus that follows. The lyrics are extremely philosophical in significance and meaning. It begins normally with 'Tere ghar abaad rahe, jaaye dulhaniya jahan rahe khushhaal rahe'. This means, 'Let your house be complete and wherever the bride goes, let her live in happiness'. But the mood switches with a chorus that follows Lata's voice and the beat and melody and lyrics broaden up to embrace the larger philosophy of life. The first two lines are slow and very sad and when the chorus joins in, there is a melodious *taan* on the soundtrack that precedes the song that spells out 'Ek ghar ujade, ek base duniya ka dhang purana iska yahan thikana yuhin rahega aana jaana'.[82]

These lines are a pointer to the break up in the home and family of the two brothers against the new home Punnu is moving to. From this point on, the very mobile camera that wandered across the two homes, captured Nilambar wiping off tears and Punnu weeping before leaving, becomes completely static. As the song goes on in the background, the

---

[80] *Bhakti Geet*—Devotional songs.

[81] A *bidayee* song is a song sung when a daughter or sister is going away to her in-law's home after marriage. The word bidayee means 'departure' which is filled with the sadness of leaving the abode the girl has been brought up in and her paternal family and is also tinged with the hope of a happy future in her husband's home.

[82] Translation—One home gets broken, one finds root, this is the old pattern (address) of the world and this is how people will move on or stay back.

camera remains fixed on a tree with its branches changing to suggest the change in the seasons. This song, visually and audio-wise, does two things at the same time. First, it clarifies and even establishes a sense of order by presenting a clearly perceived formal structure and second, it provides the underpinning for the theatrical build-up of the scene and then rounds it off with a sense of finality.

There is a mujra shaili in the film that has a beautiful prelude of the strains of a *sarangi*[83] and a tabla[84] before the song performance begins inside Deodhar's bajra. There is no dance until the clients tell the dancer to get up and dance to her own song. Her performance is filled with *adaas*[85] and the song goes 'Din yeh tujh pe sadh pe, naina tujh pe diwaane, jag saara jaane bedardi ek tuhi na jaane',[86] stretching the last line three times after each stanza. The camera cuts several times to focus on Deodhar who sports a crooked smile, panning across to move to the instrumentalists and some clients to complete the picture. The dance has not been choreographed according to the credits, but it occupies an important place in the cinematic narrative because it conveys the character of Deodhar and defines his way of life.

DEVDAS (1955)

The soundtrack of *Devdas* consists of ten songs. Some of the songs were inspired by the Baul tradition. Apart from this, it also features some thumris at Chandramukhi's place to demonstrate *tawaif*[87] culture. The music, composed by S.D. Burman on lyrics penned by Sahir Ludhianvi, is a hallmark of *Devdas*.

The first song in the film is lip-synced by the boy Devdas and the small Parvati as they wander about the fields and the gardens of the village. Devdas, with Parvati, is trying to capture a pigeon in its nest, but it flies away before he can catch it. The entire song is shot against the backdrop of the open fields filled with trees and flying birds chirping away to their heart's content. *Devdas* begins to sing and Paro joins him. Devdas's voice is lip-synced by

---

[83] *Sarangi*—It is a bowed, short-necked string musical instrument used in India and Nepal for Hindustani classical music made famous when used by courtesans and in musical soirees and also in Kathak dance as an accompaniment.

[84] Tabla—This consists of a pair of percussion instruments commonly used in Indian music of all styles; one for the right hand and another for the left hand.

[85] *Adaas*—Seduction styles practised by singing women of yore while they perform in front of their clients. Plural of 'adaa'.

[86] Rough translation—This heart is devoted to you, the eyes are crazy for you, the whole world knows this but you do not.

[87] *Tawaif* is an Urdu word for courtesans in kings' courts and courts of nawabs and zamindars who were invited to perform their music and were very classy and dignified and were treated with respect and dignity. However, many confuse this term with prostitute which is not correct.

Usha Mangeshkar and Paro's voice is by Asha Bhonsle. The opening lines are 'O albele panchi tera door thikana hai, chhodi jo daali ek baar wahan phir laut ke aana hai'[88] This is the only cheerful song that reflects the innocence of childhood where children extract happiness from the minutest of events. But there is a metaphorical meaning attached to the song if one goes looking for it. It is an irony on the life of Devdas who, like the pigeon in flight, has left the 'branch' of his tree, but will never come back another day, contrary to what the lines suggest. The song is on the one hand, an ode to nature, and on the other, a celebration of the children that reside in Devdas and Paro.

The standout number in the film is said to be the Talat Mahmood solo Mitwa. While discussing whether this song, lip-synced by Dilip Kumar as Devdas should be used at all in the film, it was finally decided that the song would be there. It is picturized in the village where Devdas comes back and Paro is no longer in his life. He sits by the pond with his stick, feeling alone and isolated and sings, slowly getting up and walking along the village roads, pausing under the branches of a tree, his face filled with the grief of having lost. The song is a very sad soliloquy which the hero sings to himself and it goes

> Mitua, mitua…
> Lagi re,
> Ek Ek chup mein,
> Sau sau baina,
> Rah gaye ansoo,
> Loot gaye raag…
> Mitua, mitua…lagi re[89]

This is very difficult to translate. But in sum, it means Oh my dear friend, your silence speaks of hundreds of demands, tears are forgotten and melodies are looted.

Another song sung by Talat Mahmood, lip-synced by Devdas in the film, which is also filled with melancholy goes as follows:

> Kisko khabar thi, kisko yakeen tha
> Aise bhi din ayengein
> Jeena bhi mushkil hoga
> Marne bhi na payenge

---

[88] Translation—Oh dear wandering pigeon, your address is far away but you will have to return to the branch you have left behind.

[89] Rinki Bhattacharya, *Bimal Roy* (Bhopal: Madhya Pradesh Film Development Corporation, 1989).

Translated, it reads,

> Who was to know, who would believe
> That such days would lie in wait
> Where it would be difficult to live
> And impossible to die as well.[90]

This song composed in *Tilak Kamod* (a classical raga meant to be sung in the second quarter of the night) is sung when Devdas is lying in a drain beside a street, drinking and sick, discovered by Chandramukhi, who, all decked up, comes looking for him in a horse carriage and locates him from the lines of this song floating in the air. She takes him home and is shocked to discover that he does not even recognize her. The choice of Talat Mahmood for the voice of Devdas is ideal even in retrospect because it blends seamlessly with the melancholy character of Devdas who just does not know how to be happy, in love or in loss. It also is in harmony with Dilip Kumar's speaking voice adopted for the film—low key, soft, subtle and sometimes so low that it is difficult to make out the words. Devdas refuses to move on, leaving his love story behind and, at one point, feels sad about not being able to respond to Chandramukhi's love.

Sahir wrote lyrics in pure Hindi for the two Baul-based numbers such as 'Aan milo aan milo shyam saware, brij mein akeli Radha khoyee khoyee phire'[91] and 'Saajan ki ho gayi gori',[92] both rendered as duets by Geeta Dutt and Manna De to fit into the situations presented ideally.[93] The first number is sung by a Baul couple when Paro is a small girl. She sits on the branch of a tree and listens to the song. Devdas has been sent away to the city and she is all alone. Towards the end of the song, she begins to cry silently. Her weeping suggests the depth of her feelings because she is just a child and pays three rupees just to hear a baul song. But the scene also suggests that she is familiar with this Baul couple and likes to hear them sing and perform.

---

[90] Akshay Manwani, *Sahir Ludhianvi—The People's Poet* (New Delhi: Harper Collins, 2013), 90–91.

[91] Translation—Oh Dear Dark Lover, please come and meet Radha who is wandering all alone in Brija.

[92] Translation—The fair one now belongs to her lover, so now the home seems to be a foreign land (to her).

[93] *Baul* is one of the few widely known and appreciated types of folk music in Bengal. Baul is not only a kind of music, it is basically a Bengali religious sect. The members of the sect are themselves called Bauls and the songs they sing are named for them, *baul-gan* (baul songs). It has been suggested that, etymologically, the word derives from Sanskrit word 'Vatula' means 'affected by the wind disease, mad'. On the other hand, it might be derived from Sanskrit word 'Vyakula' means 'restless, disordered'.

The second song, 'Saajan ki ho gayi goriab ghar kaa angan videsh laage', is sung by the same couple after her marriage has been fixed. She is still very sad because she is not in favour of marrying a much older widower and, more importantly, because Devdas is no longer a part of her life and this marriage will mark the final parting. The Baul couple is now much older and the man's hair and beard have grayed with time, though his female companion does not reveal any signs of age. The situations are different, the times are different and the backdrops are also different, but the mood is the same—two happy songs that run contrary to the sad mood of the listener. The Bauls are wandering minstrels who sing along as they travel, their lyrics talking more about the philosophy of finding God within you and also drawing from the mythological tales of love and worship often underlined with references to Krishna and Radha, but mostly singing about the abandoning of worldly life for a different kind of life altogether.

Background music is used very sparingly and effectively. This is perhaps the first Hindi mainstream film where the background music was composed by Salil Chowdhury while the song score was written by Sachin Dev Burman who requested that the background score be handled by Chowdhury. Salil Chowdhury agreed, but on one condition—his name should not appear in the credits of the film as the composer of background music. The background music is positioned beautifully and is also often edited with a rare insight into parallel movements in the life of Paro and Devdas respectively.

One example is the shot showing the transition of Parvati from a little girl to a grownup woman when she goes to fetch water in the local pond. A line of *Basant Bahar*[94] plays in the background, indicating the coming of spring as Devdas is coming back to the village. Once more, when Paro is getting married, the melodious strains of the shehnai playing out a strain of *Malkauns*[95] probably, a mandatory feature for a wedding cuts into the strains of a mujra shaili amidst the jingling of dancing bells when Devdas steps into haveli of Chandramukhi and the women who perform there. These two parallel cuts suggest the two different worlds Paro and Devdas now begin to inhabit respectively, marking a permanent schism in their tragic love story. Later, when Chandramukhi picks Devdas off the streets and brings him to her abode, off the frame, she belts out a line of the song in *Bhairavi*, a morning raga

---

[94] *Basant Bahar* is a raga in Hindustani classic music also used in Carnatic music that is sung in the middle of the night during the spring season as a tribute to the season. It is a happy raga.

[95] *Malkauns* is one of the oldest ragas in Hindustani classical music and belongs to the Shavaite musical school. It is a serious, meditative raga.

and a metaphor on the breaking of a new dawn in her life because *Bhairavi* is an early morning raga. The music also shows the change in Chandramukhi. At one point, Devdas laments, "Parvati and you are so different from each other and yet so very similar." By then, the differences between the two have blurred beyond recognition for Devdas and for the audience.

Chandramukhi's journey has already been established earlier with song–dance numbers such as 'Ab aage teri marzi'[96] through 'O jaanewale ruk jaa thodi dum'[97] to 'Jise tu kabool kar le'[98] sung by Lata Mangeshkar, a timeless number which spells out what dozens of lines of dialogue would not have been able to express. The musical interludes in 'O jaanewale' are filled with beats and ragas that go with Kathak performances while the camera focuses often on her footwork and her pirouettes. She follows Devdas with her dance as he gets up as if to leave. When the song is about to end, he opens the window and the song merges into the notes of a shehnai being played by a group of accompanists for a wedding on a *machan*[99] atop a wedding home. The music of the shehnai wipes out the notes of the song and a shocked Devdas remembers about Paro being wedded to someone else.

The dance numbers performed by Chandramukhi were not purely classical, but were based on the footwork, *tihais*, *bols* and *tukras* in Kathak choreographed by Hiralal who was Vyjayanthimala's dance teacher and guru in Bombay cinema. Hiralal and Sohanlal were brothers who were born and brought up in Rajasthan in a family steeped in Kathak. They later migrated to the South in search of work and, later, became the dance gurus of Vyjayanthimala who insisted that one of them would do the choreography of her dance numbers in the films in which she needed to dance. These dance numbers in *Devdas* are, perhaps, some of the most outstanding classical-based dances in the history of Hindi cinema. The Kathak costume and jewellery, the beautiful pirouettes she took while dancing, the music accompanists—harmonium, *pakhawaj*[100], tabla and sarangi were authentic and convincing and added to the aesthetics of the film.

'Jise tu kabool kar le wo ada kahaan se layoon, ter dil ko jo lubha le wo sada kahan se layoon' is a beautiful song sung by Lata Mangeshkar, which Chandramukhi is forced to break into when she has brought Devdas

[96] Translation—From now on, it is your wish....

[97] Translation—Oh, take a breath for a moment before you go away....

[98] Translation—Where from will I bring the style you will accept readily? Where from will I create the arrangement that will fill your mind with desire?

[99] This is a temporary chamber build atop the entrance to a wedding hall where musicians used to play the shehnai and other instruments. It is almost a forgotten part of Bengali culture today.

[100] This is percussion instrument often used to accompany Kathak performances.

back to her abode from near a drain trying to get him out of his drunken stupor by instilling some cheer into him. Later, in the same song, a couple points out the striking difference in the approaches of Chandramukhi and Devdas which Chandramukhi points out as follows:

Tujhe aur ki tamanna, mujhe teri arzoo hai
Tere dil mein gham hi gham hai, mere dil mein tu hi tu hai

Translated, it reads:

You desire someone else, I yearn for you,
Your heart is plagued by sorrow, my heart brims over with you[101]

The soundtrack is filled with the ambient music of mujra songs floating in from some other room with music and percussion instruments within the *kotha* as they enter. Chandramukhi, wearing a beautiful sari and jewellery, breaks into a dance only to music. Gone are the seductive expressions, in dance and face, of her mujra days. Her dance is a free-flowing performance done spontaneously without adhering to the grammar of Kathak seen earlier. One can see her thinking what pose to strike next because her aim is to cheer Devdas up at a time when she has already quit her trade. The performance done only to background music is graceful and poignant with the pain of trying to bring her love back to a normal state. Devdas begins to walk out not feeling good about the dance and not even fully aware of what is going on. As he walks towards the stairs and begins to clamber down, Chandramukhi breaks into a long taan and then sings 'Jise tu kabool karle'. At some point along the song, Devdas steps back into the room and collapses on the bed. The song ends and a happy Chandramukhi sits beside Devdas, a wistful smile on her lips.

In all these three songs sung and performed by Chandramukhi, Devdas is present but he refuses to look either at Chandramukhi or at her dance. He glances up occasionally, but looks away again. Is he afraid that he might begin to admire her and her performance? Or perhaps, admire the woman who loves him so deeply without expecting anything in return? Is he an escapist who voluntarily chooses to keep away from responsibilities by using drinking as an excuse which finally takes his life?

Mubarak Begum's 'Woh na aayenge palatke, unhen lakh hum bulayen'[102] is on the soundtrack, heard in the red light quarters where Chandramukhi, who has left the trade, continues to live in the hope that Devdas will come at

---

[101] Manwani, *Sahir Ludhianvi*, 91.
[102] He will not turn around and come back never mind however many times you call him.

least once. The song suggests that it is being sung by a fellow tawaif in another room to the accompaniment of string instruments and the tabla dotted with the jingling sounds of the dancing bells. This is the poignant scene where Devdas takes Chandramukhi's leave after she nurses him back to health in her abode. He insists on handing her a bundle of currency notes to help her tide over her new lifestyle where she has given up her trade completely. She, on her part, makes him promise that he will not touch alcohol again. He says he will try to but cannot promise. She requests him to come to her if he felt sick again and he keeps quiet. As he goes away, she comes to the balcony to watch the horse carriage move away and turn the corner while the song goes on in the background. This song was composed on raga *Khamaj*.

There is another background song sung by Mohammad Rafi with a chorus. The main song begins with 'Rahi o rahi' that spells out the parallel existence of the harshness of sunlight and the darkness of evening, arrival alongside departure, both of which are true because 'Yeh bhi ek roop hai woh bhi ek roop hai.'[103] It is picturized on location in the wide fields dotted with small water bodies where Paro in her palanquin drawn by four bearers moves in one direction while Chandramukhi approaches from the other side, wiping the perspiration from her face as she walks. The song is backed by the constant refrain of 'Manzil ke chaah mein raahi ke wastey'[104] by the chorus like the *hum hum* humming of the palanquin bearers and this refrain forms the beat for the main song filled with the pain-evoking taans in the mellow voice of Rafi. This song opens with the reflection of the palanquin in the water. When Paro and Chandramukhi see each other, we can see the similarity between the two where they are dressed like traditional married Bengali women, their heads covered with the end of their saris and their foreheads bearing a round bindi, and the distinction between the mainstream woman Paro and the courtesan Chandramukhi has blurred beyond recognition, the transcendence made possible by their love for the same man. This use of ambient sound, background songs and ambient music is a hallmark of *Devdas*. The music and the song here convey pace. By establishing patterns in the use of the song, music and sound effects and then manipulating these established patterns within the temporal flow, the song can be felt subjectively.[105]

Devdas, in his attempts to come to terms with the world's realities, proves to be a half-hearted rebel who, in the final analysis, sacrifices his life for the status quo. His rejection of Chandramukhi's love, in fact, can be an unconscious desire to get rid of his own feudal past. The character,

---

[103] Translation—This is one kind of beauty and that is another kind of beauty.

[104] Translation—In the desire for a destination, for the sake of the traveller.

[105] Lipscomb and Tolschinsky, 'Role of Music Communication in Cinema'.

thus, becomes the archetype of a disillusioned man who seeks his identity through self-inflicted suffering. He could see no option except the inevitable self-destruction in the face of an oppressive social milieu in which true happiness could not materialize in the physical union of the lovers. The character had—and still has—a universal appeal for the Indian mindset because the theme also represented escapism and indecisiveness, whereby the failures of the individual are attributed to external social factors.[106]

SUJATA (1960)

For a change, it was Majrooh Sultanpuri who wrote the lyrics of the songs for *Sujata* with the music composed by S.D. Burman. Originally, the film had seven songs, but today, the DVD copies of the film do not contain a song sung by Mohammed Rafi which was a satire sung in a humorous tone that went 'Andhe ne bhi sapna dekha kya hai zamana'[107] with a caustic refrain of 'Wah bhai wah' throughout the song. The picturization and positioning of the song within the film, therefore, remains out of reckoning today.

The background score of *Sujata* is also a scintillating mix of different instruments and tunes. The film opens on a blasting site with a chorus in the backdrop of workers singing a song that labourers usually do to cope with the strain of heavy work. An interaction between Upen Babu and the supervisor goes on against this low key song. As the credit titles come up, the music track changes into something else. In retrospect, this seems to have been composed by R.D. Burman because years later he composed the music for a Bengali film *Rajkumari* (1970) picturized on Tanuja and Uttam Kumar that went 'Bondho daarer ondhokaare thakbonaa'[108] sung by Asha Bhonsle and Kishore Kumar. The same melody was repeated in the Hindi musical romance *Yaadon ki Baaraat*[109] (1973) shot on Tariq who belts out 'Aapke kamre mein koyee rehta hai',[110] with Sunita (Zeenat Aman) joining him later at a hotel party sung again by Kishore Kumar and Asha Bhonsle.

As the credits end, the lines of the shehnai float across and we see Upen Babu's bungalow being decorated and lit up to celebrate his little daughter Rama's first birthday for which a grand party has been arranged. The transition of the two little girls, Upen Babu's daughter Rama and the untouchable orphan they are forced to take in named Sujata from girlhood

---

[106] Ashok Raj, *Hero*, vol. I, *The Silent Era to Dilip Kumar* (New Delhi: Hay House, 2010), 163–164.

[107] Translation—This a song filled with satire and the opening lines mean—even the blind dreamt of how the era had changed.

[108] Translation—I will not remain in the darkness of the closed doors.

[109] *Yaadon ki Baaraat*—Procession of memories.

[110] Translation—Someone lives in your room.

to womanhood, is beautifully established and edited through the sounds and visuals of speeding trains, beginning when Upen Babu is transferred from Madhupur to Dehradun and then to Bilaspur followed by Ranigunge, till he settles down with his family at Barrackpore in West Bengal in his home along the river Ganges close to the famous Gandhi Memorial. This time and place leap is effectively conveyed through trains which run through most of Bimal Roy's films.

The first song is 'Neend bhari pankh liye jhoola jhoola jaana, nanhi kali sone chali hawa dheerey aana' which is one of the most memorable lullabies (loris) in the history of Hindi cinema, sung by Geeta Dutt and lip-synced by Sulochana as she puts her little baby Rama to sleep. The cinematography and the light create just the right mood for the scene—curtains swaying in the wind, the moonlight filtering through the window in slants to fall on the floor as the mother lulls her baby to sleep. In the middle of the song, the infant in the maid's room begins to wail loudly. Hearing her cries, the mother walks to the window that peeps into the maid's room and begins to sing to the baby who slowly goes to sleep.

The second song is a nostalgia piece that functions at several levels through its picturization, placing and conceptualization. The number is 'Bachpan ke din bhi kya din they', a lovely duet sung by Geeta Dutt and Asha Bhonsle and picturized on Nutan and Shashikala playing Sujata and Rama respectively. The strains of the piano played by Rama form the prelude to the song. Sujata is on the terrace as usual, picking up the washing, when the notes of the songs float up to the terrace. She smiles and begins to hum or draw taans in the song from time to time. The song can be defined as a tribute to the beautiful synthesis between the two most gifted singers in Hindi cinema, namely Geeta Dutt and Asha Bhonsle. The camera moves back and forth from Rama to Sujata captured from different angles. The song also brings across the contrast between the two young women.

There are parallels in their movements and actions (Rama spreads her dupatta playfully across her face, and a second later, Sujata matches the gesture with the garments she is removing from a clothesline). But though their voices merge and though they are clearly attuned to each other's thoughts, they never share the frame—understandably, for Rama is indoors throughout while Sujata is on the terrace above the room. And this tells us some things about these characters and the film itself: It is short-hand for the fact that there is an invisible line separating the sisters' lives and that Sujata isn't, strictly speaking, part of the family.[111]

---

[111] Jai Arjun Singh, 'On Bimal Roy's Sujata' (and the Invisible line in bachpan ke din; 28 January 2013).

The contrast comes across in their body movements, While Rama is always jumping and running, as if always with a spring in her step, Sujata's movements are slow, cautious and disciplined as Rama points out how her placing in the home at any time of the day can be easily pinpointed by the time on the clock. Sujata is dressed in simple cotton saris while Rama is seen in a sari only at her birthday party and, otherwise, wears a *salwar–kurta*[112] and plaits her hair with ribbons as per the fashion of the time. Rama leads a full life, filled with poetry, song, badminton and participating in college dramas. Sujata is unlettered, but finds great joy in serving the members of the family. While Rama belts out the lines in the song, Sujata simply hums along or draws taans as a refrain. Rama talks nineteen to the dozen, but Sujata is quiet, and when she talks, her voice is soft and low-key. Even the way they smile is different. Rama flashes wide smiles showing the unceasing joy she draws out of life. Sujata's smile is a closed-mouth smile, soft, sweet and always reaching to her eyes.

Yet, the lyrics of the song spell out the strong bond between the two sisters, though they are not related through blood-ties and have different roots and rules in upbringing. The lines open with 'Bachpan ke din bhi kya din they, udte phirte titli ban ke'[113] which is very strong on nostalgia, carving out the strong bond they share as if they are real sisters. The narration is lucid and there is absolutely no ambiguity in the song, its lyrics, its picturization and performance. It also exudes a spirit of nostalgia. A moving scene in the film is when the little Sujata (Baby Shobha) wants to study like Rama but is not allowed to. So, she goes to the old retinue and tells him to teach her. He says he will tell her lovely stories instead. As he narrates a fairy tale of a princess, the camera cuts to animation to show what Sujata is fantasizing about—a princess, beautiful nature in all its glory against a lovely music track without any songs.

The third song is to celebrate the birthday of a grown-up Rama and it goes 'Tum jeeyo hazaaron saal saal ke din ho pachaas hazaar. The song was sung by Asha Bhonsle with a chorus. The house is decorated for the occasion, guests dropping in and so on. One lady mistakes Sujata for Rama but is corrected by Charu, Rama's mother, and Adhir who is standing by, listens to Charu's elaboration that Sujata is 'like my daughter' and is struck by the statement. The birthday song is preceded by the music of the song before a college friend of Rama begins to sing and dance while Rama sits at the piano.

---

[112] *Salwar–kurta*—Aa common form of shirt and loose trousers worn by Indian girls and women.

[113] Translation—How wonderful were those days of childhood when we would flit and fly like butterflies do.

Sujata, dressed up for the occasion, slowly walks out of the party and into the garden. She sits musing over her twisted destiny and images from the past are superimposed on her sad face—the little Rama being fed with *kheer*[114] by Charu on her birthday, Sujata demanding that her mother celebrate her birthday too because she wants to be fed with kheer from her mother's hands, crying and wailing till Charu orders the ayah to carry her and lock her up in her room. These memories now assume new meaning for a grown Sujata who now realizes why her birthdays were never celebrated—no one know when her birthday was and she did not belong to the family she grew up in.

Adhir follows her and a sweet interaction follows while in the background, there is a beautiful piece of music in raga *Bahar*[115] in keeping with the scene that depicts Sujata's surprise and happiness when she discovers that Adhir is least concerned about her parental roots and accepts her as Upen Babu's natural daughter. This piece of music was later used by S.D. Burman in the film *Dr. Vidya* (1962) with the lyrics composed by Majrooh Sultanpuri to a memorably graceful and creative dance performed by Vyjayanthimala. This song pawana deewani[116] was backed by a scintillating instrumental score with an abundance of the percussion to keep the beats of a vigorous dance number sung by Lata Mangeshkar and is counted among one of her best. But in *Sujata*, the mood is subtle and in control in keeping with the subtle character of Sujata who is so much of an introvert that she cannot bring herself to express her emotions.

The next morning, when Sujata sees dark clouds gathering in the sky, she closes the windows, latches the door to the garden from outside and steps into the garden to sing 'Kaali ghata chhaye mora jeeya ghabaraaye, aise mein kahin koyee mil jaaye re'[117] sung by Asha Bhonsale in raga *Pilu* which is a raga (melodic mode) of Indian classical music. It is mostly used in light-classical forms, like the *khayal*, of north Indian classical style. In

---

[114] *Kheer* is an Indian dessert made of milk, boiled in a low heat till it condenses to half of the original quantity with sugar added to it. It can be made in many varieties, adding rice or semiyan and dry fruits such as raisins, almonds and cashews. It has different names in different regions of India and is specially cooked to celebrate birthdays in Bengali families even today. It is considered to be auspicious for the birthday child.

[115] *Bahar* is a very popular springtime raga. During the spring, it may be sung at any time of the day. However, during any other season, it is a night time raga. *Bahar* has a very distinctive character. This raga cannot be performed straight but must be executed in a *vakra* fashion, for it is the characteristic twists which give this raga its form. Available at http://chandrakantha.com/raga_raag/film_song_raga/bahar.shtml (Accessed on 13 March 2016).

[116] Translation—Oh the crazy girl of the air.

[117] Translation—My hear thirsts (with love) when the sky is covered with dark clouds, how wonderful it would be if one could find someone in this situation.

this particular song, the raga has been toned down to cut out on the pure classical base to blend it into the situation where there is no rain but the skies are cloudy, and yet, Sujata is happy. The toning down is also in keeping with Sujata's nature.

Another tract of pure music in *Sujata* happens at Rama's college's annual function where a Manipuri dance troupe performs pure classical Manipuri only with the traditional accompaniment of the percussion instruments played by the male dancer and a predominance of the flute in the background followed by a string of dancing females who complete the dance. This performance conveys a sense of perceived energy that brings relief from the low-key narration of the story and brings in some vigour to switch the mellow mood to a more meaningful one. This is positioned before the main drama, a portrayal of the dance drama *Chandalika* based on Rabindranath Tagore's work in which Rama portrays the untouchable Chandalika. This Manipuri dance was choreographed by Little Ballet Troupe a noted institute of Manipuri dance training and performance founded by Shanti Bardhan[118] in Bombay in 1952.

Since Sujata has been asked by Charu to stay away from the college function, she stands all alone in the darkness of the evening at the Gandhi Ghat beside the river Ganges. Adhir comes away from the function when he sees that Sujata has not come and, guessing she must be at home, arrives at Bhupen Babu's house and at the Gandhi Ghat to meet Sujata. As he narrates the story of Chandalika to Sujata, the camera cuts back to the drama in the college with Buddha's chantings playing on the music track very softly with the voice of Hemanta Mukherjee.

When Adhir begins to narrate a story linked to Gandhi's views on untouchability and how he took care of the untouchable girl Lakshmi and gave

---

[118] A gifted dancer trained in Manipuri and the very rare Tipperah schools of dance for almost 12 years, Shanti Bardhan was associated with Uday Shankar for six years at his school at Almora. The Indian People's Theatre Association formed in 1942 which was the Communist Party of India's cultural wing had Shanti Bardhan as an active member. These members worked to spread awareness about India's struggle for freedom and to spread the message of the need for freedom through dance, theatre and music. But eventually, Shanti Bardhan parted ways with IPTA to form his own Little Ballet Troupe in 1952 with the core spirit of humanism, anti-imperialism and radical experimentation in form through Manipuri and other innovative performances. The first dance drama of the Little Ballet Troupe was the *Ramayana* performed by human puppets in a novel experiment.

Other members of the IPTA who became noted for their contributions to theatre, literature, cinema, art and music are Khwaja Ahmed Abbas, Ritwik Ghatak, Prithviraj Kapoor, Utpal Dutt, A.K. Hangal and Salil Chowdhury among many others. After Shanti Bardhan passed away in 1954, his wife Gul Bardhan carried the flag of Little Ballet Troupe which was later christened Ranga Shri Little Ballet Troupe till Gul Bardhan passed away in 2010.

her shelter in his ashram[119] even when his donors backed out, the soundtrack slowly fills up with notes from the Gandhian Ram-bhajan 'Raghupati raghava raja Ram, patita pawana Sita–Rama'. Somewhere in the distance, a clock strikes eight times and Sujata begins to walk towards her home, when suddenly, the beautiful notes of the 'Bhatiyali number sun mere bandhoo re, sun mere mituwa, sun mere saathi re'[120] floats in from the river where a boatman sitting on the boat with his oars is caught in a long shot in silhouette. Sujata and Adhir are held captive by the notes of the song sung by S.D. Burman himself. The boat begins to move and in the distance, as the song goes on, the boatman at the helm holds the oars while the other boatman draws the oars. The entire scene in the river is captured in silhouette while the faces of Sujata and Adhir are caught in the half-light in the gathering darkness of late evening.

The last song in the present visuals of the film is the telephone song rendered in the film by Adhir and sung in the soft and tender voice of Talat Mahmood. The song 'Jalte hai jiske liye, teri aankhon ke diye, dhoond laya hoon wohi geet main tere liye'[121] picturized on Adhir singing on a landline telephone seemed an exaggeration in melodrama at the time the film was released. But in retrospect, it was a very innovative and imaginative way of picturizing and conceiving of a song sequence that evokes opposite emotions in the one who is singing and the one he is singing to. The same song has completely contrasting impact in Adhir who is singing about his love for Sujata and in Sujata who is listening to the song over the phone because she knows that she can never marry Adhir. Adhir is confident that 'Jab talak na yeh tere ras ke bhare hoton se mile, yuhin awara phirega yeh teri zulfon ke tale'[122] and smiles as he sings, Sujata, on the other hand, keeps weeping silently at the other end. When the song ends and Sujata is still weeping, she cuts off the connection, but it begins to ring again and again. The music has been borrowed by Burman from a Bengali Tagore song that goes 'Ekoda tumi priye', but the lyrics in Hindi are not translations of the Bengali ones. The song is based on the raga *Kafi*.[123]

---

[119] *Ashrama*—Where Gandhi and his disciplines led a simple life without ostentation in food, clothing and shelter.

[120] Translation—Listen, my friends, listen my close friend, listen all my companions.

[121] Translation—The one for whom the lamp in your eyes light up, I have searched for that song only for you.

[122] Translation—Till the time this does not meet your juicy lips, this will wander like a vagabond under your loose hair.

[123] Kafi is an important raga of Hindustani classical music. Raga Kafi has a direct lineage with the folk music of India. Folk music in Tappa, Hori, Dadra, Keertan and Bhajans from different parts of India have been composed in this raga form for ages. Available at http://www.tanarang.com/english/kafi_eng.htm (Accessed on 3 March 2017).

BANDINI (1963)

There are seven song situations in *Bandini*, the last film directed by Bimal Roy. The songs are placed in different microcosmic worlds that the protagonist, Kalyani, the concrete metaphor for the title *Bandini*, inhabits over her strange and unique journey. One world is within the prison precincts where two songs are sung by a fellow female inmate, Phoolbanu and sung by Asha Bhonsle in a completely against-the-grain style and mood, and one patriotic number, mat ro mata laal tere bahu tere,[124] by Manna De.

Gulzar, when asked how his encounter with Bimal Roy began, says:

> During the making of *Bandini* in the early Sixties, S.D. Burman who was composing the music for the film and Shailendra, who was writing the lyrics, had a tiff. And there was this tune waiting to be written into. Debu Sen, who was assistant on the sets, took me to Bimal-da who introduced me to S.D. Since Urdu was my main language, S.D. had reservations about whether I would be able to infuse my son with the right Vaishnav spirit that was called for. I took up the gauntlet and my first song for Hindi cinema was born: 'Mora gora ang laye le, mohe shyam rang daye de'[125] which became a big hit. Sadly for me though, when the song was over, Shailendra and S.D. had patched up and I was left in the lurch. Bimal-da did not like this but S.D. was adamant about not taking me on for the rest of the songs. Bimal-da perhaps felt a bit sorry for me and offered me the assistantship for his next Hindi film *Kabuliwala*, based on a Tagore story.[126]

The next two songs by Lata Mangeshkar appear in the second world of Kalyani, narrated in flashback, in the village she grew up in, but left, never to return. These songs are picturized in open spaces in fields flush with corn and tall blades of grass and Kash flowers, a river on ebb and a boat anchored on the shore. This is the village where Kalyani spent her childhood and grew up in after she falls in love with Bikash Ghosh (Ashok Kumar), a freedom fighter on house arrest in the village. Of these two songs, both styled after the Vaishnava school of music tracked back to the Radha–Krishna story of love and longing, are sung by Lata Mangeshkar. Of these two, the first, 'More gora anga lai le', is the first composition by Gulzar for any film. The second song, 'Jogi jab se tu aaya mere dwaare', which is a love song veiled as a devotional with the word 'jogi' which means 'lover' in this song was written by Shailendra. But no one will be able to guess that two different lyricists

---

[124] Translation—Do not weep my mother(land), the son is yours and his wife is also yours.

[125] Translation—Take away my fair body and give me the body that shyam has—dark.

[126] Interview with the author, 2002.

had penned the two different songs because they stand united in terms of the Vaishnava spirit they carry through Kalyani who was brought up in Vaishnava teachings by her father.

'O jaanewale ho sake to laut ke aana' belted in the soft, mellow voice of Mukesh is shot when Kalyani was unable to bear the mental and social tortures inflicted on her innocent and devout father by the villagers because of the social stigma the family had acquired by the sudden disappearance of Bikash who had publicly declared that Kalyani was his wife but never came to take her back with him or kept his promise to marry her socially. This sequence is shot mainly in the dark, capturing Kalyani's hooded figure from behind as she looks back from time to time to see the village she is leaving.

One song defining the world of the prison where the story opens reflects the time of the story is a patriotic number. The time-frame is the struggle for independence when many political prisoners were jailed for their political activity, sometimes extremist and rebellious, during the last years of colonial rule. Some cells in every prison were filled with political prisoners. From time to time, the ones sentenced to death were taken to the gallows, their lives cut short even before they could properly flourish. This one song involving the men in prison widens the horizons of the story and the film's canvas by including the political scenario within which Kalyani lived, in prison or out of it.

S.D. Burman composed the music to lyrics penned by Shailendra of a patriotic paean to a political prisoner being taken to the gallows to be hanged. His mother and infant sister are waiting beyond the prison gates while the song,

> [M]at ro mata, laal tere bahu tere,
> janambhoomi ke kaam aya main
> bade bhaag hai mere…,

is sung by Manna Dey in his bass voice. Initially, it seems a bit absurd to find that the song is being lip-synced by the prisoner as he walks towards the gallows. How could a man walking towards certain death sing a song? He is a patriot and a freedom fighter, and for him, the hanging is a triumph of his love for his homeland.

In the scene there is chanting of 'Bande Mataram' by the other political prisoners as a prelude to the song, waving their hands through the bars of the prison cells till the assistant jailor tries to beat them with his stick to silence them, the sad and devastated mother waiting outside the gate with the camera closing up on a big lock, then closing on the confused, chubby face of the little sister, caught in a top angle shot to catch the walking silhouettes of the four prison guards escorting the condemned man to the gallows, frequently intercutting to the gallows where we see the silhouetted hangman waiting near the hanging rope on the platform, cutting to the jail superintendent looking at his watch till at the stroke of five at dawn, the hangman, off-screen, pulls the lever. The prisoner's mother falls in a faint and on the soundtrack and one can hear Sanskrit shlokas about the reality of life and death chanted in what sounds like the voice of Hemanta Mukherjee.

By that time, the song has ended and the soundtrack is suddenly punctured with the loud sound of the trap door under the gallows opening and closing. In retrospect, this is a beautifully picturized song and it lives to the theory that songs used in films ought to be seen within the context of the visuals which makes the meaning significant. When the same song is heard independent of the visuals, a very popular and commercially viable practice among Indian masses, it stands independent of its visual context and the narrative context of the situation in which it is placed. It is beautiful as a song per se, even beyond the parameters of the film in which it occurs. But this particular song assumes richness and cinematographic and editorial excellence when seen within the film, much more than when it is heard external to the film. This song, therefore, establishes the narrative's placement in time and serves to authenticate the era and also provide a sense of nostalgia.[127]

"*Bandini* marked the coming of age of Asha Bhonsle as a singer," writes Sathya Saran.[128] She goes on to write, "In *Bandini*, S.D. Burman gave her a new identity. Just as he had worked with Geeta (Dutt) to change her image from soulful to sexy, the teasing, flirtatious tenor of Asha's voice was shaded with pathos for a single number in *Bandini*."

The first of the two songs, 'O panchhi pyaare, saanjh sakaare bole woh kaunsi boli bataa re, bole woh kaunsi boli',[129] is lip-synced by a prison inmate Phoolbanu who sits stitching something and singing about how her wings have been clipped. She is separated from the spacious compound of the women's segment of the prison by a barred window and looks wistfully at the trees and the bird perched on a branch outside. She compares herself with a caged mynah whose wings are useless. The beat of the song is imaginatively orchestrated to keep time with the daily chores the inmates

[127] J. Stuessy and S. Lipscomb, 'Rock and Roll—Its History and Stylistic Development, 4th edn (Upper Saddle River, NJ: Prentice-Hall, 2003), 410–411.

[128] Sathya Saran, *Sun Mere Bandhu Re—The Musical World of S.D. Burman* (Noida, India: HarperCollins Publishers, 2014), 125.

[129] Translation—Oh my darling birdie, what language do you speak in morning and evening?

are engaged in, such as grinding the wheat to flour on the grinding stone, two young women beating some grains in a huge stone vessel, other women working on the sewing machine in a room and Kalyani washing clothes near the well and quietly looking at Phoolbanu as she sings, each chore beautifully keeping time with the beat of the song.

The second song inside the prison, also sung by Phoolbanu, goes 'Ab ke baras mohe bhaiya ko babul saawan ko deejo bulaaye',[130] which is a song of nostalgia that impacts on the other women prisoners who listen quietly to Phoolbanu singing as the lyrics are something they can each identify with. Though the prison is a confined area, this song and its touching rendering by Asha Bhonsle and the imaginative picturizing on screen conveys the quality of space where the complex seems larger than it actually is, with the prisoners scattered here and there, the camera capturing one face in close up and another at a distance in the same frame, a bit blurred and out of focus. Their faces are sad and pensive, but there are no tears, silent or loud. The strains of the tune of the song opens with a medium close-up of Deven's pensive face to cut to a very long shot of Kalyani seated on a platform next to the high prison walls. She looks back to where Phoolbanu sings as she grinds the corn on her huge grindstone. This juxtaposition of the camera to capture two or three figures in the same frame in different degrees of closeness and distance gives the impression of depth-of-field and enlarges to focus on the others as Phoolbanu sings. She sings about not getting any letters from her home, about youth having left her toys astray and her doll stolen. Kalyani keeps looking at the high walls of the prison as if to remind herself that they are all living in prison. All the same, the song captures the prison as a different woman's world in miniature where the audience will find it difficult to believe that these women have committed big crimes.

Mora gora ang lai le
Mohe shaam rang dai de
Chhup jayoongi raat hi mein
Mohe pee ka sang dai de

This is a song of happiness, love and cheer sung in the open by Kalyani in her village surroundings, picturized on the basis of the diary she has written about her past and given to the jailor to read. This, therefore, offers us a glimpse of the world Kalyani once belonged to, far away from

---

[130] Approximate translation—This year please carry the message to my brother about my asking him to come.

the bars and cells of a prison. She looks lovely in a coloured sari, with a round bindi decorated with dots around the bindi, romping around in the fields, walking down to a river bank, resting a bit on the helm of a boat and singing a song based on the Vaishnava philosophy that depicts the eternal love between Radha and Krishna where the very fair Radha requests Krishna to take away her fair skin and give her his dark skin so that she can hide in the darkness where the moon will not be able to pick her out when she goes to meet her lover at night. The camera wanders in the outdoors, capturing her happy face in close-up and then catching her in a very long shot along the dried banks of the river like a dot within the vastness of nature around her.

> Jogi jab se tu aaya mere dwaare,
> Mere rang gaye saanjh sakaare
> Tu to ankhiyon se jaane jee ki batiyaan
> Tose milna hi jurm bhayaare...

A bit later she sings...

> Jake panghat pe baithun mai, Radha diwani
> Jaake panghat pe baithun
> Bin jal liye chali aaye Radha diwanee
> Mohe ajab yeh roga lagaa re
> Oh Jogi jab se tu aaya mere dwaare[131]

This song also draws on the Radha–Krishna love where Kalyani identifies with Radha and imagines Krishna as a jogi. She is more simply attired in this song sequence, and both songs have to add depth to feelings the song conveyed.

'O jaanewale ho sake to laut ke aana, yeh baat yeh ghaat tu kabhi bhool na jaana' has been sung by Mukesh and marks the transition of Kalyani from her village to an unknown and uncertain future that is as dark and as dangerous as the darkness of the night she seeks escape through. Kalyani covers herself with a blanket and pulls it over her head so that she cannot be recognized or seen. The song happens on the soundtrack and functions as a bridge between her naïve past that changed from content-ment to happiness to grief and slander, and her present when the jailor is reading her diary. She of course cannot hear the song, but she turns back

---

[131] Author's note: This one is really difficult to translate as it is filled with visual metaphors that are difficult to translate in English.

to look one last time at the world, the family and the village she will never
return to. It is a very sad song of no return voiced by Mukesh with a heavy
load of melancholy to suit the mood of the scene. The song is based on the
classical raga *Jog*, belonging to Khamaj thaat. It is one of the more popular
ragas appearing often in films. Sometimes experts assign this raga to be a
member of Kafi thaat.

The last song happens in the climax, in a different world, space
and time. Kalyani is being escorted by the female warden to be taken by
train to the former jail doctor Deven who she is supposed to marry. As
she waits at the train's thatched waiting room, she suddenly discovers that
on the other side of the same waiting room, partitioned off by a straw-
thatched wall, a very sick Bikash is waiting for a steamer with one of his
followers from the party he belonged to. He is probably dying. This is the
climactic Bhatiyali number sung by S.D. Burman himself and picturized
on a singer who sits outside Good Luck Tea House just outside the waiting room and sings,

> [O]re maajhi, mera saajan hai us paar,
> main man maar, hoon is paar,
> o mere majhi ab ke baar, le chal paar le chal paar,
> mera saajan hai us paar,
> man ki kitaab se tum mera naam hi mita dena
> gun to na thaa koibhi
> avagun bhi bhoola dena…
> mere aaj ki bida kaa
> marke bhi rahega intezaar
> mere saajan hai us paar
> mat khel jal jayegi
> kehti hai aag meri manki
> mai bandini piya ki
> mai sangini hu saajan ki
> meri kheenchti hai aanchal
> man meet teri har pukaar
> mera saajan hai us paar.

Though the song is voiced by a male singer and is a Bhatiyali, almost
the exclusive domain of males because only men can be boatmen, the
song is sung from a female perspective and from a female point of view.
Words such as *saajan* (lover), *bandini* (the imprisoned woman), *sangini*
(beloved—female) and *aanchal* (end of the sari) are examples of the
female 'voice', sung by a male singer which marks a radical departure for
the Bhatiyali tradition, chosen, perhaps, as a way to strengthen Kalyani's

determination to decide on her final choice of which road to take—the train to reach Deven or the steamer to look after Bikash, the only man she ever loved This considerably expands what is commonly understood as 'film music'.

Kalyani learns from Bikash's escort that he is too sick. She finds herself in the horns of a dilemma. Bikash cannot even walk properly and has to be helped by his devoted follower. At the last minute, even as Kalyani has already boarded the train and it has sounded the whistle, the steamer's final hoot is heard. Just when the wooden plank that joins the shore to the steamer is to be pulled away, Kalyani jumps off the train and rushes to the plank to join Bikash. She has made her choice. There cannot be any 'normal' life for Kalyani because she is doomed to be a prisoner of love, of passion that compelled her to commit a heinous crime and she suffers from the guilt right through her life. The song is punctuated with the sounds of the steamer's hoot like a siren call for departure.

The song opens with the camera capturing Kalyani and Bikash in mid-long shot seated on either side of the respective waiting rooms. As the song begins, slowly, Kalyani rises to stand near the window of the room to look out. The camera closes in on her confused and sad face, as if the camera is as uncertain as she is about what to do with her life at that moment. As the whistle of the train sounds and Kalyani is walking away, she looks back again and again and the camera cuts to show Bikash painfully wobbling up the plank to the steamer, resting his body on his escort who holds him and helps him to walk up to the steamer.

CONCLUSION

The best part of the songs, lyrics, choreography and orchestration in every Bimal Roy film lies in the way they are portrayed by the 'actors' who execute the songs in action and through acting. Every single actor in Bimal Roy's films containing songs, lyrics, music, sound effects and dance is perfectly natural in their portrayal without a single note that jars or a single body language that seems out of place, loud or crude. Even the prison inmates have their dignity in *Bandini* and dignity is not the exclusive monopoly of the protagonist Kalyani. The same goes for the execution and performance of the songs within all the other films within the Bimal Roy gharana of cinema. The actors deliver precise expressions demanded of a scene even when the song is on the soundtrack and not on any actor's lips. The music and songs are universal in the way they were perceived when the audience first saw them and the way they are perceived today. You can still feel the resonance of the lyrics within you.

The music, song, lyrics and dance of these films are created in collaboration, directly or indirectly by the composer who needs to understand the dramatic requirement of a given scene that the director wishes to express. The singers involved in giving voice to the songs cannot be separated from the role of the sound designer responsible for the way in which the sound and image are synthesized to create and sustain harmony in the final audiovisual effect created on the screen for the audience. Finally, it is the actor who executes the action the song demands that influences how the audience responds to the scene and the song, its positioning within the scenario and the story and the cohesion of these factors in cinema. Not a chord goes out of tune in the cinema of Bimal Roy.

SUMMING UP: WAS BIMAL ROY A DISPLACED 'OUTSIDER'?

SUMMING UP

From *Udayer Pathey* (1944) to *Benazir* (1964), the Bimal Roy era in Indian cinema spans three decades of dedicated filmmaking. Before wielding the megaphone, Bimal Roy was cinematographer for P.V. Rao's *Nalla Thangal* (1935; Tamil), and P.C. Barua's *Devdas* (Bengali, Hindi and Tamil), *Manzil*,[1] *Mukti* and *Bari Didi*. He was a strong and silent human being with speech conspicuous by its absence. He spoke very little, about himself, about his family and even about his films. He shunned superlatives and though he was very much a part of the film industry, he kept himself aloof from parties or a loud and garish lifestyle that is the wont of film personalities everywhere. But his name was mandatory in every list of film delegations that went abroad. He was almost coerced into all sorts of associations and committees, even as he kept himself distanced from the political wrangling that formed an inevitable part of all these actions. He won awards—left, right and centre, but after some time, they did not seem to matter to him one way or another. Members of his technical crew and his acting cast won awards too, and during his time, were considered to be among the best in the industry.

---

[1] *Manzil* (Urdu)—House, sometimes it also means 'destination'.

Hrishikesh Mukherjee, editor for most of his films, who won a string of awards for his editing of Bimal Roy films, later turned into an independent filmmaker in his own right. At least two men, Basu Bhattacharya and Gulzar, who began their careers assisting him, became big names later. He gave directorial breaks to his favourite comedian Asit Sen and an old friend Arabindo Sen. Vyjayanthimala, Dilip Kumar, Kamini Kaushal, Nutan and Meena Kumari are some actors who bagged top awards for their work in his films. Salil Chowdhury, introduced as a music director by Roy in *Do Bigha Zamin*, became one of the best composers in the industry, treading a completely new path in film and other music what is known today as fusion. For a song in *Do Bigha Zamin*, Chowdhury incorporated the theme music of the Russian Red March and the song has been immortalized.

There are innumerable instances of screen performances and technical achievements never known to have been attained earlier. Though his background is traced back to the days when screen acting was directly influenced by the melodramatic exaggeration that marked theatrical performances, Bimal Roy was noted for his marked restraint. He evolved a subtle, normal mode, contributing to the richness of the tapestry of the realistic theme of his films. The visual brilliance of the filmmaker, apparent in his pre-directorial works such as *Chambe Di Kali* in Punjabi and *Nalla Thangal* in Tamil, was mature, confident and certain. He is said to have had an almost uncanny sixth sense about the positioning of the camera. Even when an independent cameraman worked for him, he would come to the set, look through the lens, and ask for the camera to be shifted at least nine or ten times. Kamal Bose and Dilip Dutta were his regular cinematographers.

Lighting, an extremely important element in his works, acquired greater vibrancy in *Parakh*, *Sujata* and *Bandini*. Whenever the narration grew nostalgic or throbbed with inner crisis, whether in anguish or in ecstasy, the mood was captured in delicate chiaroscuro patterns of black, grey and dove white. His language was painted in every possible shade of grey, white and black. One never thought of colour even in a pastoral romance like *Madhumati* nor did one miss it.

Pran, who played villain in *Biraj Bahu* and *Madhumati*, made more eloquent use of body language and facial expression than voice for both films. Bimal Roy, perhaps, is the only filmmaker of the post-Barua–Debaki Bose era who towered over the Indian cinema scenario with such consistent command over the medium. His work is a fine blend of the sophistication of P.C. Barua, the emotional lyricism of Debaki Bose and the skilled craftsmanship of Nitin Bose.

Bimal Roy's first directorial assignment under the NT banner came in the form of a 1,000-feet government sponsored documentary on the

Bengal famine of 1943. When he went on location to shoot the film, the masses turned their anger towards him, not allowing him to shoot. But he managed to win them over and got some good footage for the film. B.N. Sircar himself chose *Udayer Pathey*, an unpublished story by Jyotirmoy Roy, for Roy's debut feature film. The film turned out to be a big commercial hit and the story came out in book form afterwards. It ran continuously for one full year at Calcutta's Chitra Cinema. The story later turned into a play and the entire dialogue was transferred onto eight discs that sold very well, creating a new way of marketing dialogue. *Udayer Pathey* introduced a new era of post-World War II romantic–realist melodrama that was to pioneer the integration of the Bengal School style with that of Vittorio De Sica.

Arabinda Mukherjee, a noted director in his own right, retired from active filmmaking, said that his entire career in films was triggered by Bimal Roy's *Udayer Pathey*.

> I assisted him for *Anjangarh*. In those days, we were put through a hard, grilling process. I was already employed as editing assistant. Here, I had to train for three months in the laboratory, three months on editing and three months in sound. In the meantime, I had to learn to work under Bimal Roy. He asked me to rewrite scene number 176 from the script of the film he was then making. I was told that he had asked many people to write out the same scene but remained dissatisfied with the results. So, I approached playwright Bidhayak Bhattacharjee and he helped me out by suggesting the 'drama' element needed for the scene. I was on.[2]

Udayer Pathey soon had a Hindi version called *Hamrahi*, completely re-shot on new sets with the same artistes. However, *Hamrahi* did not repeat the success of the Bengali original. His leanings towards the poor and the downtrodden perhaps came from his basic humanism rather than from purely Leftist leanings as some critics opined. His leftist leanings of any, stemmed from conviction and not from active association because he never held any party ticket. Some of his political ideology is reflected in *Udayer Pathey's* hero Anoop's room. His walls were filled with portraits of national leaders and great thinkers as different as Karl Marx and Tagore. A few Tagore songs in the film became big hits. There was a fiery zeal in his earlier films, which was replaced with a mellow social concern in his later films. One of his most notable qualities was the total restraint he practiced

---

[2] Lecture delivered at Seminar on Bimal Roy at Nehru Auditorium, Calcutta, organized by Bimal Roy Memorial Trust, in a weeklong programme in January 2002.

in keeping away from any kind of political propaganda or pamphleteering in any of his films.

His next film in Calcutta for New Theatres was *Anjangarh* in Bengali and Hindi based on *Fossil*, a short story by Subodh Ghosh. This was followed by *Pehla Aadmi* in Hindi and *Mantra Mughda* in Bengali, based on a noted literary piece of work by Bonophool, neither of which could live up to the expectations raised in his first directorial film, *Udayer Pathey*. He also wrote Manoj Bhattacharya's *Tathapi*[3] in 1950. In the same year, he migrated to Bombay. He was invited by Bombay Talkies to make *Maa*, and had come to Bombay initially only for six months. He began to receive other offers such as *Parineeta*, based on a sweet love story by Saratchandra and produced by Ashok Kumar with beautiful music that in time turned into a signature for every Bimal Roy film. "I consider *Parineeta* to be the most beautiful and dignified celluloid metamorphosis of an original Sarat Chandra classic that has no parallel in cinema till this day," says journalist Shankarlal Bhattacharya. When he firmly established himself in Bombay, Roy decided to found his own production banner, under the name and style of Bimal Roy Productions, using as his emblem, the Rajabai Tower of Bombay University, far distanced from the more obvious and visually opulent emblems used by Raj Kapoor, Mehboob, New Theatres or Prabhat.

Do Bigha Zamin (Two Acres of Land) was released in 1953. It is a realist drama based on a story by Salil Chowdhury who loosely adapted this from a Tagore long poem of the same name. The story is about a small landowner Sambhu (Balraj Sahni), which opens with a song celebrating the rains that put an end to two seasons of draught. The song goes— 'Hariyala saawan dhol bajata aaya'. Sambhu and his son Kanhaiya (Ratan Kumar) have to go and work in Calcutta to repay their debt to the merciless local zamindar (Sapru) in order to retain their land. In Calcutta, Sambhu becomes a rickshaw-puller, facing numerous hardships that lead to his near-fatal accident, the death of his wife Paro (Nirupa Roy) and the loss of his land to speculators who build a factory on it.

He held back the release of the completed *Parineeta* in favour of *Do Bigha Zamin*, which is said to have offended producer Ashok Kumar at the time. He set up his own sound stage and an unpretentious office at Mohan Studios in Bombay's Andheri and went on to direct *Baap Beti*, *Naukri* and *Biraj Bahu* under his own banner. The films that followed are—*Devdas*, *Madhumati*, *Sujata*, *Parakh*, *Yahudi*, *Bandini* and *Prem Patra*. Eight more films came out of Bimal Roy Productions of which six were feature films—*Amanat* which Arabindo Sen was chosen to direct; *Apradhi Kaun?*, a thriller; *Parivar*,

---

[3] *Tathapi* (Bengali)—In spite of.

a family comedy; *Usne Kaha Tha* based on Guleri's short story; *Kabuliwala* based on a Tagore short story; and *Benazir*, starring Meena Kumari. The other two were documentaries—*Gautama the Buddha* and *Swami Vivekananda*, a biographical documentary he produced for Films Division. All this was done in Bombay within a brief span of 15 years, an incredible achievement for a man who stepped into a land and city that was 'foreign' to him in every sense but which he turned into his place of living, lifestyle and cinema. He saw the city and its cinema change since when he had arrived till when he fell sick. But this in no way affected his perspective on cinema.

After Partition, when Bengali literature and cinema suffered a set-back, Nabendu Ghosh joined Bimal Roy as his screenplay writer when Roy shifted to Bombay in 1950. Urdu became the state language of East Pakistan in spite of the fact that 95 per cent of the population spoke Bengali; films and books from West Bengal were banned in erstwhile East Bengal. This was a terrible setback for the Kolkata-based literary and film market. In a manner of speaking, it was this political division which brought a division in cinema and literature too, and prompted Ghosh to join Bimal Roy in Bombay in 1950. Others in the team were Hrishikesh Mukherjee, Asit Sen (comedian), Paul Mahendra and Salil Chowdhury.

One unique quality in Bimal Roy as a filmmaker is that he did not impose any political belief in his films but allowed the politics to emerge from the story, the characters and their interaction within the film. So, his films do not subscribe to any definite political ideology. Yet, there is an undercurrent of politics that emerges almost naturally as the film unfolds, cinematographically, in terms of the narrative, the characters, the incidents and the interactions between and among the characters.

BIMAL ROY—THE FILMMAKER WHO TURNED 'DISPLACEMENT' INTO A CINEMATIC STATEMENT

'Refugee?' filmmaker Ritwik Ghatak asks again and again in his films. 'Who is not a refugee?' A documentary on Ritwik Ghatak entitled *The Name of a River* by Anup Singh set out to find answers to the question Ghatak posed in and through his films, in a myriad different ways, mostly angry, often restless, reflecting the state of his schizophrenic mind, forever vacillating between his roots—Bangladesh and the city that was the base of his uprooted identity—Calcutta. Did Bimal Roy as a filmmaker who was forced to leave his roots, Suapur, in Bangladesh, to make a new career as cinematographer in Calcutta with New Theatres and then migrated to Bombay suffer from a similar sense of restlessness and frustration? If his films are any indication, he did not. His films reflect the fluidity of a river that flows to channelize frustration through stories that deal with displacement in different forms and how the characters in them cope with this displacement, immigration to a different place, be it circumstantial or self-willed or mandatory or a combination of any of these two or three.

If Bimal Roy felt distraught and frustrated by the repeated uprooting from Suapur in Bangladesh to Calcutta in India and then to Bombay, he successfully channelized his restiveness through the creative fluidity of cinema as an art form, cinema as a medium of expression and cinema as agency that could and should perpetuate social messages and reform. He had no desire to initiate any social change himself but his films, without raising slogans or holding flags, spread this need for social change or raised existentialist questions on why change should not happen to people like Shambhu in *Do Bigha Zamin* who decided to go to Calcutta to earn money to repay his debt. But for him, there was no coming back. When he did, he had already lost the money he had earned to repay the debt and he found that the mortgaged land was already somebody else's converted from agricultural land to industrial land, as if standing as an irony of the clear emphasis the Nehruvian administration placed on land reforms in the First Five Year Plan following Independence.

Bimal Roy was not a 'refugee' in the political understanding of the term as he came to Calcutta much before The Partition was to happen and India needed to gain independence from British Rule. The identity of East Pakistan had not been established. He was displaced, and as his background reveals that the uprooting from Suapur did not happen of his own will. He was forced to leave by reasons of the extended family of uncles wishing to appropriate his and his brothers' share of the land and property. The migration to Bombay happened by invitation and no one had a clue, including Bimal Roy himself, that here was a displaced artist who would write himself into the history of Indian cinema forever.

What necessitated Bimal Roy's migration from Calcutta to Bombay? The collapse of New Theatres, the pressures of the World War II on Calcutta and the advent of Bombay cinema heralded a new phase. His migration to Bombay[4] precipitated his understanding of the migration from rural areas to urban centers as one great social phenomenon of independent India. If Bimal Roy intended to make a statement upon his arrival in Bombay, he did it with *Do Bigha Zamin* and not with his first film in Bombay, which was *Maa* and which he was invited by Bombay Talkies, then going through financial bad times, to direct and which brought him to Bombay in the first place.

---

[4] Vinay Lal, 'Bimal Roy (1909–1966)'. Available at https://www.sscnet.ucla.edu/southasia/Culture/Cinema/bimalroy.htm (Accessed on 20 January 2017).

Shambhu comes back to his village to find that his 'do bigha zamin' does not exist and therefore, there is neither 'home' nor 'land' to come back to. No land reform has taken place during his absence though the nation is now an 'independent, democratic republic' where the zamindari writ has permitted the thakur to grab Shambhu's land illegally. The thakur in his turn, auctions the land and Shambhu finds a factory is being constructed on the land that was once his. He picks up a fistful of earth and stands looking through the barbed wire fencing that separate him from his land and the film ends on that note of uncertainty.

If there is no hope in the end, this reflects the reality of life for people like Shambhu, his wife Paro and their son Kanhaiya. Theirs is an ongoing struggle to find new homes, new occupations and new sources of income for the simple business of living which sets them among a growing mass of the poor, the marginalized and the downtrodden in a country that has just regained its 'independence' after more than 200 years. If they were displaced outsiders in Calcutta, they are similarly displaced outsiders in the village they left behind with the hope of coming back. Shambhu and his entire family represents a microcosm of Indian peasants who are willing to cope with displacement if necessary, as outsiders trying to grope with a new occupation, a new abode, a new neighbourhood and even a new language. But they are not allowed to because the world they once grew up in and knew as their own has changed and cannot or will not accommodate them anymore.

One may point out that one is not considering here the Freudian concept of displacement where displacement is defined as "an unconscious defence mechanism whereby the mind substitutes either a new aim or a new object for goals felt in their original form to be dangerous or unacceptable."[5] One is considering rather the immigration that an individual must go through when he or she is displaced from his or her 'place' of origin/birth/family. He or she has to begin life all over again in this new physical setting, find out new avenues of earning the basic survival needs of food, clothing and shelter followed by the extended needs of health, education, socialization and entertainment. This involves a strong coping mechanism that would help the displaced person to adjust to his or her new surroundings not only in terms of physical coping but, more importantly, in terms of emotional and social coping besides the question of adjusting to climatic, language and cultural changes.

---

[5] Eric Berne, *A Layman's Guide to Psychiatry and Psychoanalysis* (London: Penguin Books Limited, 1976), 399.

If Bimal Roy was 'displaced' in physical and geographical terms, which he really was, unlike one of his celluloid heroes, Devdas, or his peer and colleague Ritwik Ghatak, he never allowed himself to be sucked into the vortex of depression that often befalls many creative thinkers and artists who, for some reason or other, find themselves uprooted from the original roots to plant themselves somewhere else, in some other place and setting they are not familiar with. Through his films, he explored the different layers of displacement and their impact on the characters of each story that have been explained in the earlier chapters.

In order to understand the larger ramifications of the word 'displacement' as commonly understood as a shift of geographical base from point A to point B by a person X or a group of persons XYZ, it is equally important to understand what the term 'place' means. The word 'place', geographically speaking, can be defined as an area or a region which possesses some characteristic in the context of preconceived ideas, local conditions or events. But the term has varied meaning, in its myriad nuances, when it comes to literature, films, music, architecture and photography.[6]

A place does not revolve around just geography, but it has other aspects and its uniqueness is affected by its history, language, society, time and inner conflicts. More importantly, when a creative person finds himself 'displaced' in geographical terms, he does not immigrate as an individual who exists and functions in an emotional, cultural and social vacuum. He brings along with him the baggage of his past into his present, a past that has shaped him into what he will infuse into his present that will determine, in a manner of speaking, his future and his destiny. This is explained in lucid terms by filmmaker Jahnu Barua who writes:

> We see in Roy's films, a transplantation of the ethos of Bengal to Bombay and the Bengali language interpreted in Hindi much after the manner of the migrants from north-west India, particularly Lahore, after the Partition in 1947, who brought their culture and way of life to the cinema of Bombay. The filmmakers of Bengal were also victims of the Partition but an expression of this was only seen in Bengal. The cinema of Bombay of that period owes a lot to the Bengali sensibility that began with Bimal Roy and travelled through Hrishikesh Mukherjee, Basu Chatterjee, Basu Bhattacharya and even Guru Dutt, who was not a Bengali but lived in Calcutta, spoke the language and was a migrant in Bombay.[7]

---

[6] Neelabh Raj, 'Beyond Physical Realms, Life and Letters', *The Statesman* (7 February 2016), 3.
[7] Jahnu Barua, 'Bimal Roy, The Humanist', in *The Man Who Spoke in Pictures—Bimal Roy*, ed. Rinki Roy Bhattacharya (New Delhi: Penguin-Viking, 2009), 70.

Barua goes on to elaborate on how Roy's choice of three original novels by Saratchandra Chatterjee to turn into film offers just one concrete example of Bimal Roy not having shaken off his roots.[8] But he continued to make films in Hindi that gave him a larger identity as a national director of national cinema widening his canvas and his audience on the one hand and his fame as a filmmaker on the other. His native Bengali roots come across authentically in many of his films through costume, use of phrases picked directly from Bengali or translated from Bengali into Hindi, the backdrop created by nature such as the frequent use of water bodies, such as lakes, rivers and ponds, either as backdrop or as a central space for the exposition of conflict areas or areas reflecting nostalgia and homesickness, and, of course, the songs, the music for almost all of which were composed either by Sachin Dev Burman originally from the royal family of Tripura in Bengal or by Salil Chowdhury, a Bengali who migrated soon after Bimal Roy came to Bombay, on the director's invitation.

In some writers or directors, the pain of migration can lead to feelings of bitterness or regret but Bimal Roy was an exception though he had enough cause for cynicism because in one sense, his migration to Bombay soon after his *Udayer Pathey* became a big box office hit was not very welcome for him. But New Theatres was slowly going down and many young technicians who were with the studio were realising that their future was grim if they stayed on for long. His first uprooting from Suapur by his uncles must have brought in some element of pain and bitterness which he did not allow to put him down. 'On the contrary, both success and failure were irrelevant to his primary approach to cinema. This was to identify the human factor in any story that he had selected for production and to focus on it right through the making of the film.'[9]

In common understanding, the word 'place' is also referred to as dwelling or a place where someone has lived for a long time and has imbibed the social and cultural values of that region, including creating and functioning within a social network of the neighbourhood. Among some creative thinkers, writers, artists and filmmakers, dwelling as a sense of place refers to the idea of ownership. This did not apply to Bimal Roy who, throughout his life in Calcutta and Bombay, did not own or buy a single square meter of land he could call his own. He lived in rented apartments beginning with Malad, a suburb in Bombay, then shifting to Hill Road, Bandra, in Bombay where the family lived for many years in a very spacious apartment on the ground floor of a two-storey, old style bungalow with two

---

[8] Ibid.
[9] Ibid.

annexes and a lovely garden in front tended to by a gardener. He was born into an affluent family of landlords so when he was forced to leave home and homeland behind, the fact that 'ownership' does not really amount to much and power can tweak the ownership any which way against the vulnerable and the weak became a lesson of a lifetime for him.

In this sense, within a rapidly changing world where acquisition of land, flats, real estate and one's own home was growing, especially among the film fraternity with every passing day, most importantly because the terrible financial uncertainty structured into the industry as a business enterprise that could not guarantee a box office hit or had any formula to bring out one, Bimal Roy was genuinely an 'outsider' who did not believe in material possessions of long-lasting durability such as a house. He perhaps avoided a home he would never have to leave and not have to come back to, just to find that it did not exist the way he remembered it, like Shambhu in *Do Bigha Zamin*.

A place can also exist in the mind creating mind-spaces where a world of dreams distanced from reality exists, sustains and, perhaps, even enriches and entertains. If the literature Bimal Roy chose had these imaginary places and spaces, then he left a part of him behind in these worlds that he transformed from literature to cinema. This is another way in which he channelized his displacement and his feelings of uprootedness if there were any left.

This comes across in the presentation and portrayal of nature in all its ramifications and versatility in his films. Rains washing across windows, framed through the squares and rectangles of open windows, rains in an open garden drenching the sad and lonely Sujata who sits wondering about her identity, rains in *Do Bigha Zamin* that form a powerful leitmotif in the film, rains in *Biraj Bahu* backed by the sounds of thunder and lightning, drawing parallels with the crises in the lives of the characters are a throwback, perhaps, to his childhood days spent in Suapur that kept haunting him in his creative phase and found expression in his films—water bodies like lakes, rivers, ponds, the changing of seasons in prison in *Bandini* where one discovers Kalyani nurturing a garden with great care or a prisoner belting out a song as a tree blooms in spring and loses its leaves in winter, rains accompanying song sequences discussed in an earlier chapter and, of course, the village scenario sometimes transported into the city home of Sujata through the garden she tends to so lovingly and spends a lot of time in.

In *Sujata*, the orphaned girl from a very low caste, finds and makes her place in the garden in their home at Barrackpore where Upen Babu has settled down after his retirement. She is mostly found in the garden or on the terrace either hanging out the washing to dry or taking off the clothes from the clothes line or in the garden she repairs to when she is sad, happy or just so. In one touching scene, just after her adoptive mother has told her that she is an untouchable from a very low caste and is, therefore, a burden to society, she walks slowly out of the house in the midst of rains. The camera closes in on water dripping off leaves of the trees; the sound of the hooting of a steamer's horn can be heard in the distance as Upen Babu's bungalow rests along the banks of the Ganges in Barrackpore near the Gandhi Ghat. The hooting of the horn mixes with the sounds of rising thunder reflecting the storm raging in the disturbed mind of Sujata whose small world of harmony and peace is suddenly shaken as if by an earthquake. The camera pans to rest on the mural of Mahatma Gandhi on the Gandhi Ghat below which is engraved Gandhi's message against suicide. The rays of the sun slantingly filter through the trees in the garden.

In another scene, Rama brings Adhir to the garden where Sujata is tending to her pet plants and flowers. Says Rama referring to a poem she has written and which Adhir has read earlier, "I write poems on the Chandramallika (chrysanthemum) but Sujata creates real *chandramallikas*[10] in her garden."

In the only romantic scene between Sujata and Adhir near the Gandhi Ghat, after Adhir leaves, the soundtrack fills with a lovely musical composition without any song to complement it. The camera captures nature in all its glory, once again drawing parallels with Sujata's happy state of mind when she realises that Adhir does not care about her roots but loves her all the same. The camera pans across sunflowers swaying in the breeze, butterflies fluttering by, as if her garden is happy because she is happy. Rain songs and songs describing the cycle of seasons, heralding the harvest or functioning as a precursor for mystique and danger and romance (*Madhumati*) are other manifestations of nature in his films. These are the emotional baggage he brought along with him and within him to get them across so beautifully in his films.

One might find some points in common between Bimal Roy and Salman Rushdie. Rushdie believes in the integration of cultures and identities and goes on to denounce the idea of a nation, culture or even home. Living in London, the settings for most of his works are India where he was born. He refutes the idea of being on exile and accepts both places with their cultures and identities.[11] His quiet and gentle way leaves a mark in his films till this day. Bimal Roy lived in Bombay from 1951 till he passed away in January 1966, and never made a move to go back either to Calcutta or to Bangladesh, which was by then East Pakistan. But the

---

[10] Chandramallika—a flower that is called Chrysanthemum in English.
[11] Raj, 'Beyond Physical Realms, Life and Letters'.

time and place setting and the characters in his films, the stories he felt inspired by, are all deeply rooted within Bengal and within the Bengali identity. The imaginary spaces he created were in *Madhumati*, one of his last films but also the most commercially successful one, where Calcutta, Bengal and Bombay and even the Bengali identity that forms part of Bimal Roy's auteurial signature are absent. It is a film that triumphs in its celebration of open spaces, clear skies, beautiful snow-capped hills and the simple native people living in a small pocket, revelling in fairs, dances, songs and merriment.

Naukri (1954) is about a young man, Ratan, making two long journeys from his village, which is purportedly in Bengal, to Calcutta and from there to distant Bombay in order to look for a job so that he can send money home to rescue his mother from the dredges of poverty and cure his ailing sister through treatment and medicines. Though Ratan comes with hope in his heart, the teeming crowds of Bombay, the unconcerned people and the boards outside offices with their 'No Vacancy' notices make him lonelier because he is surrounded not only by strange faces but also by languages he does not know and cannot understand.[12] *Naukri* did not show the director at his best but this element of trying to find a new place to fit into and also to see that the family does not need to be geographically and culturally displaced failed so far as Ratan was concerned. So did the film despite the funny–cheerful–sad–puzzled performance of Kishore Kumar in the lead who sang his own songs beautifully positioned within the film.

The creation of 'fictional spaces' comes across touchingly in the *Naukri* song 'Chhota sa ghar hoga badalon ki chhaon mein asha diwani man me bansuri bajaaye'[13] where Ratan begins singing by creating the rhythmic beat on a cup, a saucer, two bowls and a spoon, ordinary things used at home. But with this simple accompaniment, Ratan weaves beautiful dreams of a village filled with stars triggered by the shimmer in his and his sister's eyes. Salil Chowdhury's music and the camera keep the song rooted to the definite space of the home and the village but Shailendra's lyrics take Ratan wandering off to other villages, other places, other homes. With this song, its choreography and picturization, Bimal Roy lifts the situation from its stereotypical rendering of a clichéd village home and a sick sister to bring it out in the open, where displacement brings hope and dreams instead of hopelessness, frustration and defeat.

---

[12] See http://jaiarjun.blogspot.in/2013/09/the-bekaar-in-big-city-on-bimal-roys.html (Accessed on 20 January 2017).

[13] Translation—There will be a little home in the shadow of rain clouds, as the crazy mind plays notes of hope on the flute.

In *Bandini*, the women in the prison, by some magic feminine strength, turn their displacement from the mainstream into a 'place' they reside in, albeit for some time or, maybe, forever. Just like women, they try to fit themselves into the ambience of the confined prison setting, one young girl singing a painful song filled with nostalgia while the other women sit quietly, listening in, and Kalyani sits alone to later lie down in the empty prison dormitory. This 'prison' turned into a 'shelter' somehow subverts the perceived idea of what a place should be like and also, in a subtle and indirect manner, underscores the fluidity of women to be able to fit themselves into any vessel they are poured into. Yet, most of them live in the hope that freedom will perhaps come and take them away from this confined world to reach under open skies and a real home they can go back to.

As if through some subconscious inner will, Bimal Roy never learnt to read or write Hindi and even spoke it very badly. He never tried to improve his Hindi though all his work was in this language. As if by the same logic, he surrounded himself with technicians and assistants who were either Bengali by origin or learnt to speak Bengali almost fluently because they worked within a dominantly Bengali unit and the big boss was Bengali. At home, they had Bengali food and spoke mainly in Bengali though the children interspersed their conversations with a lot of English. He was Bengali to the core. It was a close-knit family with a nurturing and loving wife, mother and housewife in Manobina Roy who formed a solid backup for her husband and the rest of the family including the household staff.

The family, in this sense, was united and in harmony in one place, geographically and emotionally speaking. He kept his two worlds—the studio and the home—separate, though close family friends like cinematographers Dilip Gupta and Kamal Bose, editor Hrishikesh Mukherjee, script writer Nabendu Ghosh, music director Salil Chowdhury, dialogue writer Paul Mahendra and Chowdhury's assistant Kanu Roy would often drop in and so would their respective families. Mrs Roy was ready to lay an extra plate or more for sudden guests for lunch or dinner.

It was a family living in harmony under the same roof for years together, and Mrs Roy lived on for many years in the same flat after Bimal Roy had passed away till the owners wanted to give away the bungalow to real estate promoters. Mrs Roy once expressed a desperate wish to convert the flat into an archival museum in memory of Bimal Roy with stills, lobby cards, posters and other technical paraphernalia on display including the still photographs he captured on his camera. But she was too old and ailing to transform this dream to reality alone, and this never happened. The heirs have been given a bungalow on a plot on the same space now, lived in by the son Joy Roy.

It would be appropriate to conclude that Bimal Roy converted his 'displaced' identity into a rich and informed creative discourse in cinema among which one may count some of the best films that will continue to dot the history of Indian cinema forever. Bimal Roy demolished preconceived Western and Euro-centric perspectives of place and displacement. Through his films, he created, invented and redefined the concept of displacement not only of a person but also of the person's existence in a given place which might be as ambiguous and ambivalent as it might be uncertain and amoeba-like, growing in every direction in every which way till one fails to pin it down with a definite identity except an essentially Indian one. Life and place settings in his films are never portrayed as a gloomy, dark place where people would not wish to stay or grow roots or both. His interpretations of place and the displaced elevate the possibilities of a lived reality that cuts across time, space and geography though they remain rooted in the culture and the language we watch them in.

If the cinema of Bimal Roy can be placed in perspective, one might qualify it as being unquestionably democratic in story, language, characterization and incidents. His cinema neither addresses nor revolves around what may be termed the 'privileged class'; it does not restrict viewing access to privileged communities and audience because, except for the spoken language in the film, everyone will be able to understand what the film is trying to say, about whom and how, even if one cannot always identify with the predicaments shown in them, without feeling distanced, alienated or alone. Bimal Roy's cinema points out again and again at the truth that place is "an amalgamation of completely independent and often, conflicting ideas. All great works of art move beyond preconceived notions of geography and frame a comprehensive construct by infusing it with the creator's individual quirks."[14] Where else can one find this truth exemplified so beautifully other than in the cinema of Bimal Roy? Where are the displaced person and the outsider? Did they ever exist?

---

[14] Raj, 'Beyond Physical Realms, Life and Letters'.

FILMOGRAPHY: THE DIRECTORIAL FILMS OF BIMAL ROY

(Compiled By: Sounak Chakraverti)

FILMS IN KOLKATA
1944 *Udayer Pathey* (**Towards the Light**)
Producer: New Theatres
Story: Jyotirmoy Roy
Screenplay: Bimal Roy, Nirmal Dey
Cinematography: Bimal Roy
Editing: Haridas Mahalanabis
Audiography: Atul Chattopadhyay
Art Direction: Souren Sen
Music: Rai Chand Boral
Lyrics: Rabindranath Tagore, Sailen Roy
Choreography: M.K. Nayar
Actors: Radhamohan Bhattacharya, Debi Mukhopadhyay, Biswanath Bhaduri, Jiben Bose, Tulsi Chakraborty, Puru Mullick, Boken Chattopadhyay, Binota Bose, Rekha Mitra, Meera Dutta, Leena Bose, Maya Bose, Smritirekha Biswas, Devbala and Rajyalakshmi.

The Hindi version of *Udayer Pathey* was released in 1946 as *Hamrahi* (Travelling companion). There were slight changes in the star cast but the technical crew remained the same.

This was probably the first time in our country when the film came before and the novel was published post-release of the film. The film was a stupendous success at the box office and the novel too became a unique bestseller. The novel was dedicated quite obviously to Bimal Roy.

1948 *Anjangadh* (Proper Noun—Name of a Fictitious Place)

Producer: New Theatres
Story: Subodh Ghosh
(The original Bengali short story is *Fossil*)
Screenplay: Bimal Roy
Cinematography: Kamal Bose
Editing: Haridas Mahalanabis
Audiography: Bani Dutta
Art Direction: Anil Bhattacharya, Sudhendu Roy
Music: Raichand Boral
Lyrics: Rabindranath Tagore, Jyotirindra Maitra, Sailen Roy
Actors: Raja Gangopadhyay, Bipin Gupta, Bhanu Bandyopadhyay, Manoranjan Bhattacharya, Indu Mukhopadhyay, Tulsi Chakraborty, Jiben Bose, Bhaskar Deb, Boleen Som, Purnendu Mukhopadhyay, Jahar Roy, Sadhan Sarkar, Prafulla Mukhopadhyay, Sunanda Devi, Amita Bose, Parul Kar, Chhobi Roy and Manorama Devi.
The Hindi version of *Anjangadh* also released in 1948. There were slight changes in the star cast but the technical crew remained the same.

1949 *Mantramugdha* (Mesmerized)

Producer: New Theatres
Story: Banaphul
(*Mantramugdha* is a play in Bengali)
Screenplay: Bimal Roy, Sudhish Ghatak
Cinematography: Kamal Bose
Editing: Subodh Roy
Audiography: Loken Bose
Art Direction: Sudhendu Roy
Music: Raichand Boral
Lyrics: Rabindranath Tagore, Banaphul
Actors: Jiben Bose, Sunil Dasgupta, Shakti Bhaduri, Kalipada Sarkar, Tulsi Chakraborty, Indu Mukhopadhyay, Jahar Roy, Bhanu Bandyopadhyay, Meera Sarkar, Reba Devi, Manorama Devi, Roma Nehru, Leelavati, Shefali Sarkar and Parul Kar.

1950 *Pehla Aadmi* (Hindi; The First Man)
Producer: New Theatres
Story: Nasir Hussain (Ex INA)
Screenplay: Bimal Roy
Dialogue: Nasir Hussain, Pandit Bhushan
Additional Dialogue: Bidhayak Bhattacharya
Cinematography: Kamal Bose
Editing: Haridas Mahalanabis
Art Direction: Sudhendu Roy
Set Decoration: Sunity Mitra
Audiography: Loken Bose
Music: Raichand Boral
Lyrics: F. Lt. Prakash (Ex INA)
Choreography: Balkrishna Menan
Actors: Smriti Biswas, Ashita Bose, Balraj Vij, Vijoy Kumar (Ex INA), Pahari Sanyal, Paul Mahendra, Hiralal (Ex INA), Asit Sen, Bhupendra Kapoor, Jahar Roy, Prem Charan (Ex INA), K.C. Sharma, Bela Bose, Sreemati, Pravat Kumar, Robins, Major Puran Singh (Ex INA), F. Lt. Prakash (Ex INA) and Capt. Nand Singh (Ex INA).

FILMS IN BOMBAY

1952 *Maa* (Mother)
Producer: Ashok Kumar and Savak Vacha (The Bombay Talkies Limited)
Story: Swaraj Banerji
Scenario: Bimal Roy
Dialogues: Nabendu Ghosh
Cinematography: Joseph Wirsching
Editing: Hrishikesh Mukherjee
Audiography: J.M. Barot
Art Direction: D.N. Jadhav
Music: S.K. Pal
Lyrics: Bharat Vyas
Actors: Leela Chitnis, Bharat Bhushan, Shyama, Nasir Hussain, Kumud, Paul Mahendra, Manju, B.M. Vyas, Kusum Deshpande and Achla Sachdev.

1953 *Do Bigha Zamin* (Two Acres of Land)
Producer: Bimal Roy Productions
Story: Salil Chowdhury
Scenario: Hrishikesh Mukherjee
Hindi Dialogues and Dialogues Direction: Paul Mahendra

Cinematography: Kamal Bose
Editing: Hrishikesh Mukherjee
Audiography: Essa M. Suratwala
Art Direction: Gonesh Basak
Music: Salil Chowdhury
Lyrics: Shailendra
Choreography: Prem Dhawan
Actors: Balraj Sahni, Nirupa Roy, Ratan Kumar, Murad, Rajyalakshmi, Nana Palsikar, Noorjahan, Nasir Hussain, Rekha Misra, Chitra, Jagdeep, Tiwari, Sarita Devi and Meena Kumari (in a guest appearance).

1953 *Parineeta* (Married Woman)
Producer: Ashok Kumar Productions
Story: Sarat Chandra Chattopadhyay
Scenario: Bimal Roy
Additional Dialogues: Nabendu Ghosh
Hindi Dialogues: Vrajendra Gaur
Cinematography: Kamal Bose
Editing: Hrishikesh Mukherjee
Audiography: Sherali Pabani and J.M. Barot
Art Direction: Jadhav Rao
Music: Arun Kumar Mukherjee
Lyrics: Pt. Bharat Vyas
Choreography: Gopi Kisan
Stage Dance: Gopi Kisan and Roshan
Actors: Ashok Kumar, Meena Kumari, Asit Baran, Baby Sheela, Nasir Hussain, Badri Prasad, Pratima Devi, Rekha, Manju, Manorama, S. Bannerji, Nayane, Sarita, Bhupen Kapoor, Vikram Kapoor, Sailen Bose, Shivjibhai, Omprakash, Colin Pal, Baby Rehana, Baby Mumtaz and Tiwari (guest artiste).

1954 *Naukri* (The Job)
Producer: Bimal Roy Productions
Story: Subodh Basu
Screenplay: Nabendu Ghosh
Hindi Dialogues: Paul Mahendra
Cinematography: Kamal Bose
Editing: Hrishikesh Mukherjee
Audiography: Dinshaw Billimoria
Art Direction: Sudhendu Roy
Music: Salil Chowdhury

Lyrics: Shailendra
Actors: Kishore Kumar, Sheila Ramani, Kanhaiyalal, Noor, Achala Sachdev, Bikram Kapoor, Krishnakant, Tulsi Chakravarty, Bhupen Kapoor, Sunil Das Gupta, Iftikar, Jagdip, W.M. Khan, Samson, Moni Chatterji, Sheojibhai, Sailen Bose, Mahmud, Dubey, Girdharilal, Shakuntala Devi and Collin Pal.

1954 *Biraj Bahu* (Proper Noun—A Wife Named Biraj)

Producer: Hiten Chaudhury
Story: Sarat Chandra Chattopadhyay
Scenario: Bimal Roy
Screen Adaptation: Nabendu Ghosh
Hindi Dialogues: Nasir Hussain
Cinematography: Dilip Gupta
Editing: Hrishikesh Mukherjee
Audiography: Essa M. Suratwala
Art Direction: Sudhendu Roy
Music: Salil Chowdhury
Lyrics: Prem Dhawan
Actors: Kamini Kaushal, Abhi Bhattacharjee, Shakuntala, Pran, Randhir, Manorama, Kammo, Bikram Kapoor and Iftikhar.

1954 *Baap Beti* (Father Daughter)

Producer: S.H. Munshi
Story inspired by Guy de Maupassant's *Simon's Papa*
Adaptation: Nabendu Ghosh
Scenario: Bimal Roy
Dialogue Translation: Mohanlal Bajpai
Cinematography: Kamal Bose
Editing: Hrishikesh Mukherjee
Audiography: B.M. Saha
Art Direction: Gurjit Singh
Music: Roshan
Lyrics: Pradeep
Choreography: L.C. Mathur
Actors: Ranjan, Baby Tabassum, Sunalini Devi, Nasir Hussain, Nana Palsikar, Baby Naaz, Sabita, Nalini, Anju, Kanta Kumari, C.L. Shah, Krishnakant, Anwaribai, Dolly and Mridula.

1955 *Devdas* (Proper Noun—Name of the Protagonist)

Producer: Bimal Roy Productions
Story: Sarat Chandra Chattopadhyay

Screenplay: Nabendu Ghosh
Hindi Scenario: Rajinder Singh Bedi
Cinematography: Kamal Bose
Editing: Hrishikesh Mukherjee
Audiography: Essa M. Suratwala
Art Direction: Sudhendu Roy
Music: S.D. Burman
Lyrics: Sahir Ludhianvi
Choreography: Hiralal
Actors: Dilip Kumar, Vyjayanthimala, Motilal, Suchitra Sen, Nasir Hussain, Murad, Kanhaiyalal, Moni Chatterjee, Iftekhar, Nana Palsikar, Baby Naaz, Pratima Devi, Kammo, Sarita Devi, Shakuntala, Pran and Johnny Walker (as guest artistes).

1958 *Madhumati* (Proper Noun—Name of the Protagonist)
Producer: Bimal Roy Productions
Story: Ritwik Ghatak
Dialogues: Rajinder Singh Bedi
Dialogue Direction: S. Paul Mahendra
Cinematography: Dilip Gupta
Editing: Hrishikesh Mukherjee; Associate: Das Dhaimade
Audiography: Dinshaw M. Billimoria
Art Direction: Sudhendu Roy
Music: Salil Chowdhury
Lyrics: Shailendra
Choreography: Sohanlal, Satyanarayan, Sachin Shankar
Actors: Dilip Kumar, Vyjayanthimala, Johnny Walker, Pran, Jayant, Tiwari, Misra, Sheojibhai and Tarun Bose.

1958 *Yahudi* (The Jew)
Producer: Savak B. Vacha
Screenplay: Nabendu Ghosh
Associate Screenplay: R.K. Soral
Dialogues: Vajahat Mirza
Cinematography: Dilip Gupta
Editing: Hrishikesh Mukherjee
Audiography: Dinshaw M. Billimoria
Art Direction and Costume Design: Sudhendu Roy
Music: Shankar–Jaikishan
Lyrics: Shailendra, Hasrat Jaipuri
Choreography: Suryakumar, Vinod Chopra, Satyanarayan

Actors: Sohrab Modi, Dilip Kumar, Meena Kumari, Nigar Sultana, Nasir Hussain, Anwar Hussain, Minu Mumtaz, Murad, Bikram Kapoor, Baby Naaz, Helen, Cuckoo and Kamala Laxman.

1960 *Sujata* (**Proper Noun—Name of the Protagonist**)
Producer: Bimal Roy Productions
Story: Subodh Ghosh
Dialogue: Shailendra
Dialogue Direction: Paul Mahendra
Cinematography: Kamal Bose, Montu Bose
Editing: Amit Bose
Audiography: Essa M. Suratwala
Art Direction: Sudhendu Roy
Music: S.D. Burman
Lyrics: Majrooh Sultanpuri
Choreography: Satyanarayan
Manipuri Dance: Little Ballet Troupe
Actors: Nutan, Sunil Dutt, Shashikala, Lalita Pawar, Tarun Bose, Sulochana, Asit Sen, Ashim Kumar, Paul Mahendra, Baij Sharma, Brahm Dutt, Moni Chatterjee, Sabitri, Sheojibhai, Master Sohni, Baby Farida and Baby Shobha.

1960 *Parakh* (**The Test**)
Producer: Bimal Roy Productions
Story: Salil Chowdhury
Dialogue: Shailendra
Dialogue Direction: Paul Mahendra
Cinematography: Kamal Bose
Editing: Amit Bose
Audiography: George D'cruz
Art Direction: Sudhendu Roy
Music: Salil Chowdhury
Lyrics: Shailendra
Choreography: Badri Prasad
Actors: Sadhana Shivdasani, Durga Khote, Leela Chitnis, Sheela Rao, Ruby Paul, Mumtaz Begum, Sarita Devi, Meherbanoo, Nishi, Vasant Chowdhury, Nasir Hussain, Kanhaialal, Jayant, Rashid Khan, Asit Sen, Paul Mahendra and Motilal.

1962 *Prem Patra* (**The Love Letter**)
Producer: Bimal Roy Productions
Story: Nitan Bhattacharya

(This was adapted from the superhit Bengali film *Sagarika* (1956), starring the golden pair of Bengali cinema, Uttam Kumar and Suchitra Sen)
Screenplay: Salil Chowdhury, Debobrata Sen Gupta
Dialogues: Rajinder Kishan
Cinematography: Dilip Gupta
Editing: Amit Bose
Audiography: M.R. Pitle
Art Direction: Sudhendu Roy
Music: Salil Chowdhury
Lyrics: Rajinder Kishan, Gulzar
Actors: Sadhana, Shashi Kapoor, Seema, Rajendra Nath, Sudhir, Chand Usmani, Parveen Chowdhury, Padma Devi, Bela Bose and Sarita Devi.

1963 *Bandini* (The Prisoner)
Producer: Bimal Roy Productions
Story: Jarasandha
(The original Bengali novel is *Tamoshee*)
Screenplay: Nabendu Ghosh
Dialogues: Paul Mahendra
Cinematography: Kamal Bose
Editing: Madhu Prabhavalkar
Audiography: Dinshaw Billimoria
Art Direction: Sudhendu Roy
Music: S.D. Burman
Lyrics: Shailendra, Gulzar
Actors: Ashok Kumar, Nutan, Dharminder, Raja Paranjape, Tarun Bose, Asit Sen, Chandrima Bhaduri and Moni Chatterjee.

DOCUMENTARIES OF BIMAL ROY

1943 *Bengal Famine*
1961 *Immortal Stupa*
1963 *Life and Message of Swami Vivekananda*
1967 *Gautama the Buddha*

BIBLIOGRAPHY

INTRODUCTION

Ahmed, Omar. 'Do Bigha Zamin.' *Senses of Cinema* 47 (27 January 2009).

Arora, Poonam. 'Devdas: India's Emasculated Hero, Sado-Masochism and Colonialism'. *Journal of South Asian Literature* 30, no. 1 & 2 (1995): 253–276.

Bhattacharya, Rinki, ed. *The Man Who Spoke in Pictures—Bimal Roy*. New Delhi: Penguin-Viking, 2009.

Bhattacharya Roy, Rinki. *Bimal Roy's Madhumati—Untold Stories from Behind the Scenes*. New Delhi: Rupa Publications, 2014.

Chakravarty, Sumita S. *National Identity in Indian Popular Cinema, 1947–1987*. Oxford University Press, 1996.

Dasgupta, Chidananda. *Seeing is Believing—Selected Writings of Cinema*. New Delhi: Penguin Books, 2008.

Khan, Amir Ullah, and Bibek Debroy. *Indian Economic Transition Through Bollywood Eyes—Hindi Films and How They Have Reflected Changes in India's Political Economy*. Working Paper, August 2002.

Lewis, David, Dennis Rodgers and Michael Woolcock, eds. *Popular Representations of Development: Insights from Novels, Films, Television and Social Media*. Routledge, 2014.

Masud, Iqbal. 'The Great Four of the Golden Fifties'. In *Frames of Mind: Reflections on Indian Cinema*, edited by Aruna Vasudev. New Delhi: UBS Publishers, 1995. Quoted by Khan, Amir Ullah and Bibek Debroy. *Indian Economic Transition Through Bollywood Eyes: Hindi Films and How They Have Reflected Changes in India's Political Economy*. Working Paper No. 2.

Mazumdar, Ranjani. 'Figure of the Tapori: Language, Gesture and the Cinematic City'. *Economic and Political Weekly* 36, no. 52 (29 December 2001): 4972–4980.

Phutela, Rohit. '*Do Beegha Zameen*: Textualizing Subalterns in Post-Independence Indian Cinema'. *Journal of Literature, Media and Cultural Studies* IV, no. 7 & 8 (January–December 2012): 195–203.

Valicha, Kishore. *The Moving Image—A Study of Indian Cinema*. Orient Longman, 1988.

Vasudevan, Ravi. *The Melodramatic Public—Film Form and Spectatorship in Indian Cinema*. Ranikhet, India: Permanent Black, 2010.

Wood, Robin. 'An Introduction to the American Horror Film'. In *Movies and Methods*, Vol. II, edited by Bills Nichols, 199–200. Calcutta: Seagull Books, 1993.

CHAPTER I

Astruc, Alexander. 'Fire and Ice'. *Cahiers du Cinema*, no. 1, 70–71.

Banerjee, Sumanta. 'Paradoxes in Inventing Bengali Identity'. Accessed 28 February 2017, from http://www.indiaseminar.com/2013/645/645_sumanta_banerjee.htm

Bazin, Andre. *Cahiers du Cinema*, no. 70, 1957.

Buscombe, Edward. 'Ideas of Authorship'. In *Theories of Authorship*, edited by John Caughie, 22–34. London: Routledge and Kegan Paul, 1981.

Buscombe, Edward. *The Construction of Authorship—Textual Appreciation of Law and Literature*, edited by Martha Woodmansee and Peter Jaszee. Durham, NC: Duke University Press, 1994.

Chatterji, Shoma A. *Parama and Other Outsiders—The Cinema of Aparna Sen*. Kolkata: Parumita Publications, 2002.

Corrigan, Timothy. 'Auteurism'. Accessed 1 March 2017, from http://www.oxfordbibliographies.com/view/document/obo-9780199791286/obo-9780199791286-0009.xml

Dey, Sumit. 'Authoring Space, Gender and the Past: A Film Called *Shuvo Muhurat*'. *Journal of the Moving Image* no. 10 (September 2012).

Kael, Pauline. 'Circles and Squares: Joys and Sarris'. In *Perspectives on the Study of Film*, edited by John Stuart Katz, 154. Boston, MA: Little, Brown & Company, 1971.

Lal, Vinay. 'Bimal Roy (1909–1966)', 2008. Accessed 1 March 2017, from https://www.sscnet.ucla.edu/southasia/Culture/Cinema/bimalroy.htm

Nag, Amitava. 'Hrishikesh Mukherjee's Makaan, Book Review in Marquee'. *The Statesman*, 31 October 2015.

Rangoonwalla, F. *Life and Work—Bimal Roy—A Critical Study*. NFAI, 1991.

Sarris, Andrew. *Perspectives on the Study of Film*, reprint edn, edited by John Stuart Katz, 132–133. Boston, MA: University of Illinois Press 1974.

Staiger, Janet. 'Authorship Approaches'. In *Authorship and Film*, edited by Janet Staiger and David A. Gerstner. 27–60. London and New York: Routledge, 2003.

Thompson, Kristin and David Bordwell. *Film History: An Introduction*, 3rd edn. New York, NY: McGraw-Hill, 381–383.

CHAPTER II

Ahmed, Omar. '*Do Bigha Zamin*/Two Acres of Land'. *Senses of Cinema* (27 January 2009).

Sahani, Balraj. *Balraj Sahani: An Autobiography*. Hind Pocket Books, 1979.

Biswas, Moinak. 'Bengali Film Debates: The Literary Liaison Revisited.' *Journal of the Moving Image* 1, no. 1 (1999).

Chaudhuri, Nirad C. 'The Autobiography of an Unknown Indian'. In *Memory's Gold: Writings on Calcutta*, edited by Amit Chaudhuri. New Delhi: Penguin, 2008.

Chowdhury, Indira. *The Frail Hero and Virile History: Gender and the Politics of Culture in Colonial Bengal*. New Delhi: Oxford University Press, 1998.

Chowdhury, Romit. 'Bengalis but Not Men? Bhadralok Masculinities in Adda'. *Sub/Versions, A Journal of Emerging Research in Media and Cultural Studies* 1, no. 1 (2013): 146–170.

Dasgupta, Chidananda. 'Precursors of Unpopular Cinema'. In *Seeing is Believing, Selected Writings on Cinema*. New Delhi: Penguin-Viking, 2008.

Gangar, Amrit. 'Do Bigha Zamin? Two Acres of Land and Migration in Indian Cinematography'. *Café Dissensus*, 1 August 2014. Accessed 7 March 2017, from https://

cafedissensus.com/2014/08/01/do-bigha-zamintwo-acres-of-land-and-migration-in-indian-cinematography/

Khan, Amir Ullah and Bibek Debroy. *Indian Economic Transition Through Bollywood Eyes: Hindi Films and How They Have Reflected Changes in India's Political Economy*. Multimedia Presentation by the authors at the April 2002 seminar on India's Political Economy held by the Rajiv Gandhi Institute for Contemporary Studies, Working Paper No. 2, August 2002.

Mani, Lata. 'Abstract Disquisitions: Bhadralok and the Normative Violence of Sati'. In *Contentious Traditions: The Debate on Sati in Colonial India*. London: University of California Press, 1998.

Phutela, Rohit. '*Do Beegha Zamin*—Textualizing Subalterns in Post Independence Indian Cinema'. *Journal of Literature, Culture and Media Studies* IV, nos. 7–8 (January–December 2012).

Raj, Ashok. 'The Pen and the Camera—The Influence of Literature on Cinema'. In *Hero*, Vol. I. New Delhi: Hay House, 2009.

Ramakrishnan, Nivedita. '*Udayer Pathey* (1944), Bimal Roy's Realistic Inference of Socialism', *Dear Cinema.com*, January.

CHAPTER III

Arora, Poonam. 'Devdas: India's Emasculated Hero, Sado-Masochism and Colonialism'. *Jouvert, a Journal of Pre-Colonial Studies* (1997).

Bandopadhyay, Jayanta. *Sharat Shahitye Byakti O Samaj*. 15, Kolkata: Karuna Publications, 2000.

Chattopadhyay, Sharat Chandra. *Narir Mulya, Sharat Sahitya Samagra*, Vols. I and II [The value of women, collection of Sarat literature]. Kolkata: Ananda Publishers, 1986.

Creekmur, Corey K. 'Remembering, Repeating and Working Through *Devdas*: Sarat Chandra's *Devdas*'. In *Indian Literature and Popular Cinema: Recasting Classics*, edited by Heidi P.M. Pauwels, 173–190. London: Routledge, 2007.

Jana, Soumen. 'The Problematics of "Dalit space" in Sarat Chandra Chattopadhyay's "Mahesh" and Mahasweta Devi's "Shikar"'. *The Criterion: An International Journal in English* 4, no. VI (December 2013).

Maitreyee, Mishra and Manisha Mishra. 'Marriage, Devotion and Imprisonment: Women in Bimal Roy's Devdas and Bandini'. *Commentaries: Global Media Journal* 3, no. 1 (June 2012).

Mukherjee, Manidipa. 'Such a Long Journey'. *High Spirits* XXVII (September), 1995.

Mukherjee, Meenakshi. *Realism and Reality: The Novel and Society in India*. Reprinted. New Delhi: Oxford University Press, 1985.

Purakayastha, Madhumita. 'Cultural Relativism and Feminist Discourse in Sharat Chandra Chattopadhyay's Fiction vis-à-vis His Concepts on the Worth of Women'. *IOSR Journal of Humanities and Social Science* 16, no. 2 (September–October 2013): 58–63.

Raj, Ashok. *Hero*. Vol. I of *The Silent Era to Dilip Kumar*. New Delhi: Hay House, 163–164.

Roy, Dilip. Speech at seminar on *The Influence of Sarat Chandra Chattopadhyay on Cinema*, January 2004, Panitrash, Bagnan, Howrah District, West Bengal.

Sen, Sukumar. *History of Bengali Literature*, rev. ed. New Delhi: Sahitya Akademi, 1979.

Thompson, Theodosia. *Introduction to Srikanto Part I*. London: Oxford University Press, 1922.

CHAPTER IV

Chakravarty, Sumita. *National Identity in Indian Popular Cinema—1947–1987*. New Delhi: Oxford University Press, 1996, 112.

Chatterji, Shoma. 'Men Directors—Women's Voice'. PhD thesis. Netaji Subhas Open University, Kalyani, Kolkata, 2007–2008.

Ghosh, Shohini. 'Deviant Pleasures and Disorderly Women—The Representation of the Female Outlaw in Bandit Queen and Anjaam'. In *Feminist Terrains in Legal Domains—Interdisciplinary Essays on Women and Law in India*, edited by Ratna Kapur, 167–168. New Delhi: Kali for Women, 1996.

Mishra, Maitreyee and Manisha Mishra. 'The Outsiders: Women as Social Outcasts in Bimal Roy's Films'. Paper presented at International Conference on Communication, Media, Technology and Change, Istanbul, Turkey, 9–11 May 2012.

Sridhar, Lalita. 'Films and Femininity, An Interview with Film Scholar Venkatesh Chakravarty', *Info Change News and Features*, December 2003.

Ziya Us Salam. 'Bandini', *The Hindu* (1 October 1, 2009).

CHAPTER V

Bhattacharya, Rinki. *Bimal Roy*. Bhopal: Madhya Pradesh Film Development Corporation, 1989.

Chakrabarti, Shyamal. 'Sachinkarta'. In *Smarika*, edited by Mohan Swaroop Maheshwari. Jaipur: Sachin Dev Burman Smriti Samaroh, Film Society of Jaipur and Sangeet Natak Akademi, 4–9 April, 2009.

Chatterji, Shoma A. 'The Influence of Tagore on Indian Film Music'. Paper presented at Tagore Conference, Calcutta University, Alipur Campus, 11 February 2011.

Gorbman, C. *Unheard Melodies: Narrative Film Music*. Bloomington, IN: Indiana University Press, 1987.

Lipscomb, Scott D. and David E. Tolschinsky. 'Role of Music Communication in Cinema'. In *Music Communications*, edited by D. Miell, R. MacDonald and D. Hargreaves. London: Oxford University Press, 2005.

Manwani, Akshay. *Sahir Ludhianvi—The People's Poet*. Noida, India: HarperCollins Publishers, 2013, 90–91.

Raj, Ashok. *Hero*. Vol. I of *The Silent Era to Dilip Kumar*. Hay House, 2010, 163–164.

Saran, Sathya. *Sun Mere Bandhu Re—The Musical World of S.D. Burman*. HarperCollins Publishers, 2014, 96.

Singh, Jai Arjun. 'On Bimal Roy's Sujata (and the Invisible Line in Bachpan ke Din)'. 28 January 2013. Accessed 4 April 2016, from http://jaiarjun.blogspot.in/2013/01/on-bimal-roys-sujata-and-invisible-line.html

Stuessy, J. and S. Lipscomb. *Rock and Roll—Its History and Stylistic Development*, 4th edn. Upper Saddle River, NJ: Prentice-Hall, 2003, 410–411.

SUMMING UP

Barua, Jahnu. 'Bimal Roy, The Humanist'. In *The Man Who Spoke in Pictures—Bimal Roy*, edited by Rinki Roy Bhattacharya, 70. New Delhi: Penguin-Viking, 2009.

Berne, Eric. *A Layman's Guide to Psychiatry and Psychoanalysis*, 1976, 399.

Lal, Vinay. 'Bimal Roy (1909–1966)', 2008. Accessed 1 March 2017, from https://www.sscnet.ucla.edu/southasia/Culture/Cinema/bimalroy.htm

Raj, Neelabh. 'Beyond Physical Realms, Life and Letters'. *The Statesman*, 7 February 2016, 3.

INDEX

ABOUT THE AUTHOR

Dr Shoma A. Chatterji is a freelance journalist, film scholar and author based in Kolkata. She has won two National Awards for Best Writing on Cinema—Best Film Critic in 1991 and Best Book on cinema in 2002. She won the Bengal Film Journalists Association's Best Critic Award in 1998, the Bharat Nirman Award for excellence in journalism in 2004, a research fellowship from the National Film Archive of India in 2005–2006 and a Senior Research Fellowship from the PSBT Delhi in 2006–2007. She has authored 22 books on cinema and gender and has been a member of jury at several film festivals in India and abroad.

She holds a master's degree in Economics and in Education; PhD in History (Indian Cinema) and a Senior Research Post-doctoral Fellowship from the ICSSR. In 2009–2010, she won a Special Award for 'consistent writing on women's issues' at the UNFPA–Laadli Media Awards (Eastern region), was bestowed with the Kalyan Kumar Mitra Award for 'excellence in film scholarship and contribution as a film critic' in 2010 and the Lifetime Achievement SAMMAN by the Rotary Club of Calcutta-Metro City in July 2012.